The 100 Mile City

The building boom of the late 1980s, along with money from Japan, ensured that Los Angeles, a city the rest of the world had always underestimated, metamorphosed into what was undeniably a world city.

With its seemingly endless spread of low density settlement, from which high rise towers erupt at apparently random intervals, Los Angeles is perhaps the clearest example of the hundred-mile city

Deyan Sudjic
Photographs by Phil Sayer

The 100 Mile City

A Harvest Original
Harcourt Brace & Company
San Diego   New York   London

Library of Congress
Cataloging-in-Publication Data
Sudjic, Deyan.
The 100 mile city/by Deyan Sudjic;
photographs by Phil Sayer.—1st U.S. ed.
p.   cm.
Includes bibliographical references
(p.) and index.
ISBN 0-15-642357-X
1. Metropolitan areas. 2. Sociology, Urban.
3. Cities and towns.
I. Title. II. Title: Hundred mile city.
HT330.S83   1993
307.76—dc20   93-17359

Printed in the United States of America
First United States edition

A B C D E

Contents

Introduction

The thesis of this book is that a whole range of fundamental urban changes whose causes had been building up for some time took effect in the course of the 1980s and resulted in the recasting of the shape and character of the city. Some of these changes concerned the way people lived, some had an influence on the physical form of the city, and others were connected with the relationship of one city to another.

This book deals with five cities in particular: London, Paris, Tokyo, New York and Los Angeles, though it touches on many others, and it seeks to make sense of the forces that are shaping all western cities. The five are the largest, the furthest evolved, and the most important of the industrial cities, a species that went through its most violent period of growth in the nineteenth century, but which then, in many cases, atrophied. In these five however, while there has been some decay, their metamorphosis into a system of interlinked, but also antagonistic cities has been the real legacy of the 1980s. Together they dominated the world's economy and cultural life, but they also had to struggle to maintain their position, against each other and potential competitors.

A city of ten or more million people is a complex organism, one which can be experienced by its inhabitants at many different levels, and any attempt at coming to grips with the essence of what it is like to live in one, or the forces that are shaping it must itself work on a variety of different levels. Thus this book deals with housing statistics as well as with the changing nature of museums. It looks at the exhibitionistic tendencies of expos and Disneyland, and the role of airports as contemporary stand-ins for the city square. It analyses architecture as well as the demographics of population, and transport. It looks at the impact of different attempts to control the form of the city, from the autocratic politics of Paris, to the apparent *laissez-faire* of Houston.

It is in three parts. The first deals with the attitudes of various different groups such as theorists, developers, architects and politicians towards the city. The second discusses a series of urban issues: transport, housing, and employment. The final section attempts to draw all these aspects together to paint a picture of the way that life is actually lived in the city beyond its historic core.

Overleaf: The historic crust of the European city – the picture postcard views that serve as logos for London and Paris – is under threat not so much from the wave of redevelopment, but from the changing reality of the nature of the modern city. The historic core is no longer the focus for the lives of the majority of the city's inhabitants

I

Theory and practice

1

The world's great cities are still too close to the explosive dislocation of the last decade for the smoke and dust to have settled. But it is already clear that the eighties were the decade in which the industrial city finally shook off the last traces of its nineteenth-century self and mutated into a completely new species. Migration and economic development changed it beyond recognition. Technological innovations eliminated traditional industries and scattered new ones in unpredictable places over ever wider distances.

Culturally, the successful cities have distanced themselves from their national contexts. Paris and London now have much more in common with each other than they do with their respective nations. Shops in the Rue St Honoré and Bond Street, or for that matter Madison Avenue, Rodeo Drive and Aoyama, have exactly the same names, and carry the same merchandise. In Knightsbridge and Beverly Hills the dentists and the tax lawyers lead similar kinds of lives, protected by the same burglar alarms, driving back and forth in the same late-model Mercedes. At the other end of the scale, the stress of daily life for the jobless of Brixton and Watts is similar too. And the concerns of middle-class citizens in big cities – for better schools and hospitals, lower property taxes and limits to the pace of development around them – are equally international.

Despite the fluctuations of the boom and bust cycle, the property market, dominated as never before by international rather than local money, has rebuilt the skylines of the big cities. While the timing of these changes coincided in America, Japan and Europe, their impact has not been uniform. Some cities have declined while others have prospered.

As the decade opened, the big cities that had emerged from the nineteenth century remained substantially intact. Despite motorcars and air-conditioned offices they still clung faithfully to the traditional organisation of the city. All of them had a market district, a financial centre, and university and legal precincts. Each of them was defined by a network of decaying but still intricately ordered neighbourhoods which pursued their distinctive daily rituals just as they had for centuries.

Well into the 1970s, giant steamship funnels still closed the view down side streets on Manhattan's Lower West Side and London's Rotherhithe,

New York has struggled to come to terms with a rapid fall in the population of the inner boroughs, and the idea that a life and death battle for control of the world's financial markets is its best hope for economic survival. In the process the city's skyline has been rebuilt, the glass slabs of the 1960s replaced by stone-faced monuments to the corporate ego of the banks an unmistakable reminder of the international trade which once underpinned their respective cities' economies. In New York you could still see the piers for transatlantic shipping jutting into the Hudson, just as they had since the days of Ellis Island. As late as the 1960s, there were six hundred sailings a month in and out of New York harbour. In London the gaunt brick walls of the enclosed docks that once accommodated ocean liners and freighters lived on, even though the ships had vanished.

The wholesale food markets still worked through the night in a blaze of lights, their cafés opening before dawn to feed blood-stained meat porters. Fresh produce, fish, livestock and flowers still came into the city every morning, feeding markets that operated much as they always had done, even if some of the merchandise might now be flown in from Alaska and the Seychelles. Harley Street and Savile Row were still potent addresses, bestowing the kind of legitimacy on their occupants that can only come from the concentration of generations of doctors and tailors in the same street, drawn together for much the same reasons that the silversmiths and the tanners of the middle ages clustered together on the same streets.

The building of suburban railway networks allowed the nineteenth-century city, shaped by the endurance of pedestrians, to spread far beyond its pre-industrial limits. Significant though that growth was, it did not fundamentally alter the ancient pattern of the city, radiating out from its historic core. But in the 1980s, when even the most conservative banks joined department stores and corporate headquarters in the exodus from the old city centres, the city changed out of all recognition.

Eclipsed by upstart competitors and even their own suburbs, at least three of the world's five greatest cities began the decade apparently in the worst of shape. New York, Paris and London, previously the most successful of the mature metropolises, had lost the dynamism of the nineteenth century. Tokyo and Los Angeles, the two most significant newcomers who made up the rest of the group, offered entirely different physical and historical models, and looked to be their most threatening rivals.

New York's economy, like London's, seemed to be stagnating dangerously. In the 1970s, both cities failed to spend enough to maintain even their sewers let alone their public transport systems. The gloss of their monumental buildings faded, their streets were potholed, and the plate-glass store windows began to disappear behind plywood. New York City, having narrowly escaped its first brush with bankruptcy, was overshadowed by catastrophic dereliction in the South Bronx, Harlem and large parts of Manhattan and Brooklyn. The city centre was losing people so quickly that even the wider conurbation around it, taking in northern New Jersey and Long Island, slipped below eighteen million in 1986 – down nearly two per cent in a decade, a change that hid a far steeper drop in the city's core and the inner ring of suburbs, where the population had shrunk by 800 000 between 1960 and 1980.

London followed an uncomfortably similar pattern. More than a million people left the inner boroughs in twenty years, their departure officially encouraged by the Westminster government through such agencies as the Location of Offices Bureau, which went so far as to advertise the joys of out of town life on the Underground. They left behind a population that, despite the arrival of the international super rich, was poorer, darker-skinned and increasingly likely to be without a job.

The statistics were more than remote abstractions. Their physical effects could be seen in derelict schools and abandoned factories. Particularly in America, inner city population decline had a multiplying effect on economic decay. Detroit, for example, faced the prospect of being cut off from federal funds and losing the right to levy its own taxes as census returns showed the city's population falling below the essential one million mark. The fact that many former residents moved no further than just beyond the city limits cut no ice with state legislators preparing to take control of the purse strings.

The City of Paris – as distinct from the Parisian region – had also seen its population fall steeply in the 1970s – by nearly twenty per cent. As in London and New York, its traditional employers were moving out. Such former mainstays as the wholesale produce market at Les Halles and the old Citroën factory on the Quai Javelle, under the shadow of the Eiffel Tower, vanished. Les Halles was replaced by a new market at Rungis, while Citroën moved to modern plants outside the capital. Or perhaps it is more accurate to say that the old definition of the boundaries of Paris shifted to take in these new outlying markets and factories. As in so many cities, jobs, particularly manual jobs, were evaporating as a centralised industrial system, one which dealt with physical things, their manufacture, processing and movement, gave way to a decentralised, quicksilver economy that dealt chiefly with information.

The middle classes in Paris, London and New York found themselves driven out by the polarisation of the city between the very rich and the very poor. They fled from blight, runaway house prices and school systems in crisis. The ambitious tended to move to the inner suburbs, displacing their blue collar residents in the name of gentrification. The less affluent were forced further and further out into new suburbs inadequately served by public transport, while migrants from the Third World moved into the old city. In London they came from India, Bangladesh and the Caribbean, in New York and Los Angeles from Indochina, Korea and Central America,

Tokyo is both the city that has gone furthest towards the shapeless, formless sprawl that characterises the late twentieth century metropolis, and also the one which retains unexpected remnants of its nineteenth century incarnation. While the markets of Covent Garden and Les Halles have migrated to suburban business parks, the floors of Tokyo's Tsukiji wholesale market still run red with the blood of giant tuna fish each morning

in Paris from North Africa and Iberia. The move to the cities from the countryside had turned into a more general move from the poor south towards the rich north.

The big corporations, looking to capitalise on the value of their city centre property holdings or to reduce their rent bills, began to leave. Corporate offices moved to business parks, rural enclaves and smaller cities. At the same time, what had been suburbs began to take on the characteristics of the old city centre.

The outflow did not stop in the suburban ring. In London, for example, the old Covent Garden wholesale vegetable market which had moved to Nine Elms on the south bank of the Thames in the 1970s after 150 years on its original site, was already looking at moving again less than a decade later. The market's Nine Elms site, seen as a prime business area by the late 1980s, was already being stalked by property developers who wanted to turn it into an office tower and move the wholesale market even further out to the M25 orbital motorway.

In New York, many of the big corporations did not stay long in the palaces they had built for themselves in suburban Connecticut during the 1970s. Lower taxes and more amenable workforces lured them as far afield as Texas, Florida and Colorado. The counterpoint to all this was the explosive growth of the American sunbelt cities – Phoenix, Miami, Atlanta, Houston, Dallas and, most of all, Los Angeles. Seventy-five years on, they echoed the rapid urbanisation of their forerunners in the nineteenth century, but they grew in a different way to the older cities. Development was in scattered clusters and on orbital roads, rather than in concentric rings or along railway tracks radiating from an established core. It looked as if the new cities were growing at the expense of the old ones. And if that was so, there were few signs that anyone knew how to deal with the post-industrial problems of the rustbelt's cities.

Even as late as the 1960s, Los Angeles was seen as irredeemably provincial. Now its size and its financial and cultural clout make it undeniably a great city, yet by the lights of the more conservative of urban theorists, it is still not a city at all. When Peter Hall, in homage to Patrick Geddes, the visionary Scots academic who became the father of regional planning, wrote *The World Cities* in 1966, Los Angeles didn't even merit a chapter. Certainly, its success seems to place the very existence of urbanism of the traditional kind under threat.

Some argued that the old cities were becoming decentralised and shapeless to look like the new ones. Los Angeles, on the other hand, was actually starting to acquire the characteristics of an older city. It grew denser in some areas, though not necessarily the original core, and started to worry about planning and its environmental context. Its population grew with the frenzied haste of a Third World city, putting on at least three million people between 1970 and 1986, a population explosion that brought water rationing in its wake. Miami also almost doubled its population in the same period, while in Houston the ten thousand new arrivals who came pouring in each week for months on end in 1981 overstretched the sewage system, which led to a moratorium on new building in large parts of the city and sharply underlined the constraints on growth even in such bastions of *laissez faire* as Texas.

On the other side of the Pacific, Tokyo, as dependent as a nineteenth-century city on its suburban railways, and with a delirious mixture of traditional qualities and rampant innovation, is seeing the same forces at work as its western counterparts. Its centre is still dominated by the Imperial Palace, department stores very much like the one that Zola described in *Au Bonheurs des Dames*, and a vast central fishmarket whose floor is stained each morning by the blood of giant tuna. It is also seeing a drop in the population of its innermost wards, as people shift westward, but Tokyo at least is prepared to accept the logic of those changes. In 1991 the city government moved out of Marunochi to a new gothic skyscraper home in Shinjuku, following the drift of its citizens.

While many of the bricks and mortar traces of the past are still intact, their significance for cities that are now shaped by freeways and airports, tourism and services, has become more symbolic than real. The changes that have taken place are not simply a question of degree. They go beyond the temporary fluctuations of economic cycles or the replacement of the superannuated architectural mannerisms of one decade with those of another. They are qualitative in their results as much as quantitive.

This book is an attempt to provide a framework for an understanding of the multilayered new city. To do so it is necessary first to look at how the theorists have attempted to come to grips with the modern city. For most observers and interpreters, the point of formulating a theory to account for the way that the city has developed has been to initiate change. Their work has been based on the supposition that the urban world as it is presently organised is fatally flawed and that there is a pressing need for improvement. Apart from the most dogmatic of Marxist planning theoreticians, they have always assumed that improvement is actually possible. For them the city is not merely an inanimate organism to be studied like some meteorological phenomenon, but is susceptible to treatment.

The modern profession of planning got a kick start from the shock of the discovery of an urban underclass by nineteenth-century reformers. In

Theory and practice

the wake of cholera epidemics like that of 1832 which killed 20 000 people in Paris and 5500 in London, clergymen, commissions of inquiry, poets and journalists were all in their own ways horrified to find a parallel world out of sight of the comforts of the respectable middle class. In London, Paris, New York and Berlin, families spent their lives sharing a single room. So-called improved tenement design had elevated congestion to an applied science, while makeshift drains poured raw sewage into the streets.

To rescue a population rotting, as they saw it, in sinful squalor, at the mercy of disease, alcohol, crime and, according to their political prejudices, socialist agitators or monopoly capitalists, the Victorians set in train their onslaught on the city. While pragmatic engineers built waterborne sewage systems, the philanthropists and social reformers took their direction from William Morris and his mentor Ruskin. They shared a sense of aesthetic disgust at the products of industrialisation, and dreamed of a return to the middle ages as an alternative to the hideous night of the nineteenth-century city. Conditions were so bad that anything, even the destruction of the city, appeared to be an improvement. Blending nostalgia and anarchism in a particularly British way, Morris painted a picture of a post-industrial England, where depopulated cities disappeared into the forests, their citizens restored to bucolic delights.

The consequences are still being felt today. Ruskin and Morris longed for a return to the world of medieval guilds and gothic spires, but they set in motion a process that culminated eighty years later in the building of new towns such as Milton Keynes in Britain and Marne-la-Vallée in France, and eventually even to the suburbanisation of southern California, hardly the outcome they had in mind.

The effects of the remedies offered by planning have turned out to be quite different from those promised by their proponents. To save the city, nineteenth-century reformers argued in effect for its destruction. In an attempt to reorder it along more democratic lines, present-day radicals have focused their attention on maintaining existing streets and advocate new homes which are facsimiles of the efforts of speculative builders from the past.

Urban theorists with an architectural bias have put many different glosses on their strategies for shaping the city, but there have been two fundamental and sharply opposed recurring themes in their models: the high-density city set against the decentralised, low-density city. At one extreme are those who want to see existing urban densities maintained, or even intensified, and at the other are the decentralists. Both sides blame each other for all the perceived ills of the modern city.

Sir Frederic Osborn, for many years the manager of Welwyn Garden

City, and one of the more effective propagandists for the garden city movement, wrote to his influential American sympathiser Lewis Mumford in 1943, a moment at which the debate over the direction of London's postwar reconstruction, polarised between the construction of new towns and the extension of the existing city, was at a crucial point:

'The London County Council has a Labour majority, rather more than ordinarily under the thumb of a party junta – partly because of its precarious position, and of a very poor rank and file personnel – which again (as you will understand better than most people here) is due to the filtering out from the County of London (our Manhattan) of the prosperous and enterprising elements of society and the best of the intelligentsia, who have moved to the outer suburbs. Such intelligentsia as is left is, as you would expect, of the over-urbanised café-lounging, quasi-communist, quasi-technocrat type – right out of touch, not only with the sanity of the countryside but with the psychology of ordinary, home-centred workers. They mistake the highly organised and commercialised theatre etc for culture; and mass meetings of unrelated people for democracy. And being right inside a huge city, they cannot see it as a whole.' From the opposing camp, *The Architectural Review* declared war in the 1950s on the suburban dream, a counter-attack on what it termed 'Subtopia', aimed not just against casual urban ugliness but sprawling suburbs and the entire garden city movement. 'The higher the population, the neater and more defined should be the cities, and the more rural and countrified should be the country,' argued its leader writer. The magazine kept up its campaign over two decades, and in 1971 put forward its own alternative, *Civilia*, billed as the end of suburban man, an antidote to what it called the dreadful consequences of Geddes and Mumford and the city-region. *Civilia* was a high density model for a new city built on derelict urban land. It was presented in the form of a strangely compelling set of photographic montages, collaging images of Britain's new plate-glass universities with shots of Brasilia. It was both the highest and the most absurd point of the campaign for congestion, an urban fantasy launched at a moment when all but the most myopic had realised that suburban life was an overwhelmingly popular choice for those who could afford it, and that every restriction on development outside the city simply raised the price of decent housing. But that did not stop *Civilia*'s partisans from declaring that 'The need today is not to expand, but to contract urban development'.

The low-density garden city, with its roots in Morris's writings, was codified in 1898 by Sir Ebenezer Howard in his book *Tomorrow: A Peaceful Path to Real Reform*. It was far more an organisational and political strategy than it was an architectural one. Howard, whose formal education ended when he was fourteen, was very much the nineteenth-century autodidact. He made a living as a shorthand clerk after a miserable spell as a would-be emigrant to the United States, farming in Nebraska. Town planning was by no means his first interest. He was a dedicated amateur inventor, an Esperantist and spiritualist. In fact, towards the end of his life he was using his shorthand skills transcribing spirit messages he claimed to be receiving from his deceased first wife.

He saw a bleak future for the city unless radical changes were made, and he put forward a programme that envisaged the old city supplanted by alternative settlements that were neither country nor town. Not a suburb, but a garden city offering jobs as well as homes, a blend, as he saw it, of the best of all possible worlds.

Howard's book is a densely detailed prescription for the building of a garden city, packed with financial and legal fine print. His style does not run to flights of rhetoric and oratorical flourishes. Perhaps because he assumed that the shortcomings of the contemporary city were self-evident, he confined himself to reproducing criticisms of it made by others, culled from a thick file of newspaper clippings. He cites Lord Rosebery, for example, a one-time chairman of the London County Council, confessing that: 'there is no thought of pride associated in my mind with the idea of London. I am always haunted by the awfulness of London, by the great appalling fact of these millions cast down as it would appear by hazard on the banks of this noble stream. A tumour, an elephantiasis sucking into its gorged system half the life and the blood and the bone of the rural districts'. The violence of his view should make enthusiasts for what is called the 'traditional city', by which is almost inevitably meant its nineteenth-century version, pause for thought.

Howard saw himself as simply providing the technical means to realise the vision of others. He quotes Ruskin with approval and explains that his chief aim was 'the spontaneous movement of the people from our crowded cities to the bosom of our kindly mother earth, at once the source of life, of happiness, of wealth and of power'. Evidently his bleak experiences in Nebraska had not dimmed his enthusiasm for the land. But despite his meticulous legalisms, Howard was a species of anarchist. Under the spell of Patrick Geddes, who had first formulated the notion of the city-region, the garden city was essentially a syndicalist vision for a federated community. Howard hoped that a network of cooperatively organised garden cities, pegged to populations of thirty thousand each, would reverse the unwholesome rush of people from the country to the towns.

Howard has exercised a continuing fascination for planners on both sides of the Atlantic. In America, he inspired Lewis Mumford and

Clarence Stein to set up the Regional Planning Association in 1943. Of his present-day disciples, Peter Hall, Professor of Urban and Regional Planning at Berkeley and one-time Professor of Geography at Reading, is the most prolific. Hall claims that Howard accurately predicted the actual pattern of city development in the twentieth century, in particular the de-densification of the inner city core and its absorption into a network of satellites, a pattern in which Los Angeles must be considered the most advanced and extensive example. But though there are indeed striking similarities in the emerging structure of the big cities to the diagrams that Howard drew, there is also an essential flaw. Howard saw the garden cities as the first step towards rebuilding London itself. He believed that de-densification would lead to falling land values in the inner city, thus allowing it to be replanned to lower densities, which certainly has not happened. And without that vital linkage, Howard's whole theory comes apart at the seams. It may be a recipe for building attractive suburbs, but it is not a blueprint for the future of the city.

There was no single architectural model for the garden city. It appeared garbed in the style of the vernacular revival, as well as neo-Georgian and even modernist. But Camillo Sitte's 1889 study, *City Planning According to Artistic Principles*, provided the imagery that Howard's earliest architectural disciples, Barry Parker and Raymond Unwin, used to shape the first new towns, Welwyn and Letchworth, and later the garden suburb of Hampstead. Sitte, outraged at what he saw as the careless and crude extension of the Vienna of his day, set out to formulate a set of rules for aesthetic city planning based on personal observation. He toured the ancient cities of Europe, Baedeker and notebook in hand, seeking out vantage points from which to gather material on the historical precedents for urban spaces, and from these to establish a set of general prescriptions to apply to new buildings. He spent years peering down from steeples and city walls to see how the anonymous builders of the past had fitted entrances into civic squares and had positioned prominent buildings in relation to them.

'How can there result an artistically harmonious plaza when each architect is self-consciously trying to eclipse the work of his colleagues, and if possible, to rob them of any effect?' Sitte asked. A question that to many still sounds as pertinent as it did when Sitte first asked it, a century ago. 'Such an attitude,' he continued, 'must inevitably destroy the plaza ensemble, just as effectively as a great scene in drama is killed when actors in secondary roles obviously want to be in the limelight and the director and stage manager are too weak to put them in their place.'

The most seductive high-density, café-lounging model of urbanism in the nineteenth century, standing at the opposite pole to the city as both Howard and Sitte saw it, was Baron Georges-Eugène Haussmann's rebuilding of Paris in the 1860s.

In the eighteen years that Haussmann, a career civil servant more versed in government than aesthetics, was prefect of the Seine for Napoleon III's Second Empire, Paris was transformed from a city that still bore the stamp of the middle ages, into what even fiercely jealous foreign contemporaries conceded was the most modern, and the most handsome capital of Europe. Wholesale demolition, massive engineering projects and rigid aesthetic controls constituted a comprehensive redevelopment as ambitious as anything that the twentieth century has attempted. More than twenty thousand structures were demolished, whole areas, including the winding medieval streets of the Ile de France, being reduced to rubble. Haussmann claimed his purpose was to stimulate the national economy, as well as to improve Paris's sanitation and security. The new boulevards sliced through the working-class slums that had been breeding grounds for the insurrection of 1848, but also involved the demolition of many houses belonging to the well-to-do. Haussmann was the model disinterested technocrat. He spent a year mapping Paris, the results of which were engraved at the scale of 1:200 and mounted on screens that stood permanently in his office, like a field marshal's campaign maps.

He provided a dazzling demonstration of how the state could harness the legal system and the private economy to remake an entire capital. His programme was financed in three tranches, the first two being borne jointly by the state and the city. But when the courage of the National Assembly finally ran out, Haussmann set up his own bank to fund the acquisition of land and the building of the new boulevards. La Caisse des Travaux de Paris raised money by selling annuities backed by the expectation of increasing city revenues, that is to say tax increment financing, very much as it is practised in the redevelopment of downtown Los Angeles in the 1990s.

Building lots acquired for Haussmann's road building projects were sold subject to stringent conditions on the form of development that could take place on them, just as they had been a hundred years earlier when Edinburgh built its new town. Very often they were reacquired by their original owners, and rebuilt using the generous compensation Haussmann had paid. His approach, within a classical architectural vocabulary, was based on a view of the city that depended on calculation rather than sentiment. He created a Paris of stone-faced buildings, six and seven floors high, where homes were piled up on top of shops, restaurants and offices. Rather than conceiving of streets as made up of isolated individual buildings, he produced an urban landscape in which streets were defined by

blocks disposed as sculptural elements and focused on landmarks and distant views. The lesson was noted enthusiastically as far away as contemporary Chicago and Buenos Aires, and it provided the model for half-baked megalomaniacs like Nicolae Ceausescu as well as more enlightened interventionists.

Haussmann's ruthless single-mindedness was to win the admiration of Le Corbusier, who copiously acknowleged the debt he owed him. Haussmann was equally a model for the French civil servants who implemented De Gaulle's infrastructure investments for Paris in the 1960s. Their work represented a bold attempt at shifting the centre of gravity first of France, and then of the whole of Europe, which foreshadowed François Mitterrand's Grands Projets of the 1980s. Not much had changed since the days of the Sun King, or for that matter, the pharaohs: Haussmann was using architecture to impress. And Mitterrand in his own way has tried to do the same. In the hands of Haussmann, Howard and Le Corbusier, development was a political issue – the purpose of building had as much to do with a vision of a certain kind of state as it did with the pragmatic concerns of civic life.

When, in an attempt to define the modern city, Le Corbusier began to formulate *La Ville Radieuse* in 1918, twenty years after Howard published his garden city blueprint, it was Haussmann who was the real influence. Le Corbusier saw the massive growth in population of the nineteenth century and the impact of the motorcar and the aeroplane as the imperatives shaping the city. His frenetic plan-making was directed towards the creation of a city that maintained its essential urban qualities while addressing the changing world. His high-rise towers floated above lush green parks like obelisks in an arcadian landscape. Le Corbusier's city plans were a riposte to the low density garden city. For better or worse, he attempted to provide a continuing sense of the kind of urbanism that Howard's low density utopianism threatened to extinguish. If it was ambiguous in its relationship to Howard, it was conspicuously at the opposite extreme to Camillo Sitte's gentle comforts in its imagery. Yet the legacy of Le Corbusier's work, which can be traced to the anonymous business districts of countless modern cities, was as far from his intentions as the results of Ruskin and Morris's love affair with the middle ages were from theirs.

Despite the monotonous regularity with which Le Corbusier has been represented as a malevolent, all-powerful force for evil by everybody from Prince Charles to Tom Wolfe, he was by no means the simple-minded megalomaniac that he is often depicted as.

'It is no longer possible, as in Haussmann's day, to throw whole districts into confusion, drive out the tenants and make a desert in the crowded

Theory and practice

heart of Paris over a space of three or even five years,' Le Corbusier cautioned in his book, *La Ville Contemporaine*, in 1922.

And it was only years of wartime destruction that finally provided an opportunity for the ideas of both Le Corbusier and Howard to be put into practice at last. After the war's end in 1945, Le Corbusier started designing high rise apartment blocks, the kernel of the *ville radieuse* idea, outside Marseilles, at Berlin, in Nantes, and at Firminy-Vert. Simultaneously, and with the prompting of Howard's supporters in the Town and Country Planning Association, the British threw a ring of new towns around London.

America also went through a bout of renewal and rebuilding. Encouraged by the Regional Planning Association and Lewis Mumford, federal funds poured into slum clearance, redevelopment authorities and urban highway building. With Robert Moses in New York setting the pace, America's big cities systematically set about demolishing the blighted, and not so blighted inner suburbs. While they were quick to clear sites, they were by no means so successful in persuading private developers to rebuild them, and in many cases existing populations were displaced with no provision made to rehouse them.

The paternalism of New Deal Liberalism had ushered in a surprisingly authoritarian planning system. The brave hopes of the federal programmes for interstate highway building and slum clearance foundered in a welter of recrimination, pork barrel politics and out and out racism. Too often, those areas demolished to qualify for Washington's subsidies were the very places that black communities concentrated. At the end of America's first infatuation with planning, four million people lived in public housing, the vast majority of them black, trapped in conditions of extreme squalor in vast projects that were often slums before they were even finished.

The reaction was not slow to materialise. Less than fifteen years after post-war reconstruction got under way, the whole premise on which modern city building was based, whether of the Howard or the Le Corbusier camp, started to be questioned in an increasingly urgent fashion. No critic of the twentieth-century city attracted more attention than Jane Jacobs. Originally a small-town journalist, she had graduated to the position of associate editor on the now defunct magazine *Architectural Forum*. Jacobs wrote *The Death and Life of Great American Cities* in 1961 when she was forty-five. It became an immediate bestseller, perhaps the first genuinely popular book on city planning since Howard's cranky-looking garden city pamphlet. Jacobs set out to slay what she saw as the double-headed demon of town planning, glibly eliding Ebenezer Howard and Le Corbusier, two vastly different and mutually antagonistic thinkers, into a single entity.

Howard believed in drastically lowering the density of the city, Le Corbusier just the reverse, yet to Jacobs they had both 'set spinning powerful city destroying ideas'.

'Town planning,' she maintained, 'starts more or less with Ebenezer Howard. He not only hated the wrongs and mistakes of the city, he thought it was an affront to nature; his prescription for saving the city was to do it in.' The garden cities were 'really very nice towns if you were docile and had no plans of your own'.

To Jacobs, planning and urban design is a pseudo science, one she compares to the habit of nineteenth-century surgeons of leaching their patients. 'If it appears that the rebuilt portions of cities and the endless new developments spreading beyond the cities are reducing city and countryside alike to a monotonous and unnourishing gruel, this is not strange. It all comes first, second, third or fourth hand from the same intellectual dish of mush: a mush in which the qualities, necessities, advantages and behaviour of great cities have been utterly confused with the qualities, necessities, advantages and behaviour of other, and more inert types of settlement,' she wrote, perhaps somewhat overestimating the power of the planner.

There was a savage reaction from Lewis Mumford, who sympathised with her view of Le Corbusier, but saw Howard as a hero. Jacobs, whatever else she believed, was clearly in favour of the high density city, which Mumford was not. But despite Mumford's stinging rebuke in the pages of *The New Yorker* in 1961, where he denounced Jacobs's 'comic school girl errors' and her 'visual philistinism' as 'home cures for cancer', Jacobs's ideas have stuck. Even a neo-Marxist such as Marshall Berman in *All That is Solid Melts into Air*, swallows her line. Her tract was one of the first attacks in the onslaught on professionals of all kinds that characterised the political climate of the late 1960s and early 1970s. Both the radicals, such as Robert Goodman in his overexcited blast against professionals as imperialists in *After the Planners*, and the ultra-conservatives, such as those who later advised the Thatcher government in Britain, poured scorn on the very idea of planning. To Marxists, planning could never be a disinterested technocratic solution since the development of the city embodied class conflicts that could only be resolved politically, while the champions of the free market distrusted the social engineering proposed by planning. Much of the popularity of Jacobs's book is in its ambiguity. It can be interpreted as supporting either left- or right-wing positions.

Jacobs was by no means the first, nor the most sophisticated critic of the conventional norms of planning wisdom. But the passion of her book, and the timing of its publication, just at the point at which the first American

Theory and practice

urban renewal schemes were starting to come unglued, gave it enormous currency. Jacobs was the prototype for every activist, advocacy planner and community architect.

She turned the conventional wisdoms of 1950s planning upside down, and produced a new set, one which is still being dusted down and rediscovered by the likes of the Prince of Wales. Jacobs objects to large scale redevelopments as being more likely to create problems than solve them. She argues instead for diversity and street life, the recurring theme of urban writing in the last two decades, and her approach, based on the close observation of her immediate surroundings, set the agenda for William H. Whyte and Oscar Newman.

Between them, Whyte and Newman were the Yin and Yang of social observation. The former looked at the positive aspects of street life – the street traders, the lunchtime picnickers, the schmoozers and the more cheerful type of bag lady – and tried to establish how the physical qualities of public places affected them. The latter wrote *Defensible Space*, which is mainly about lift lobby rapes, violent crime, and its relationship to the design of public housing.

Jacobs's *Death and Life* was written from the perspective of a middle-class activist at the end of a bruising, but successful campaign to curb the power of Robert Moses, the man who as Commissioner for Parks and holder of a fistful of obscure but powerful city and state offices, did more to reshape New York than Baron Haussmann did to Paris. Moses built bridges, roads, parks, schools and housing on a massive scale, he was behind the United Nations complex, the Lincoln Center and the Coliseum. Whole sections of the city, many containing plenty of perfectly sound dwellings, were demolished on his orders, to be replaced with the brick barracks that characterise public housing in New York, all without even the minimum of public involvement, and often without political control either.

Jacobs was an effective lobbyist and a dedicated petition raiser. By helping to mobilise the residents of a rapidly gentrifying Greenwich Village, she played her part in stopping plans for a highway across Manhattan. Yet her book is no more and no less than an examination of the minutiae of the pavement life of her corner of Hudson Street in Lower Manhattan. Jacobs's message was at heart simple. She had taken over a run-down house in West Greenwich Village, returned it to middle-class comfort with her architect husband and three children, and did not want to see a motorway driven past her front door. Clearly she enjoyed the life of Hudson Street, with its delicatessens and bars, its familiar corner grocery store with its friendly – but not too friendly – proprietor, ready to look

Caught between the skyscrapers of Midtown, and the lofts of SoHo, Hudson Street still looks outwardly much as Jane Jacobs left it in 'The Death and Life of Great American Cities'. This was the street – and the book – that launched a thousand neighbourhood activist-campaigns to stop the road builders, and keep out the developers. But the White Horse Tavern, where Jacobs claimed to find dockers mingling with literary critics has declined into a tourist trap and where the neighbourhood store once stood, smart little shops now offer gourmet delicacies while outside paraplegics beg for small change

after her front door keys but not to pry into the details of her domestic arrangements.

It was a district whose character closely paralleled London's Covent Garden in the late 1960s, when it too was threatened by major roadbuilding schemes, and Les Halles in Paris. British squeamishness stopped the demolition of Fowler's market building in Covent Garden, while French autocracy refused to bow to popular protests against the destruction of the old Les Halles. Yet both places have evolved in almost identical fashion, not because of any shared architectural ideology, but because refrigeration and giant articulated trucks put paid to the need for city centre wholesale food markets. Once they had gone, no amount of aesthetic control could recapture the authentic vitality of a lost way of life. Covent Garden's buildings remain intact, but its working-class residents have largely been dispersed, and its specialist stores and its workshops have vanished. Les Halles lost the remarkable complex of cast iron pavilions of Baltard's old market, and its streets have since been worn smooth by the shuffle of countless millions of tourist feet, while lurid fast food restaurants swarm around its underground shopping centre.

Jacobs ridiculed suburbia in the conventional manner of the metropolitan intellectual of her day, and she scorned the attempts of the planners to reconstruct the city in its image. Curiously, much of the West Village around Hudson Street, with its small scale tree-lined streets, is closer to an English suburb than it is to the kind of metropolis she praises.

In essence, her position as advanced in *Death and Life*, though she appears to change her mind in later books, notably in *Economy of Cities*, is a nostalgic one. She argues for a way of life that, if it ever existed, has disappeared. She looks back to the vitality of urban neighbourhoods that she assumes were a vital part of the city in its youth. But economically and ethnically, cities are never static; rather they are in a constant state of flux – as her very presence in Hudson Street at the start of the 1960s testifies. Beyond the nostalgia, much of her writing is concerned with the ill-concealed sense of threat she feels from the city. She sounds like a pioneer from the old West, guarding her homestead in hostile territory. Her description of what, with an uncharacteristic lapse into purple, she calls the daily ballet of the Hudson Street sidewalk, celebrates 'the allies whose eyes help us natives keep the peace of the street'. Despite her ostensible celebration of diversity and community, the underlying message is of unblinking paranoia.

Jacobs was perceptive about the impact in the inner city of gentrification. Even before the word was invented, she identified the birds of passage who would not help defend the stockade. She disapproved of them

Theory and practice

with all the strong, silent scorn of John Wayne in *Stagecoach* contemptuously dismissing a lily-livered carpet bagger.

Hudson Street in her day – as it is now – was a wide, but modestly scaled thoroughfare. It has the width of an avenue more than a street, made up mostly of three- and four-storey houses, interspersed with taller blocks of flats with 'the high rent tenants most of whom are so transient we cannot keep track of their faces'. At street level, there are bars and restaurants, stores, a butcher, a greengrocer and a barber.

The street, six lanes wide and heavy with traffic, was a busy link between the canyon of downtown skyscrapers and the then still undeveloped midtown. It was shaped by its public characters. There was Joe Cornacchia who kept the delicatessen, Mr Goldsmith at the hardware store, Mr Halpert at the laundry, Mr Lacey the locksmith, Mr Slube at the cigar store, and Mr Koochagian the tailor. 'We have a bar in our street made famous by Dylan Thomas. Morning and early afternoon it's used by the old community of Irish longshoremen. From the mid afternoon it takes on the air of a college bull session with beer combined with a literary cocktail party,' she wrote of the White Horse Tavern.

All of this vitality she saw threatened not by economic change, but by the malevolent influence of planners and politicians bent on clearing away diversity and replacing it with the suburban dream. In fact Jacobs herself opted to move out altogether, quitting New York for Toronto at the start of the 1970s. Twenty years later Hudson Street outwardly still looks much as Jacobs left it. But the wharves on the river three blocks away are derelict, and around the corner in Christopher Street, you find yourself in the heart of what is New York's most determinedly gay neighbourhood, whose members apparently did not figure in Jacobs's sidewalk ballet.

Mr Lacey the locksmith, though somewhat frail, is still hanging on at number 559 in his bleached dungarees and his white stubble, looking as if he has stepped out of Grant Wood's *American Gothic*. He inhabits a chaotic world of rusting keys, caught between decay and gentrification. The Hudson Street fruit market calls itself a gourmet delicatessen, and is run by Koreans. In the White Horse Tavern, thickset men in leather trousers nurse their glasses of Scotch. Outside, a demented and legless woman in a wheelchair begs unsuccessfully for small change. The tailor and the hardware store have long since gone, but across the street at number 634 is Myers of Keswick, an arch little place run by two smart young Englishwomen with Scottie dog brooches selling tins of baked beans, suet pudding, mushy peas and Lucozade to dispossessed Anglo-expatriates. Close by is a shop offering pet portraits, and the Gay Treasury Video – sale or rental. In Hudson Street News, run by the Patels, fat, unshaven old men leaf through rack upon rack of magazines depicting fellatio from every angle.

Set against the high rise condominium rabbit hutches east and west of Central Park, this is still an attractive area for certain types of people to live, from ethnic and sexual minorities to affluent gentrifiers. But it is hardly the urban Eden that Jacobs suggested. It offers low rent diversity, but there are costs. But Hudson Street was clearly never the soft focus idyll that Jacobs portrayed. The city is a tougher, darker reality than she ever allowed. In the apartment buildings of Hudson Street, frail and incontinent widows die alone on urine-soaked beds, left forgotten for weeks before the super calls the police to tidy them away.

Jacobs is a self-proclaimed enemy of suburbia, but the image of the big city advanced by *The Death and Life of Great American Cities* is as sentimental as the corny vision of utopia cherished by the boy scout garden city types she scorns. Oscar Newman, who pays her great regard, is not nearly so sentimental in his chilling analysis of the dangers of apartment block corridors and the darker corners of public parks.

Despite the much advertised charms of the densely built metropolis, whatever policy the planners and politicians have pursued, the inescapable background to the evolution of the city in the last twenty years has been accelerating decentralisation. The population of the central core of every major city in Europe, America and Japan has fallen while that of the constantly spreading outermost ring around them has continued to grow. The shift in population has been accompanied by the weakening of the centre, as department stores have closed, and even libraries have turned from civic buildings into circuits of anonymous sheds set on out of the way industrial parks, linked to reading rooms by shuttle buses. Dockers don't work in Manhattan anymore, let alone relax in the White Horse Tavern. They have been displaced not by the long arm of Le Corbusier, nor by the garden city propaganda of Ebenezer Howard, but by the shipping container.

Jacobs reserves special scorn for Los Angeles, a deprived city, she claims, because it has no street life and lacks a conventional urban centre: a casual inaccuracy of such a degree to suggest either breathtaking ignorance or blind prejudice. She professes surprise that its bankers don't know film people. Were they meant to bump into each other on the pavement, and thereby form life-long friendships? She seems to suggest that just such a thing is possible on the pavements of Hudson Street. Yet Los Angeles, a city hardly affected by the spirit of utopian planning, has continued to attract newcomers, providing them with jobs and homes, while New York has wasted away.

Enthusiasts for Los Angeles in the 1960s looked at the city through the knowing eyes of pop art to find intrinsic merit in the banal, making high culture out of low. Not surprisingly, Reyner Banham, the English architectural historian whose book on Los Angeles, *The Architecture of Four Ecologies* of 1967, remains one of the more illuminating studies of the city, was a member of the Independent Group, the fathers of pop art. But what Los Angeles really has to recommend it as a subject for urban study is that it forces the observer to look beyond the historic crust that monopolises attention in older cities. All big cities have suburbs like those that make up the greater part of Los Angeles. To lovers of the picturesque they have little to offer, so they pass quickly by, to return yet again to the grids and piazzas of the centre. But it is the apparently amorphous periphery of the city that testifies to the real nature of twentieth-century urbanism. And Los Angeles is almost entirely organised in this way.

Until Banham, a doctoral student of Sir Nikolaus Pevsner's and a historian of the modern movement, turned his attention to California, Los Angeles was always presented as a textbook example of what not to do urbanistically. The sprawl, the freeways and the mushrooming strip growth of boulevards seventeen miles long were regarded as planning horror stories. Banham, by clearing his mind of prejudice and looking at Los Angeles for what it was, discovered a sensuous city with a remarkable landscape and climate that offered its citizens enormous freedom. It was a city in which you could get from your ocean-front bungalow to your workplace in ten minutes, overwhelmed by the scent of citrus fruit as you drove through the orange groves with the top down. Twenty years ago it was a dream that was still within reach of the mass of the Californian working class.

Los Angeles's other leading academic enthusiasts, Robert Venturi and his wife Denise Scott Brown, went still further, swallowed hard and decided that actually even Las Vegas wasn't so bad. Los Angeles had at least got Frank Lloyd Wright, and the European émigrés to give it a respectable architectural pedigree. Las Vegas on the other hand had drive-in weddings at the Hitchin' Post chapel, and enough winking neon to scare the pants off the primmer moderns. The Venturis wrote *Learning from Las Vegas* to try and prove their point. They saw strip development, with its giant illuminated signs, forecourt car parks and artless buildings, as a vernacular, one moreover with more popular relevance than the Essex farmyard look favoured by British planners to camouflage out of town shopping centres – the difference between folk and country and western perhaps. To the Venturis, the Las Vegas vernacular is there to be quoted by the academically trained, and even translated into the basis for a literary form, while still retaining its familiarity and accessibility for a wider audience. But for all

26   *Theory and practice*

the radicalism of *Learning from Las Vegas*, Venturi and Scott Brown are full of nostalgia for redundant technology. The light bulbs of the flashing signs of the Las Vegas strip from the 1950s appeal to them, but the vacuum-formed, back-lit perspex which has replaced them – just as Burger King has taken over from the diner – does not. The Las Vegas they wanted to learn from is no more the real Las Vegas than Jane Jacobs's nostalgic view of Greenwich Village was the real New York.

'Many people like suburbia, this is the compelling reason for learning from Levittown,' they wrote in the 1973 edition of *Learning from Las Vegas*. Like Banham, they turned the attitudes of the townscape people upside down, though Colin Rowe argues they simply adopted them for their own purposes. 'We can learn from sprawl and strip as well, we must go to the suburban edges of the existing city that are symbolically rather than for-malistically attractive. The archetypal Los Angeles will be our Rome, and Las Vegas our Florence. Total design is the opposite of the incremental city that grows out of the decisions of many. Total design includes a mes-sianic role for architects.'

They claimed to be formulating an urbanistic approach that worked on the level of both high culture and low. Venturi professes to believe that a living city cannot be created by building monuments to architectural ego. Only by allowing for vitality and diversity can you create the complexity of genuine urbanity. But that vitality is disappointingly absent from the Venturis' own architectural work.

At the other extreme from the Venturis and their inclusiveness is Leon Krier, who does indeed believe that the architect has a messianic role as a total designer. Krier is one of those who see the changes that the twentieth century has brought to the city as so negative and destructive that they argue for its complete reversal. Krier is a Luxembourg-born architect now based in London who, for a while at least, had the ear of the Prince of Wales. He urges with the quasi-religious passion of a Pugin that the tech-nology we have developed to build high rise structures should be aban-doned, and that in future cities should be constructed as they were before the invention of the steel frame, the lift, and air conditioning.

Krier is the heir to a tradition of looking at cities as works of art that in its modern form can be traced back to Camillo Sitte. For him, the most damaging effect of modern development has been the way in which it has outlawed mixed uses. Cities, as he sees them, have been turned into rigid diagrams, with dormitory housing areas segregated from the work place and the civic functions of the centre. His self-appointed mission has been to break down this segregation, insisting, against opposition from all quar-ters, on the virtue of mixed uses in new developments. Yet from the planners of Chicago who see zoning as the only way to protect job-creating factories from encroaching gentrifiers, to the councillors of Dorchester who do not appreciate the idea of living next door to workshops even if they are being built by the Prince of Wales, Krier's anti-zoning crusade is by no means the simple, populist good sense he represents it to be.

Krier believes that if a sufficiently subtle set of development rules is formulated, it will again be possible to build towns with the conventional urban qualities of pre-industrial Europe that he and the Prince admire so much. To date, Krier's experiments in this direction bear a strong resemblance to Camillo Sitte. He has softened the stand he took in the 1980s of refusing to build at all, and has drawn up proposals for the Prince of Wales's land on the edge of Dorchester. But the town councillors of Dorchester have roundly condemned the Krier scheme for mixing workshops with homes (somewhat of an embarrassment, given the Prince's commitment to participatory planning), and his plans have proved too expensive even for the Prince to underwrite.

With perhaps more direct importance to day-to-day development, Krier was the mentor for Andres Duany and Elizabeth Plater-Zyberk's master plan for the holiday community of Seaside in Florida. Seaside is a testament to their belief that in the American sunbelt, the isolated urban monument is not the priority. 'This place doesn't need masterpieces, it needs fabric,' they told the English critic Jan Abrams. Like latter-day Sittes, Duany and Plater-Zyberk spent months touring the small towns of the American south looking for precedents on which to base guidelines to recreate the urban character of the pre-modern era. They developed what they hoped would be an easy to follow code on a single sheet, aimed at generating 'controlled heterogeneity'. It specifies such things as building types, and lays down maximum roof heights and minimum extents of lot frontage that must be built on in an effort to create an overall sense of coherence to the town. Despite the rapture with which it was received at the time, attracting such distinguished visitors as the Prince of Wales, and the rush of America's sheep-like developers to hire them to repeat the trick, it is pretty conventional fare in the lexicon of American zoning practice.

As it turned out, their priorities were to recreate the traditional principles of Beaux Arts composition, axes and vistas culminating in landmark public buildings, and carefully dimensioned streets and sidewalks, like Haussmann's Paris in miniature. To recreate the diversity of small towns that grew organically, they looked to use a variety of different architects to build individual structures. Seaside is minute: it is planned to have no more than a few hundred houses, a couple of hotels, shopping facilities, a confer-

Theory and practice

ence centre and recreation areas to be built over a period of ten to fifteen years. Unlike Howard's Garden City, it is purely residential, with no provision for jobs for its residents. As a summer resort, Seaside is hardly a real test of the power of Duany and Plater-Zyberk's approach, yet on this slender basis they have been declared urban geniuses, and have been deluged with work from New Jersey to California. In Los Angeles, where they are working on another masterplan for a project close to Los Angeles airport, known as Playa Vista, they face an altogether more challenging commission.

The Santa Monica-based developers Maguire Thomas have acquired nearly one thousand acres of land from the estate of Howard Hughes. Nearly five million square feet of offices, 680 000 square feet of retail space and 11 000 homes, along with a marina and a hotel are planned, to be designed in small parcels by a team of different architects. The height limit of twelve storeys already puts it way beyond the pale as far as Leon Krier is concerned. And it is hard to see how Duany and Plater-Zyberk can deal with all the parking structures and road layouts that such developments conventionally require within the constraints of their approach at Seaside.

Duany and Plater-Zyberk compare themselves with the Venturis. 'Their main street is ugly, ordinary and messy, ours is plain but dignified, and rather pretty.' But the question that really faces them is the troublesome one of just how much relevance harking back to Sitte has for the present-day urban realities of a city such as Los Angeles, with its population of more than fifteen million, projected according to some estimates to reach twenty-two million by the end of the century. What can such an approach offer Houston, a raw new city still in the grip of the booms and busts of a Victorian metropolis, where the main street is effectively Loop 610, a 44-mile-long eight-lane freeway that circles the city ten miles out from downtown? Duany and Plater-Zyberk are associated with a controversial scheme to demolish Freedman's Town and West Allen Parkway, displacing one of the city's stable black communities, which will do them no good with those who have sought to present them as heroes of community architecture.

For that matter, what relevance has the Sitte tradition in Tyson's Corner outside Washington, two decades ago nothing more than a strip off the capital beltway, now the fastest growing office focus on the eastern seaboard? Or indeed Tokyo, which is amongst the world's most dynamic cities, a place where the pressure of population density is so high that every subway passage is full to bursting with shops and restaurants, and the city's main railway station is permanently flooded with humanity?

To suppose that some sort of a picturesque dream of the city based at third hand on Camillo Sitte's explorations of Central Europe at the end of the nineteenth century is going to offer anything to such cities is pure fantasy.

The agenda for urban theory has always been set by the European experience. But it is a model which has less and less relevance even for the cities from which it was developed. In the century since the Victorians discovered the grim state of their cities, countless billions have been spent on renewal and reconstruction. But it is hard to be sanguine about the outcome. While in absolute terms deprivation in late twentieth-century industrial cities has certainly abated, there are still too many haunting images of poverty, too many homeless people sleeping in Manhattan doorways, under London bridges, in the metro subways at Tokyo's Shinjuku station, even at Chicago's O'Hare airport, for complacency. There is a dispiriting similarity between the accounts of deprivation in the Victorian city and the conditions on the contemporary housing estates built to sweep away the old slums.

The continuing shock of middle-class researchers discovering unpalatable home truths has a familiar ring, too. In her *Utopia on Trial*, published in 1984, Alice Coleman, a London University geographer and follower of Oscar Newman's *Defensible Space*, is appalled at the realisation that what she had assumed was the product of stray dogs around public housing schemes is in fact human excrement. In shock that is almost comical, she sets teams of doctoral students to work counting its incidence, and attempting to draw up guidelines for the design of improved social housing on the basis of their results. It is a measure of the desperation of the British planning system at the height of the Thatcher years that her prescriptions should have been taken seriously enough for the Department of the Environment to employ her as an advisor.

There have certainly been material gains. Unlike the slums of the 1880s, the slums of the 1980s – built in the fifties and sixties – were designed with adequate sanitation, sunlight and space, even if they may have been so poorly constructed that they are impossibly damp, and so flimsy that every domestic argument, every 3 am coughing fit, is clearly audible to four sets of neighbours. But the indignities of life on a post-war housing project infested with armed drug-dealers, ravaged by AIDS, and in the grip of real poverty, are scarcely preferable to those of the past. Indeed, so serious are the problems of the modern city, despite the massive scale of investment and renewal, that the theorists of whatever camp would do well to draw breath before offering too many fresh insights. So many strategies have been attempted, and so many found at fault, that the truth may be that the urban crisis will prove not to be susceptible to any simple physical solution.

Theory and practice

Present-day conventional wisdom has it that high density, high rise towers cause social problems, and low density bungalows with gardens and street frontages solve them. Yet in Tokyo and Paris, high density housing functions perfectly well, while in East Los Angeles there are bungalow ghettoes more dangerous than any high rise tower. Perhaps the truth is that formal issues are of only marginal relevance. The poor are poor because they have no money, not because they have poor housing.

The dark side of the nineteenth-century metropolis horrified the Victorians, but it was a world not so different from contemporary Bombay or Mexico City, with their teeming rookeries, densely packed with new arrivals from the countryside, drawn by the prospect of the better life that even the meanest city offers a landless peasant.

The city is a complex organism, never entirely comfortable, always a place with its dark corners and suffering. But it is precisely that edge of danger and instability that makes the city such an extraordinarily powerful force. In the final analysis it is in its role as an engine for change that the city is at its most alive.

The developer at work

2

When the frenzied development boom that swept across Western Europe, America and Japan in the 1980s boiled over, Canary Wharf, London's biggest building site in a century, was still a forest of tower cranes sprouting from a strip of mud half a mile long. More than two thousand construction workers swarmed over it, pouring concrete foundations for the seven separate office towers that formed the first phase of the development, fitting out a shopping centre, building a mass-transit rail station, erecting parking garages for 6500 cars, laying new roads, and planting trees in a public open space the size of Trafalgar Square.

Designed three thousand miles away in Chicago and New York at the height of the first flush of enthusiasm for post-modernism among self-consciously up-to-date developers, Canary Wharf aspires to town making in the grand manner. But as the cranes winched wafer-thin slivers of masonry and steel up into position at the rate of three floors a week, they unwittingly betrayed its apparently massive walls as no more solid than the icing on a cake.

Despite their enormous repercussions for the future shape of Europe's largest city, these prodigious efforts were triggered not by any civic master plan – London had none – but by the conviction of the Canadian developers, the $20 billion conglomerate Olympia and York, that this was a project that would turn out to be highly profitable. As Olympia and York's paternalistic owners, the three Reichman brothers, René, Paul and Albert, saw it, the figures spoke for themselves. Tokyo had 400 million square feet of offices, New York 300 million, so London, as the world's third financial centre, with only 160 million was clearly underprovided for. As long as London retained its position as Europe's financial capital, paying £190 million for Canary Wharf's seventy-one acres and risking another £2 billion on building up-to-date office space, would stand them a good chance of making money, even if the location was a long way from what was conventionally regarded as London's business centre. It was a bet that the British government could not afford to see Olympia and York lose. Despite Conservative antipathy to public spending, £900 million was hastily committed to extending the subway system into the Docklands by 1996 to ensure Canary Wharf succeeded. But a sharp downturn in the property

Pelli's atrium for the World Financial Center collects up all the social amenities of the complex – the shops, the cafés – and puts it all under one glass roof, suggesting that urbanity is an endangered species, capable of flourishing only under the watchful eye of security guards. With the exception of the palms, shipped fully grown all the way from the California desert, the mall at Canary Wharf looks just like it market turned the project into a white knuckle gamble that required the coolest of poker-playing skills. After attracting a clutch of well-known tenants, from *The Daily Telegraph* to American Express, the Reichmans were forced to tour the international banks cap in hand to raise the money they still needed to finish the complex.

While Canary Wharf was shaped by unabashed commercial opportunism, its closest contemporaries, the World Financial Center in New York, and California Plaza in Los Angeles, paid at least lip service to the strategic planning guidelines set for them by city governments. But planned or not, all these schemes served to demonstrate that it is the property developer, not the planner or the architect, who is primarily responsible for the current incarnation of the western city. Large scale speculative developments – offices, shopping centres, hotels and luxury housing – shape the fabric of the present-day city, not public housing or civic buildings. The developer, or more likely the institutions that fund his projects, pays the price for the land on which development will take place, determining far more rigidly than any zoning ordinance the range of activities that it may be used for. He chooses the architect and he sets the budget. When height, density and form is dictated, by a combination of the developer's economic strategy and zoning restrictions, architecture easily becomes little more than a cosmetic. Yet ever since Christopher Wren so conspicuously failed to understand the practical self-interest of the landowners of a burnt-out London who spurned his baroque plans to rebuild it for them, professionals have shown a marked reluctance to grasp the realities of development.

The modern practice of property development has its roots in the relationship between the builders and the big urban estates, who between them shaped the eighteenth-century British city. The builder-architects responsible for much of Georgian Bath, Edinburgh and London were certainly speculators. But venal though many undoubtedly were, on occasion, using shoddy materials and questionable methods, they nevertheless provided an unequalled model for urbanism. Their successors, nineteenth-century builders such as the Cubitts, worked hand in hand with the gentlemen landowners whose grip on London's West End is still strong. Through the Grosvenor Estate, the Duke of Westminster retains control of large parts of the most valuable areas of the capital. The estate's policy ever since the eighteenth century, when its London holdings were first laid out with streets and squares carved from agricultural land, has always been to hold on to freeholds and sell leases. Development in this sense is closer to farming than trade. It aims to produce a rent roll that provides a regular income, not to accumulate capital by selling assets. Of course, this means

The developer at work

taking a long view on the economic health of the properties and the careful management of tenants and the uses to which they put their premises. It amounts to a private system of zoning, which is not to say that the dukes have exactly been guided by a sense of *noblesse oblige* to their tenants. The estate is old enough to have seen its leases fall in more than once, and even to have reclaimed the land it sold to St George's Hospital in 1820, all of 167 years later, for the original price of £18 000, thereby depriving the National Health Service of badly needed millions. The present duke, by no means coincidentally the richest man in England, has seen fit to go to the European Court of Justice protesting, unsuccessfully as it turned out, that his human rights had been infringed by the leasehold reform acts passed by the British government.

It was only in the 1860s that the City of London Real Property Company gave birth to the idea of development in the modern sense. For the first time, buildings and land were traded as assets in their own right rather than regarded as long-term investments. In the years after 1940, property development quickly became a byword for ruthless short-term deal making, in which Britain led the world. As the Blitz came to an end, a handful of opportunists began acquiring land at knockdown prices ready for the eventual rebuilding of the City of London. In the midst of post-war shortages, and tightly enforced restrictions on building permits, their strategy was to assemble sites and secure planning permissions rather than to build. To achieve the maximum return for the minimum outlay, sites were often sold on without any construction taking place. The inflated values that this kind of horse trading put on the more desirable sites allowed developers to claim that any but the most mundane structures, and the most simple-minded letting policies were uneconomic.

When the deal makers did get as far as building, it was a hit-and-run affair. What developments looked like or how they affected the environment did not figure in their calculations. The fallout from that period still gives the very word developer a pejorative ring. The fires that destroyed many of London's historic dockland warehouses in the early 1970s, conveniently making room for more profitable new buildings, the unequal bargains some developers drove with local authorities, the aesthetically worthless rent slabs many built, and their occasionally criminal attempts to evict sitting tenants, are well publicised aspects of the post-war development boom – the urban equivalent of the destruction of the rain forests.

Twenty years later, the newly respectable property business goes out of its way to distance itself from that period. Most development companies now affect patrician surroundings for their offices, rather than keeping their records under a hotel bed as one notable sixties developer did. In

Britain, the Civic Trust, founded in 1959 to combat the worst excesses of the developers, is now sponsored by property companies and, as a result, pursues thoroughly uncontentious policies. In New York, developers fund exhibitions of avant garde architecture at the Museum of Modern Art. This, however, has not insulated them from the sudden downturn in the market which saw a wave of bankruptcies and a glut of office space in New York and London in the early 1990s that shook the banks that financed them.

The negative public perception of the developer, shaped in the 1960s by such flamboyant figures as Jack Cotton, who got within an ace of building a high rise at Piccadilly Circus and was a major investor in the daunting Pan Am building on top of New York's Grand Central Station, is not easily dispelled. The sheer size of the fortunes made during the property booms with so little apparent effort, as much as the havoc the developers caused, offended a lingering puritanical streak in the British.

But while a great deal of passion was expended on furious polemical assaults on developers, society at large came to depend on them. Pension funds in particular rely on property – so much so that even as radical a group as the British mineworkers were once the owners of the Watergate complex in Washington through the proxy of the Coal Board pension fund.

Yet this focus on property as a vehicle for institutional investment has also helped to erode the manufacturing base of those countries which show the most enthusiasm for it. It is scarcely a coincidence that Britain, which was the first country to see the emergence of international property development companies in the 1950s, has suffered the sharpest decline in its manufacturing industries as capital has been diverted into property. When returns on property development run far ahead of those from manufacturing, even such remaining industrial giants as British Aerospace devote a substantial amount of their attention to realising the potential of their property portfolio.

Paradoxically, the health of these investments depends on the long-term performance of the economy as a whole. Office and shop rents are essentially a tax on success which rises faster than the ability of tenants to pay. Soaring office rents in international financial centres have the effect of diminishing the diversity of their employment base. The City of London, for example, is now home to the restricted range of businesses, accountants, lawyers, bankers, investment companies and insurance underwriters, who alone can afford to be there. Even corporations as wealthy as British Telecom find it difficult to justify the cost of offices in the City of London, no longer a natural location for headquarters offices. Rents are amongst the highest in the world, and even when companies own their freeholds, the money to be realised by moving out is too tempting to forego.

It is a pattern which is precisely mirrored in New York. In both cities large corporations which have no overwhelming reason to stay in the centre have moved out rather than pay high taxes and rents. In America, the exodus of large corporations is not confined to the big East Coast cities, but has spread to California where companies are ready to leave the luxury of expensive premises in San Francisco and Los Angeles for inland obscurity.

Those multinational law, accountancy and financial services companies who do need city centre offices look for the same kind of space whether they are in Tokyo, New York or Bogotá. Any developer attempting to attract them as tenants must provide the same marble foyers and air conditioning. This may not produce great architecture or urbanism, but it does result in a certain professionalism, just as McDonald's, though it cannot supply a meal to remember, invests an enormous amount of effort to ensure that its food is served quickly, in spotless conditions and, above all, in identical portions throughout the world.

It is just this model of development that the Reichman brothers' Olympia and York have made their own. They arrived in Canada in the 1950s by way of Tangiers as refugees from Europe. Their assets now include oil wells, lumber forests, railways and department stores. At its peak, just before the property crash of 1990, Olympia and York owned forty million square feet of offices in North America, with ten million more under construction. The family's rise to prominence was remarkably swift. Olympia and York's first big development was First Canadian Place in Toronto, a five million square feet office tower of numbing banality built between 1970 and 1975. They used their profits to buy eight Manhattan office blocks for a bargain basement $320 million in 1977, the bleakest moment of New York's first financial crisis when the city was threatened with imminent bankruptcy. Ten years later Olympia and York valued them at $3 billion.

In its size and organisation the company has come more and more to resemble its clients, giving the Reichmans, or so they hoped, the worldwide spread of resources to ride out the busts that inevitably follow local property booms. It's a strategy that came badly unstuck in the simultaneous American and European downturns of the early 1990s.

All its developments, from Toronto to New York and London, and now in Tokyo, Moscow and San Francisco, are aimed at the same kind of occupiers. Olympia and York tenants around the world are the same – Amex, Dow Jones, Salomon Brothers, Goldman Sachs, Daiwa and Nikko. In the traditional sense of oak-lined parlours crowded with Pooterish clerks working at high desks, its buildings are hardly offices at all. They aren't even corporate Taj Mahals, the preferred headquarters of the modern tycoon, set on country estates with lavish amenities. Rather they are financial factories where workers toil in the twentieth-century version of a cotton mill. The hands may be well paid, but they are still tethered to their workplace just as much as their Victorian predecessors on the shop floor were. The average broker or financial analyst spends his working life in a tightly prescribed space, defined by the reach of a five-wheeled office chair, propelling himself from one corner to another like a hyperactive laboratory mouse. It may be carpeted and air-conditioned, but because the machines that make possible the information technology on which modern finance depends demand it, the office is as open and desolate as a string of football pitches.

Canary Wharf typifies O&Y's approach. With its eventual ten million square feet of offices – enough for 46 000 workers, and its 500 000 square feet of retail space, it is larger than the entire business district of Edinburgh or Detroit. It amounts to nothing less than the creation of a fourth office centre for London, alongside Croydon, the City and the West End. Its growth has echoes in all the major cities, as new commercial centres leapfrog old ones. In Paris, the allotments of La Défense became the city's major business district in a single generation. In New York, midtown Manhattan suddenly emerged as the city's high rent business location in the 1960s, Century City eclipsed Los Angeles's old downtown, and Shinjuku challenged Marunouchi as Tokyo's leading business district.

According to conventional wisdom, Canary Wharf was far too ambitious to have a chance of success. Even when the cranes finally arrived, after three years of complex financial and political foreplay, the recurring whisper among rival developers, who might be considered to be less than objective, was that perhaps the project might be partly built, but that it would never be finished, and would certainly be impossibly slow to let.

Canary Wharf was initially greeted with outright hostility by all but the most determined enthusiasts for Mrs Thatcher's version of the enterprise culture and her cheerleaders in the Murdoch-owned press. The economically deprived dockland boroughs surrounding the development saw nothing in it for their hard-pressed residents beyond a few low-paid, unskilled cleaning and maintenance jobs, though in fact the agreement eventually signed by Olympia and York promised two thousand jobs for local residents, and training schemes to go with them. The conservationist lobby, led as usual by the Prince of Wales, regarded the project as an unsightly blot on the skyline. 'Why', the Prince asked of Cesar Pelli, architect of

Canary Wharf's largest tower, 'does it have to be so tall?' The answer, which Pelli was too polite to give, was that Canary Wharf needed a skyscraper for the irrational, but real need to overawe the sceptics and impress the banks.

After the breathless enthusiasm for change of the 1960s, when flyovers and skyscrapers were the popular symbols of progress, the scepticism surrounding development of any kind in the early part of the 1980s was hardly surprising. But the reaction to Canary Wharf was more than simple disenchantment with the results of development. Rather it showed how well the wider public understood that the line dividing sober, calculating developers from loud-mouthed fantasists pursuing impossible dreams with nothing more substantial than a colourful brochure and a site option, is a very narrow one. Donald Trump was just such a fantasist who briefly turned out to be able to work the requisite sleight of hand that turns an idea into a profitable building. But most would-be developers are even less successful. The option to redevelop Jesse Hartley's magnificent Albert Dock in Liverpool, Britain's largest group of grade one listed buildings, for example, was held for several years by Gerald Zisman, a man who conducted his business affairs from the kitchen table of his mother's suburban home. He claimed that his restoration scheme could only be viable if he were allowed to drain the water from the dock basin and fill it with concrete. According to Zisman, Liverpool's chronic unemployment problems made any attempt to prevent him from having his way the height of elitist irresponsibility. It was an argument that continually recurs around the world, including (as we shall see) in Donald Trump's corner of Manhattan, and one that Liverpool, to its credit, ignored.

For all the scepticism, Canary Wharf duly did get under way. There was no need to wait until the completion of its monolithic eight hundred feet-high skyscraper centrepiece to see what it was going to be like. No need to peer at the developer's model, the size of an adventure playground, while Canary Wharf's cultural figleaf, Sir Roy Strong, former director of the Victoria and Albert Museum, fussed over the finer points of the purpose-made street furniture and the full-grown plane trees imported from Belgium to line its boulevards. For on the other side of the Atlantic, in an eloquent demonstration of the international nature of the development business, New York already had its own Canary Wharf.

Also built by Olympia and York, and also making extensive use of Cesar Pelli, the World Financial Center is at the tip of Manhattan Island and forms the commercial core of Battery Park City. Completed in 1988, thirty years after Governor Nelson Rockefeller first floated the idea of building a huge office development there, the eight million square feet development

New York had its own Canary Wharf before work was finished on the London version and it came from the same team. Pelli designed the stubby towers of the World Financial Center with geometric tops for easy recognition, and Olympia and York had the muscle to build it. As in London, this was a case of the authorities abdicating responsibility for city building to the private developer

is made up of exactly the same kind of space as Canary Wharf – office buildings filled mainly by men in shirt sleeves working at computer terminals. The major buildings in both schemes are interchangeable to a dismaying extent: both have pyramidal silhouettes, designed to play off the domes and ziggurats on top of the attendant towers as well as to offer obvious landmarks for disorientated visitors. But even the suave facades fail to hide the brute size of the complex.

Neither of these places has much in common with the conventional image of a diverse and sociable city. The bankers, lawyers and accountants who make up the majority of the workforce of the four stolid office towers at the World Financial Center vanish soon after 6pm, despite its gestures towards urbanism. The winter garden contained in a soaring glass vault that hosts symphony concerts and squash matches, is there to entice the public, and its spending power, inside during the lunch hour only. The cafés, decorated in bright pastel colours, spill out onto its marble floors, and two tiers of smart little shops that feel like an up-market out-of-town mall, are empty during the rest of the day.

Yet the World Financial Center is born of an era which is not entirely without insight into the subtleties of urbanism. The winter garden opens onto a riverside plaza looking out over the Hudson towards New Jersey and the Statue of Liberty. You can walk along an iron fence into which has been cast, letter by letter, a line from Walt Whitman: 'City of the Sea, city of wharves and stores, city of tall facades, of marble and iron, proud and passionate city, mettlesome and extravagant city,' it declaims. And then another from Frank O'Hara: 'One need never leave the confines of New York to get all the greenery one wishes. I can't even enjoy a blade of grass unless I know there is a subway handy, or a radio store, or some other sign that people do not totally regret life.' Clearly there are some here who do not simply see the city as an awkward and anarchic inconvenience, best replaced by tidy well-regimented order. It is the gap between that perception and the mundane reality which makes the development so poignant. Architecturally it is disappointingly crude. From the outside, the winter garden resembles nothing so much as one of the pieces of engineering equipment that litter the banks of the Hudson, ventilating the tunnels to New Jersey. It is the only obvious fragment of urbanity associated with the centre, preserved under glass and protected by watchful security guards, like an endangered species sheltered in a more than usually enlightened zoo.

Canary Wharf will have something very similar, a long, vaulted mall enclosing a food court designed by Sir Terence Conran to seat six hundred people, offering a dozen different cuisines. No doubt it too will have palms as splendid as the World Financial Center's sixteen full-grown Washingtonia Robusta, transplanted all the way from the California desert. But though it is substantially larger and more ambitious, there is no sign that Canary Wharf will have any more to offer in terms of urbanism. Indeed, the World Financial complex includes apartment buildings, consciously patterned on the pre-war New York model, and profits from the development have financed the construction of affordable housing elsewhere in the city, while Canary Wharf supports no housing at all.

Olympia and York salvaged Canary Wharf from the failing grip of one of the property industry's more flamboyant fantasists in the summer of 1987. G. Ware Travelstead, an otherwise obscure property consultant to Credit Suisse/First Bank of Boston, with a disconcerting taste for gold jewellery, was a man with more vision than experience, and with more of either than access to the lines of credit that alone could realise his dreams. But in the absence of any strategic planning authority for London as a whole, Travelstead must take the credit for the British capital's biggest lurch to the east since the building of the docks in the nineteenth century.

Property development is a curiously anachronistic industry. In an era of corporate giganticism, when a massive investment is needed to break into any manufacturing market from dog food to portable computers, property speculation is one of the last businesses that allows an individual with no resources beyond a sense of his own worth to amass huge wealth in a very short period, and then to lose it equally quickly. It is an edgy, maverick undertaking, requiring successful practitioners to make the difficult adjustment from street corner huckster to pin-striped corporate responsibility. The naked realities of guile, bravado, aggression and ego, tactfully concealed in more mature, not to say anaemic businesses, are still disconcertingly close to the surface in property. It is not only the confidence men of the property business who have perfected the technique of adopting a convincingly serious tone when announcing that things which they know perfectly well to be impossible are, in fact, entirely practicable. In the early stages of the creation of a property empire, bluff, hyperbole and vainglorious publicity seeking are as much a part of the developer's repertoire as financial skill.

The derelict Thameside wharfs were seen as a lost cause. Before it was abolished by the Conservative administration of Mrs Thatcher, the Greater London Council went as far as debating turfing over the whole area to create a giant park. In an attempt to salvage the situation, the government suspended the planning responsibilities of the local authorities and handed the area over to its own appointees at the London Docklands Development Corporation. With massive grants, and a bit of luck, the

The developer at work

government hoped that the LDDC might succeed in turning Docklands into a location for low rise business parks and industrial sheds. Indeed, that is exactly how the first steps in the Canary Wharf development were taken. In February 1985 Dr Michael von Clemm, chairman of Credit Suisse/First Boston toured Docklands looking for a site for a five thousand square feet warehouse for a restaurant business in which he was a shareholder. Walking along the derelict berths of Canary Wharf, he was hit by a sudden flash of opportunistic intuition. This was a place in which to build his own bank's back offices. Clemm talked to Travelstead about the possibility, who in turn transformed the back office idea into a full-blown financial centre. Nobody had foreseen that Travelstead could seize on the enterprise zone incentives for Docklands – the tax advantages and lack of planning restrictions – as a chance to build a massive high rise office complex. What he was proposing was on the face of it impossible, but then if he admitted that to himself, he was admitting that he was going to remain an obscure property consultant in Manhattan for the rest of his days. If only he could project enough confidence to make everybody else, and especially the banks and investment funds, believe in his project then Travelstead could become rich.

He came back to London six months later, carrying a set of plans drawn up for a contingency fee by a clutch of American architects keen to break into a city that was fast becoming the world's construction honeypot. With nothing to lose there was no point in being modest about things. New York architects Kohn Pedersen Fox drew up an arresting perspective showing what would have been, until they were pre-empted by Frankfurt, the tallest building in Europe, more than half as tall again as the National Westminster Bank tower, slap in the middle of the site. Scribbling away on yellow detailing paper in his studio on West 57th Street, KPF's design partner Arthur May persuaded himself that the paperback he kept near his drawing board on the churches of Hawksmoor was sufficient reference material for him to produce a development that lived up to London's traditions. For reasons that remain obscure, he gave the tallest of his three towers a top that could easily have been designed by Frank Lloyd Wright in his Midway Gardens period.

I.M. Pei and Skidmore, Owings and Merrill's Chicago office lent their names to the master plan for the project, and in the process gave it a much needed whiff of credibility. The boy scouts running the London Docklands Development Corporation were beside themselves with delight. Of course it wasn't possible, people just didn't build this kind of thing in London. But, just supposing, what if they did? Here at last was a chance, as Reg Ward, the LDDC's ambitious chief executive at the time saw it, to break out of the toy town of crinkly tin sheds that were mushrooming in the Docklands enterprise zone, a chance to see the slice of real city planners long to build, but which they can never achieve.

Just as work was about to start on building a range of modest, but securely funded projects on the site, the LDDC went back on the agreements it had already concluded. There was of course not a shred of evidence that major financial companies would actually want to move to Docklands on the scale Travelstead's plans suggested. Still less was there the transport infrastructure to get the expected 46 000 office workers to and from their desks every day. But by sheer persistence Travelstead made influential people take him seriously. He got to talk to government ministers. He had an elegant company logotype drawn up, sponsored a show at the Royal Academy and staged a ground-breaking ceremony that was elaborate but, with no chance of an immediate start to construction, purely symbolic. And suddenly Limehouse Studios, the first successful new employer in the area, whose converted banana warehouse inconveniently happened to stand in the middle of the lift lobby of Travelstead's biggest skyscraper, found its days were numbered. In the event Travelstead couldn't come up with the money, despite being given extension after extension to find time to do so. But by this time the development corporation's prestige was at stake too, and its chairman, Sir Christopher Benson, also the chairman of MEPC – one of Britain's most prosperous developers – took it upon himself to find someone who could handle the project. He talked to the Reichmans, and persuaded them to take over. And with their resources and reputation, Travelstead's fantasies could finally become realities. Flawed though it was, the shape of the scheme is fundamentally as Travelstead planned it.

So it is that the shape of great cities is determined in the closing stages of the twentieth century. The developer is the prime mover, and yet he can only operate within the tight constraints of the economic system. Developers have the last word in shaping the city, but their room for manoeuvre is severely limited by what the market will bear. They have to work with the current, rather than struggle against it. They are subject to all kinds of pressures, from the changing whims of the banks, to the planners and the activists who try to frame legislative means of forcing developers to take the wider urban picture into account.

But building a slice of authentic city is a task that is beyond the old-fashioned developer, typically an estate agent turned tycoon, given to prowling the city in his limousine looking for likely prospects, and with few resources beyond a telephone. Traditionally the developer has no interest in the city or the public realm; he concentrates instead on creating manageable chunks of development – an office building, or a shopping centre, or an industrial park. Land tenure tends to encourage sterility too. If you want to build offices with shops at ground level, or to mix flats and offices, the funding institutions will be unenthusiastic, as mixed use is very hard to finance because of legal technicalities. Retail leases are traditionally much longer than office tenancies, thus a floor of shops on the ground floor of an office block can substantially reduce the resale value of a development.

In its newest incarnation, property development is characterised by what might be called internationalisation and corporatisation. As Olympia and York demonstrate, not only do the biggest developments around the world take on an ever more similar shape, the money that builds them comes from the same places too. The finance for office towers and business parks comes increasingly from Japan, which seeks a home for its financial surpluses; some comes from the pension funds of Sweden, anxious about being shut out of the rest of Europe by the customs union of 1992; and some, rather less so now, from the Arabs. The international nature of development focuses investment on just a few cities where hot money pours in to rebuild skylines. When Norwegian tanker owners, or Asian despots syphoning money out of their national treasuries, looked for safe investments in the 1980s, they put property in New York and London high on their shopping list. And that is a view the major banks used to share. Property in London and New York looked to be a far better bet than Latin American governments. But banks are given to violent mood swings. After over-lending for property in New York and London, the banks cut back savagely at the start of the 1990s when vacancy rates climbed rapidly. Indeed, many have found themselves forced to take over projects from bankrupt developers. But the next twist of the boom/bust cycle will bring them back into the market.

Property in the major world cities has a continuing appeal to cash-rich economies with little scope to recycle funds at home. At the time of the Iraqi invasion, the Kuwaiti investment office, for example, had two million square feet under development in London on the Hay's Wharf site alone, which was just the most conspicuous part of its property portfolio in London. The hotel and office development on the St George's Hospital site at Hyde Park Corner has been owned successively by the Australian Alan Bond and the sheiks of Abu Dhabi. Hong Kong buyers are also important. The Hong Kong and Shanghai Bank fuelled the residential development market in London's Docklands with soft loans to developers. And after the impact of Arab money in the 1970s faded, Japanese funds established themselves as major property investors in the big world cities.

In New York, Mitsubishi snapped up the Rockefeller Center in 1989. In London, Kajima – a company that was building a hotel in East Berlin even before reunification - acquired the Euston Station site, the old *Financial Times* building and many others. In Los Angeles, just one of the many Japanese property companies active in the city went on a buying spree that netted a dozen of the city's most prominent landmarks in the course of a single week.

When the Bank of England cautioned British banks against lending to what it saw as an overheated property market, overseas money poured in to fill the gap – at the rate of almost £3 billion in 1989. The long-term interests of the domestic economy take second place when large quantities of liquid cash are in search of a home.

The other main characteristic of the new development business has been the way in which some developers have broadened the scope of their interests. The universal pattern for American retailing is the shopping centre, with its two or three anchor department stores at each end of a mall. Both department store and developer are well aware that it is the traffic generated by the big stores that attracts the bulk of tenants, allowing department store chains to exert highly favourable terms to move into such developments. Property companies specialising in such centres have now moved to acquire retailers in order to be able to guarantee captive anchor tenants for their centres.

The concentration of investment on the property sector has fuelled a change in the way that it operates. The different types of developer have converged. Despite the buccaneers, property companies have begun to mature into subtler businesses, while the old estates now operate more like developers. The Grosvenor Estate, for example, builds speculative shopping centres and business parks in Canada, America and Australia, while Olympia and York, Land Securities and others attempt to take a longer view on their properties. Olympia and York has deliberately set out to build on a larger and larger scale. In doing so it has become a model for the future direction of such companies. The experience of failed shopping centres, badly managed business parks and unsuitable office building developed by others has encouraged O&Y to act like a hybrid of an old-fashioned landed estate and a civic planning authority, albeit one geared up to maximising financial returns. To succeed it must involve itself more and more in issues such as transport planning, and long-term economic forecasting. It has had to co-opt the kind of people who would once have worked in public city planning offices. Ron Soskolne, former city planner for Toronto, for example, was recruited as development director after he encountered the Reichmans when they put forward their plans for First

The developer at work

Canadian Place. And Meyer Frucher, chairman of the Battery Park City Authority when the Reichmans acquired the land for the World Financial Center, is another employee.

While London has a reputation as a city with a strong conservation movement and a highly interventionist planning system, O&Y's big New York development at Battery Park had a much more thorough and well worked-out planning strategy behind it than Canary Wharf. A development brief had been drawn up by Cooper Eckstut, architectural consultants working for the Battery Park City Authority, set up by the city through the Port Authority to direct the project. They stipulated the inclusion of housing and retail space in the scheme, as well as offices, and went as far as specifying the type of buildings that were to be included, their density and mix. They even attempted to insist that development should take place in small parcels using different architects to introduce an element of diversity.

By the time New York tried to interest commercial developers in the project, they were faced with a seller's market. One local politician called Battery Park's landfill site the Sahara off Lower Manhattan. And in 1979 the Battery Park City Authority faced the prospect of defaulting on $200 million worth of bonds it had issued to fund the scheme. When Olympia and York promised to assume immediate responsibility for the debt repayments if they got a free hand on the project, the authority was only too happy to cave in and accept their terms.

The fine print of Cooper Eckstut's plans went by the board. Olympia and York insisted on building fewer, and larger buildings than the master plan indicated so that they could accommodate 40 000 square feet dealing rooms for prospective tenants such as American Express and Dow Jones. Nor did O&Y accept the stipulation insisted on by the masterplan, that development should be carried out in small parcels by different companies. They argued that unless they were allowed to take on the whole project, their entire investment would be at risk. Otherwise how could they be sure that their buildings would not remain marooned in the midst of the Sahara below Wall Street?

After an architectural competition, O&Y selected Cesar Pelli as the designer for the project. Pelli's appointment in 1978 marked a landmark of another kind. He was one of the first academically respectable architects to work for a major developer since Gropius's disastrous involvement with the Pan Am tower, and I.M. Pei's years as house architect for William Zeckendorf. Until then, most developers' work in America, as in Britain, was carried out by cynical plan factories. Pelli was something else: a well thought of architectural educator, who maintained a small office, relying on an associated firm to churn out the detailed drawings. It is a division of responsibilities that has appealed to Olympia and York and many other developers.

With Pelli's help, Olympia and York have tried to develop on an urban scale, to densities that have the scale and variety of city blocks rather than suburban business parks. World Financial Center is a knowing pastiche of the Art Deco skyscrapers of the 1930s, but unlike the Rockefeller Center with which O&Y's publicists make continual comparisons, it is not an organic part of the rest of the city around it. An eight-lane highway cuts it off from the streets to the east, forcing pedestrians up off the ground and into a network of bridges and enclosed malls. It was an attempt at post-Jane Jacobs city planning, launched at a time when most developers, even of the most egotistical Donald Trump variety, were prepared to pay at least lip service to the idea that variety, lively streets, and neighbourhoods were a good idea.

Trump, who was beginning to succeed in his well-orchestrated publicity campaign to become New York's highest profile developer at about the same time that Battery Park was getting under way, had plans for an even larger development on the old railway yards north of the Lincoln Center. Bread, not a commodity that Trump is in the habit of slipping out to buy too often, would apparently be a staple of the huge supermarkets he wanted to build in front of the apartment towers that formed the bulk of the development. With a straight face he suggested in his autobiography, *The Art of the Deal,* that 'it is easier to buy a pair of gloves than a loaf of bread' on the Upper West Side. He claimed that he would be able to remedy this shortcoming by building a row of six monstrous high rises, flanking the tallest structure in the world, a vacuous doodle produced by Helmut Jahn.

Trump had high rise, fortified towers behind a stockade looming over the neighbourhood in mind, and with the easy populist confidence of his sort, he could breezily tell himself that what was good for Donald J. Trump was good for the city: 'I believed tall buildings would make the project more majestic and alluring. I also envisioned a huge retail shopping promenade along the riverfront in front of the buildings.'

With uncharacteristic modesty, Trump did not immediately name the scheme after himself but, with an eye on potential tenants, was pleased to call it Television City. It was a diagram that had the psychotic, parade ground-neat logic of Milo Minderbender's *Catch 22.*

As if to prove that there is nothing to choose between one developer and another, Alex Cooper, who as a partner with Stanton Eckstut had helped draw up the supposedly enlightened development strategy for Battery Park, was hired by Trump to take over the master plan for Television City

The developer at work

from Richard Meier and Helmut Jahn.

Developers make their living out of change, by deducing ahead of time which cities and which city areas are going to present them with opportunities. They attempt to predict changes in the character of cities, and by doing so they accentuate what they have detected. So, for example, the shift from light industrial manufacturing space to residential loft use in Lower Manhattan was seized on by developers as a business opportunity, and the flight from the area of the old sweat shops that had provided a pool of unskilled jobs accelerated. Like sheep, developers follow each other in the pursuit of faddish enthusiasms that often end in disaster. Seeing the early profits made by some developers in building homes in London's Docklands, so many attempted to follow them that the whole area is now glutted with luxury apartments, so much so that some of them are being converted into offices of which there is now also a glut. Similarly, in the United States, the Rouse Corporation's success in recycling old industrial buildings for specialist retail use attracted far more imitators all around the world than the market could stand.

Developers like to present themselves as tooth and claw, red-blooded capitalists, giving the market what it wants and living on their wits. In fact throughout the Western world developers rely on public subsidy to make their activities profitable.

Behind Donald Trump's schemes for Television City was a bid to persuade New York City to underwrite the project with massive tax subsidies. Trump seized on the fact that the NBC TV network was talking about leaving New York in the same year that Mobil and J.C. Penney had both moved out of the city. He offered NBC two million square feet of space in the project at a discounted rate. And he asked New York City for a twenty year tax holiday on the entire project to pay for it. Since his earlier real estate projects in New York had been heavily underwritten by the public purse, he had no reason to believe that he would be anything other than successful in his demand for subsidies. The Trump Tower condominium complex depended on air rights transfers, and Grand Central Hotel enjoyed massive tax subsidies too. For the Big Apple, the spectre of large companies leaving is the worst anxiety – a blow as much to civic ego as a threat to the city's employment base. How could anybody not want to stay?

In the event, Mayor Koch said no and the site remained empty into the Dinkins era. While Olympia and York may appear to represent the opposite development pole to Trump, they too have based their business in London on public subsidies. The enterprise zone of Canary Wharf enjoyed one hundred per cent capital write offs on any building started before 1992, as well as a property tax holiday until that date. Subsidies of

this kind ostensibly provided to combat decay and dereliction have been attacked from both ends of the political spectrum for exacerbating the problems that they claim to attempt to solve. In Chicago, for example, so desperate was the city to keep Sears Roebuck that it went into a bidding war of subsidies with the State of Illinois when the company announced its intention of quitting its skyscraper in The Loop, the tallest in the world, for a suburb sixty miles away. In the event, the leafy suburb chipped in $250 million to persuade Sears to move into its neighbourhood: good for business but, since such tax privileges were designed to encourage employers to move to disadvantaged areas, not prosperous suburbs, hardly an appropriate use of public money.

Sharon Zukin's book *Loft Living* presents a carefully constructed argument to suggest that the subsidies provided over more than twenty years to maintain the historic fabric of the old cast-iron industrial buildings in New York have had the effect of driving out productive industry, and only help developers providing luxury housing make larger profits. The defunct GLC put forward a similar critique of the massive investment by the British government in the London Docklands Development Corporation. Public infrastructure investments did little more than provide windfall profits for developers, they argued. Tax avoidance schemes such as those proposed for Trump's TV City project penalise those who do pay city property taxes, while at the same time cutting the city's income, thereby reducing still further its ability to provide the services on which its lower income residents depend, and at a time when the new developments place an even heavier demand, a particularly vicious spiral of decline.

Modern developers profess to deplore municipal interference in their activities, and Olympia and York is no exception. Indeed, the company's first attempt to build up a presence in the British property market came to an abrupt end in the early 1980s when the Reichman brothers sold their British subsidiary, claiming that it was no longer possible to do business in what they called the restrictive planning climate in Britain. Interestingly, it was to Sir Christopher Benson's MEPC that they sold their stake, and only two years later Benson, in his other role as chairman of the London Docklands Development Corporation, played an important behind-the-scenes role in persuading the Reichmans to take on the Canary Wharf project. When the Reichmans were firmly established at Canary Wharf, they changed tack, with a lobbying campaign, both public and private, for more not less government intervention in the area. They pressured Whitehall to provide £900 million extra funding for the road and rail links without which the project is not viable.

London's Canary Wharf typifies more or less *laissez-faire*, developer-led planning. It's the nearest thing in Britain to an edge city on the North American model, but for once located within an existing city. With London's chronic lack of strategic planning, it is the developers who are in the driving seat, a state of affairs that is the product of unparalleled disillusion with the effects of post-war planning, coupled with a Thatcherite distaste for interventionism in all forms.

But *laissez-faire* planning has had such manifest drawbacks that even development specialists have begun to call for some form of strategic planning authority. The way in which Canary Wharf's unpredicted leap from business park to financial centre made the Docklands Light Railway system obsolete before it was even opened has left considerable scars, and is in stark contrast to the way in which La Défense, Paris's business district, was developed on top of a major subway station, providing a properly financed high-speed link to the city centre long before the development was complete.

The same crude mistakes can be seen everywhere in the *laissez-faire* system of America, where there is no reason to suppose that you can get from one side of a freeway cloverleaf to the other without detours many miles out of your way. These are hardly sophisticated urbanistic issues, they are not the missing alchemical ingredients to rediscover the lost formula for building Florence; they are simply pragmatic expediency, and yet they seem to require a degree of coordination that is beyond the capacity of even the most sophisticated developers.

The truth is that while it is commercial development which shapes the city, it is in the hands of those who have no interest in using their powers for the long-term future. The commercial developers are in business to respond to opportunities. They are not interested in, or equipped for planning cities. Yet that is just what they are doing by default.

Messenger boys
of change

3

Rising above the sea of autoroutes, red and white electricity pylons and anonymous crinkly tin sheds that aimlessly laps against the farther shores of Parisian suburbia, a twice life-size version of the Coliseum bursts through the blue gasoline haze over Marne-la-Vallée. It has the jarring but unforgettable impact of the floodlit revolving lobster equipped with six guns you can see on the road into Houston from the airport.

But this is not an advertising sign for a Tex-Mex seafood restaurant. It's the grandiloquent Palacio d'Abraxas, the most exhibitionist piece of domestic architecture that Europe has seen in twenty-five years. Its architect, Ricardo Bofill, optimistically calls it an inhabited monument. In fact it is three distinct buildings, skewered on an axis that runs right through the complex. Bofill has put a ten-storey-high, crescent-shaped block at the end nearer Paris with cypress trees and grass sprouting from its roof alongside the sewer vents. From the upper floors you can see the towers of La Défense and the Eiffel Tower on the horizon. The main entrance is through a slot in the centre of an elephantine eighteen-storey, U-shaped block, that has been hollowed out to create a dark shadowy Piranesian space, crisscrossed by access bridges and staircases. Caught between the crescent and the U is a toy-like version of the Arc de Triomphe adapted into a block of flats – overlooked from all sides, its windows closed, their blinds permanently drawn.

When it was designed at the end of the 1970s the scheme seemed to be literally impossible. The taboo against such wilfully eclectic architecture was so strong that the project was widely assumed to be not only too outrageous to take seriously, but unbuildable as well.

But a decade of academic doubts, coupled with the all too obvious shortcomings of post-war reconstruction and sheer boredom with the architectural status quo, had opened up architecture to an unprecedented period of questioning and introspection. In the face of its public humiliation, the architectural profession suffered a kind of collective nervous breakdown. Everything that it had previously held to be good was suddenly seen as bad with the same apparently decisive finality that the high Victorians overturned classicism with the pointed arch. What had once been virtues – consistency, simplicity and flexibility – were suddenly vices.

The boom of the early 1980s that turned to bust, costing Houston two hundred thousand jobs, has left conspicuous architectural casualties in the city. Philip Johnson's Dutch gable skyscraper remained occupied, even if the bank that commissioned it had to be taken over to stay in business. Other equally conspicuous monuments of that era were not so fortunate, and stood empty for years before finding tenants

Bofill's building in Marne-la-Vallée is only the most extreme and conspicuous manifestation of the search for an architecture that offers a wider emotional range than the prim rationalism that was the dominant means of architectural expression for half a century. Its close contemporaries were Michael Graves's Humana Tower in Louisville, Kentucky and Philip Johnson's AT&T tower in New York, with its notorious broken pediment. Graves was able to move from academic respectability at Princeton to international celebrity status on the strength of his city hall for Portland, Oregon, a dumpy wedding cake decked with joyless plaster garlands, famous more for the hostility of the local followers of Mies van der Rohe than its intrinsic qualities. Humana, his next major project, was a much more impressive building. It's a polished marble and granite-clad tower that addresses both its site and its context. Graves designed the building to make an obvious impact on the city skyline, hence the distinctive pyramidal outline of the tower. But rather than rising sheer from the pavement, the tower is set back from a relatively low street facade to maintain the existing character of Main Street.

The language that Graves used to name the parts of his building – loggia, rotunda, aedicule – suggest a despairing, nostalgic attempt to rediscover old architectural certainties. But the reality of the building has nothing to do with the past. Graves knows how to set up powerful, rhythmic compositions in his facades using square windows punched out of stone. He knows how to handle colour and texture, and to use motifs that have a dreamlike quality. Graves's design at its best is a reinvention of the present: he constructs buildings that look modern the way that modern would look if modernism had never been thought of. Johnson, by contrast, has none of Graves's deftness. He is more interested in building didactic propositions than in the physical qualities of a building. His arcade for the AT&T is anaemic, his lift lobbies look stiff and wooden, and his wilfulness grows tiresome.

Despite the lurid headlines that Michael Graves and Philip Johnson attracted, and the obvious relish they took in the controversy their work aroused, Marne-la-Vallée represents a far sharper somersault in aesthetic values than the adoption of post-modernism as corporate America's style of choice. The public face that large companies choose to present to the world is, in the nature of things, rather less of an emotive issue than the identity of a whole town.

When the new towns were young, they captured both the professional and the popular imagination to the point that, despite their faintly collectivist ethos, even America built a few. For forty years, the new town remained the paradigm of the modernist utopia, a place in which the perceived ills of the metropolis – lack of planning, unrestrained commerce, social inequality – would be redressed by a more humane new order. Hierarchies and monuments were anathema to this view of the world. The reductive aesthetics of modernism seemed to be the only way to express its values. Received wisdom now has it that new towns are socially impoverished, and architecturally deprived. But the truth is more complex. The new town movement never really managed to decide whether it was urban or anti-urban in its ambitions, whether it was in the business of building sculptural Corbusian metropolises rising from cornfields, or pandering to the sentimentality that pushed the British new towns into an epidemic of saccharine-sweet brick and tile.

The French new towns around Paris were modelled partly on the British example, but were conceived on a much more ambitious scale. Where British new towns in general were planned for populations of tens of thousands, the French masterplans drawn up from 1965 onward were for hundreds of thousands of people. And, unlike London's essentially suburban ring of new towns, Paris intended to reduce the congestion of Haussmann's city by reproducing its own high density on its outskirts.

The result, however, has not been the extension of the boulevards, but the creation of a curious, state-sponsored version of one of the North American edge cities, the formless agglomerations of offices, shopping malls and hotels that sprawl along the Washington beltway and the New Jersey turnpike. Centralised French planning has mysteriously contrived to echo North American individualism run riot. Mirror-glass office buildings erupt from pavementless roads in Marne-la-Vallée just as they do in Tyson's Corner, and corporate jogging tracks are often the closest such places come to having a public realm. In this setting urbanism appears more as a process of crystallisation along the line of least resistance, as Victor Gruen, the father of the shopping mall once put it, than the positive act of an individual architect or planner.

This was the context for Bofill's housing schemes in three of the Parisian new towns – Marne-la-Vallée, Cergy-Pontoise and St Quentin-en-Yvellines. His projects in each town were deliberate attempts at subversion, designed to cut across masterplans as he found them. Rather than treat urbanism as the product of a pragmatic balance between road layouts, low-budget construction, and neatly zoned neighbourhoods centred on primary schools well away from factories, Bofill sacrificed everything to the pursuit of the historical resonances that twentieth-century planning – setting aside such isolated cases as Port Grimaud – all but obliterated.

Bofill sees himself treating the city as a work of art. He disposes of streets, squares, circuses and terraces as elements in an overall composition

Previous page: For
monumental classicism to
become the style of choice
for corporate ego trips was
one thing; for it to appear
in the Parisian new town of
Marne-la-Vallée in the guise
of social housing was quite
another. Ricardo Bofill's
pre-cast concrete version of
Piranesi produced dismal
spaces and awkward
interiors, but did get the
place talked about which
was the chief object of the
exercise

whose principal goal is to achieve a picturesque effect. Unblushingly, he has claimed that his work in the Parisian new towns is an attempt to build Versailles for the people: 'I believe that in the present phase of our culture, man should be at the centre of daily life. That is why housing must provide him a monumental context.'

Instead of accepting, in approved modernist fashion, the limitations of construction technique and using them to provide clues to the design of architectural facades, he has put the technical achievements of modernism to work to overturn its visual premises. Unlike the vast majority of prefabricated concrete structures which for the last sixty years have set out to show off their essentially repetitive nature, Bofill has tried to give his buildings the massive character of stone, going to considerable trouble to devise a system which camouflages its character.

Bofill's team was able to create an inventive repertoire of rusticated walls, elaborately moulded cornices and pedimented windows, ingeniously fashioned from precast concrete panels, allowing them to be built quickly and economically. The essential flimsiness of modern building materials was to an extent mitigated. Bofill managed to convey at least the impression that he was working with an architecture of depth and mass, rather than merely redecorating paper-thin facades.

Marne-la-Vallée is constructed around a tiered garden modelled on an amphitheatre which does its unsubtle best to suggest that it is an agora built for some ancient civilisation. But since this is not in fact an imperial palace, nor a venue for gladiatorial combat or even worship, but a low cost apartment building, Bofill has had an uphill struggle. The antique references are in any case unlikely to mean much to the refugees from Indochina and Francophone Africa who have made their homes here in large numbers. And even though the block is photogenic enough to have formed the backdrop for countless fashion shoots, it is approached not by some triumphal way, but through a mundane underground parking garage, its polished concrete floor painted an unappetising shade of peach.

The inner face of the crescent-shaped block is adorned with a sweep of massive columns, rising almost the full height of the building. Far larger than anything the classical world ever saw, they are rendered in mirror glass, and used alternately as entrance lobbies and to provide a stack of bay windows, piled one on top of another. Their sheer size can hardly fail to impress. But they are the skin for a warren of meanly proportioned apartments contorted to accommodate Bofill's scenographic ambitions. Privacy is poorly provided for and dark internal corridors proliferate.

When the shock value wears off and the realisation dawns that behind all the prefabricated concrete megalomania is nothing more than several hundred dispiritingly small flats, geared to the pockets of would-be home-owners of limited means, it's hard to understand how Bofill came to be asked to repeat the formula so often. Not just in France, but in America, Sweden, and even Iraq. All the money that has been lavished on cornices, pilasters and pediments would have been better spent on making the apartments a little larger, reducing their density, or producing a more agreeable plan. It is an extravagance and indulgence that might have been acceptable, if only the results had more to offer. But even in its own terms, though the streets at Marne-la-Vallée are presumptuously named after architects as distinguished as Etienne-Louis Boullée and Charlotte Perriand, Bofill's work is hardly a match for Diocletian's Palace, the Roman monument that metamorphosed into the town of Split, nor even for John Nash's Regent's Park. Indeed, if kitsch is defined as the distance between ambition and achievement, then Marne-la-Vallée is kitsch on a heroic scale.

Yet the very fact that such a development was attempted at all has enormous symbolic importance. It demonstrates as nothing else could the confused state of the architectural world at the start of the 1980s, and the complete absence of shared assumptions about what constituted appropriate architectural imagery. Above all, it shows just how desperate was the search for an architecture that could provide some sense of meaning and identity in the city. It is a theme that has for better or worse preoccupied architects in the last decade.

What is intriguing about Marne-la-Vallée is that it is not lacking the social resources that could have been expected to create the diversity and intensity of a traditional city. The French call it a technopol, and its development is part of an enormously ambitious plan to make Paris the effective capital of Europe. Under the direction of a committee set up to consider the future of the entire Parisian region, Marne-la-Vallée has been designated part of an office corridor that stretches all the way north from La Défense, by way of the new finance ministry at Bercy. Unwinding aimlessly from its narrowest point, the RER red line station at Noisy-le-Grand, fifteen miles from Place de la Nation across the flat, featureless fields east of the French capital, Marne-la-Vallée fans out eastward like the plume of fallout marking a nuclear accident to form an extruded wedge, a mile wide at its broadest point. The railway, with five stations from Noisy to Marne-la-Vallée at the end of the line, is the town's spine. Its northern edge follows the Marne, winding away to the north-east. The autoroute towards the German frontier, black with articulated lorries, carves its way through the town to the south. IBM France is here, and Europe's first Disneyland opens in 1992, two developments that neatly encompass the twin poles of late twentieth-century economic life.

The highly centralised French way of doing things has seen to it that a whole crop of research institutes, university departments and high-tech employers have been directed here. Far from being segregated from each other by zoning, there is a physical proximity between occupants that ought to, but doesn't gladden Leon Krier's heart. Renault's regional office is on top of the Carrefour hypermarket, which shares a car park with Bofill's apartments two minutes' walk away. But proximity is not enough to create the public life that architects dream of in their drawings. Office workers do not in fact wander the amphitheatre, engaged in a discourse about the meaning of life, looking like the School of Athens in the way that Bofill seems to imagine. Most of the day the place is all but empty, save for the universal symbol of low income housing, knots of abandoned supermarket trollies, signs of families struggling to and from local shops without a motorcar. True, Marne-la-Vallée does not suffer from vandalism or muggers in the way that public housing in the South Bronx or Cabrini Green or Southwark does. There are no abandoned flats yet, no packs of three-quarters wild dogs fouling the walkways. But nor does Marne-la-Vallée have the pavement cafés and philosophers of the Left Bank, the promise of which was responsible for the high density of the development in the first place. There aren't even the political posters or pissoirs of the Boulevard Saint Michel to remind the town of what it's missing.

Whether it was Bofill's intention or not, he has created the empty shell of a city rather than an authentic slice of urbanism. As such it threatens to be the worst of both worlds. It is built to densities that make life difficult – enforcing proximity with the neighbours to the point that you can smell their toothpaste in the mornings – without offering any obvious compensations.

Like advertisements, Bofill's buildings serve to draw attention to new towns competing for jobs, people and investments. They are the exact counterparts of François Mitterrand's Grands Projets in the centre of Paris.

The president's taste is for slick, sensational geometry such as Pei's pyramid for the Louvre, Spreckelsen's cube at La Défense and Perrault's upturned table for the Bibliothèque Nationale. Bofill's patrons on the other hand, of whom Mitterrand's predecessor, Valéry Giscard d'Estaing was the foremost, obviously set great store on his equally sensational skills as an ornamental pastry cook. But in their detachment from their surroundings, and their elevation of form above content, the Palacio and the Cube are one and the same.

Bofill succeeded in making Marne-la-Vallée a tourist attraction long before the Euro Disney projects were thought of. But an architectural freakshow isn't much of a basis for establishing a city in the long term.

Bofill's palaces, just like John Portman's bankrupt mirror-glass fortresses in Detroit, Atlanta, San Francisco and New York, lose their appeal as quickly as the novelty of precast baroque facades and glass wall-climber lifts begins to fade.

Once you have built something as overtly image conscious as the Palacio, you need to go on continually raising the visual stakes if you are going to avoid looking old hat. It was the urge to stay in the headlines that was behind Marne-la-Vallée commissioning Bofill's one-time collaborator Manolo Nuñez Yanowsky to design another big housing complex nearby which takes the elements of Bofill's project, and heightens them to a delirious fever pitch. Yanowsky has constructed two large discs of housing, conveying an authentic hint of the megalomania of Boullée, embellished with creepy science fiction decorative detail that seems to have been inspired by *Dune* as much as anything. Circular windows give the twin discs the look of beehives as they face each other across a courtyard and six fat white nude sculptures.

Milton Keynes, in some ways Marne-la-Vallée's English twin, takes the opposite approach. Instead of using a few show-stopping gestures to try to make something out of the unpromising sprawl of housing, shopping and factories that characterise both towns, Milton Keynes opted for consistency. It was laid out by a generation of planners who had been to California and saw Los Angeles, with its grid of freeways and boulevards, as the salvation for English parochialism. Their architectural strategy was to dignify a diffuse collection of buildings by using a common vocabulary of flat roofs and orthogonal layouts. It was an attempt to make a whole that was more than the sum of its not very promising parts. Red pillar boxes and the occasional telephone box provide the only memory of the world outside this attempt at the platonic ideal.

In fact, Milton Keynes quickly lost its nerve. Its high-mindedness petered out even before a tide of rip-roaring Thatcherism turned a new town that began as a sickly child of the welfare state into a rampaging commercial success – with its brash leisure centres, its carpet warehouses, drive-in McDonald's, and brand new thatched houses.

The unreality of Bofill's approach is glaringly apparent in his only project in central Paris, an apartment complex close to the station at Montparnasse, in the working-class fourteenth arrondissement, where large-scale redevelopment in the 1950s and 1960s had seen the destruction of a network of streets to make way for parallel slab blocks in approved Corbusian fashion.

Bofill laid out a sequence of monumental spaces. There is a circus, looking out over a traffic island that doubles as a giant water sculpture. Beyond are two partially private courtyards, one elliptical, the other a crescent that deploys pediments and giant mirror-glass columns, familiar from Marne-la-Vallée. Watching its residents opening windows in the columns, as litter blows across the lawn, is to experience a disconcerting disruption of scale. This is a doll's house inflated to monstrous proportions. Apologists cite the Woods' work in Bath as a worthy precedent, but there every house has its own front door, a fact that was clearly expressed in the facades, and which anchors the composition to a familiar scale, something that virtually all of Bofill's projects lack.

The street facade, designed by others to Bofill's layout, though suggesting the traditional city in its form, has compromised on the details. There are shops and cafés at ground level, but there are too many cracked panels and floor tiles for the place to be completely convincing. Bofill's project at Montparnasse is pitched several notches quieter than Marne-la-Vallée. The former is an attempt to recreate a slice of a monumental city within a context that contains fragments of the genuine Haussmann article. Marne-la-Vallée, on the other hand, is a full-blast bid to build a monumental landmark to give definition and focus to an apparently amorphous urban agglomeration. Bofill's greatest significance is as the architect who has pursued the nostalgia for the monumental city to its ultimately futile conclusion. And in the wake of his failure to resurrect the past, we have begun to see the first steps towards an urban architecture that accepts the contemporary city for what it is, a fractured, incoherent place.

Bofill's is just one of many architectural approaches to the impossible task of monumentalising the sprawling periphery that is now the inescapable accompaniment to every major city, and many small ones too. At Tsukuba, Tokyo's science-based new town, Arata Isozaki was commissioned to create a focus for a township that was so unpopular with the academics required to work there that many preferred the three-hour commute from central Tokyo to spending the night. Isozaki's centrepiece, which combined shops and restaurants with a hotel and theatre, grouped around a town square, was a remarkable fusion of baroque and modern motifs, including a plaza modelled on Michelangelo's Capitoline Hill in Rome overlooked by a shopping arcade complete with a branch of McDonald's, just like the Roman original. The architecture includes quotations from Loos, Ledoux, and even Isozaki's own earlier works. It is very much indebted to Colin Rowe's book, *Collage City*, in that it attempts to create an architecture of depth and complexity by collaging different architectural elements and different kinds of space.

On the edge of Toronto, the English architect Edward Jones plundered

Messenger boys of change

the imagery of the vernacular architecture of the prairies – water towers and silos – and reassembled them in monumental form to suggest a classical pedigree for his city hall for the new municipality of Missassauga. His aim was to provide an urban focus for a sprawling suburb which previously had none. He did his best to construct a civic mythology for a place that did not exist before 1972. Its founding father was the developer who decided to build a shopping centre here. Missassauga's blue-domed council chamber, decorated with a constellation of names spelling out a roll call of local settlements, uses rich timber veneers and marbles to create a sense of occasion. Jones went well beyond the merely picturesque, employing a harsh yellow industrial brick and an exposed steel frame for the clock tower, with the bleak melancholy of an Edward Hopper painting.

In a previous incarnation, Jones was part of the team that designed a competition-winning, though unbuilt design for Northampton's city hall in England, in the form of a glass pyramid. He was responsible for aligning the borough treasurer's office so that the rising sun would light up his desk on budget day each year. Missassauga represents a far subtler attempt to reclaim the flotsam and jetsam of the edge city, and co-opt it for the traditional urban hierarchy of streets and squares, than Bofill's megastructures.

Clearly it is informed by an attitude that has progressed several steps forward from the neuroses of the 1970s, demonstrated by Hillingdon's town hall, built in a low density suburb of London, a building with a similar brief to Missassauga's. There the response of the architects Robert Matthew, Johnson-Marshall was to deny the monumental aspects of local government altogether, opting to camouflage the whole complex in a skin of brick-faced pseudo-domestic architecture.

Where once architects were intimidated by the very idea of monumentalism, they now pursue it with unabashed enthusiasm. But in less sure hands the collage and the myth-making of Isozaki, Jones and others, such as James Stirling, degenerates into the facile, and the facetious.

The question remains how relevant a model is Bofill's approach for the outskirts of modern Paris, or for that matter any other sprawling metropolis? Much of the initial power and notoriety of his work at Marne-la-Vallée came precisely from the outrage that it caused. But there was also a symbolic significance to his building. Marne-la-Vallée's left-inclined administration wasn't unsympathetic to Bofill's self-appointed mission to restore classicism to the working class, to rescue it from the authoritarian connotations of Speer, and Stalin.

But underneath all the rhetoric about classicism, there are worrying signs that Bofill has simply indulged in the same sterile formalism that blighted the 1960s. He has assumed that simply by adopting a classical vocabulary he can recapture the qualities of the past. But his pedimented window mouldings look like picture frames hung onto a wall. The late Romanian dictator Ceausescu adopted the same vocabulary for the rebuilding of Bucharest.

In his enthusiasm for classicism, Bofill resembles the English architect Quinlan Terry who, after designing a series of Palladian country houses, has begun to build classicism at an urban scale too. Bofill's messianic sense of mission is close to Terry's. Both men clearly believe that they have been vouchsafed a great architectural truth, one which it is their duty to reveal to a sceptical world. But where Bofill differs from Terry is in his attempt to turn classicism into a modern form of expression. Bofill embraces contemporary materials, mass production and industrialisation with enthusiasm. Terry on the other hand makes it perfectly clear that modern architecture represents only a small part of his disenchantment with the twentieth century. To Terry, even the lift and the curtain wall are the inventions of the devil. Despite graduating from the Architectural Association in the 1960s, and having been a one-time employee of James Stirling, Terry sees himself conducting a lonely crusade against abstract art, technology, motorcars, Godless architecture, and the twentieth century in all its forms. It is a peculiarly English conceit, one that stretches from the Luddites to Ruskin and Morris. Of course the Palladianism that Terry happens to have espoused would have been anathema to the last two, but their attitudes have much in common.

Terry's most conspicuous piece of urbanism is the redevelopment of the Richmond riverfront, west of central London. After a local outcry at developers' plans to build a conventional commercial scheme, Terry was brought in to head off a costly delay on the project, giving it a new architectural form without changing its content. His strategy was to restore a number of Victorian buildings, demolishing others to make way for a large office block treated as a series of classical pavilions. They were modelled in no particular sequence on Palladio, Borromini, Chambers, Wren, the Greek Revival, and Venetian Gothic in a partially successful attempt to suggest that they had grown organically over the years. But though the development is well mannered, it leaves you emotionally unmoved. It is an elaborate blend of archaeology, stage scenery and literary parlour game. The weakness of Terry's case for claiming that the practice of the Georgian builders provides a complete model for the present day is cruelly exposed by the interiors. Terry seems to have little or no interest in creating architectural space. All his energies have been invested in the facades. Palladio, as interpreted by Terry, stops at the lobbies and foyers. The offices beyond are crude, open plan, marred by unsympathetic striplighting and, despite

Messenger boys of change

the sliding sash windows, fully air conditioned.

For all Terry's appeals to tradition, the Richmond scheme is far less 'traditional' than Sir Richard Rogers's headquarters building for Lloyd's of London, say. For while the latter is built in an apparently ruthlessly contemporary manner, with a maximum of technological imagery, and seems to represent the very antithesis of tradition, it is actually a building in which tradition is very important. It is tailor-made for the insurance brokers of London, who have worked in this part of the city for three hundred years. It's a Savile Row suit, even if the cut is eccentric. And in Rogers's view at least, the decision to festoon its plumbing on the exterior has given him the chance to model the building in a way which creates a broken up, picturesque silhouette that is less of a disruption to the twisting lanes that form the City of London's fabric than the simple-minded 1960s slabs all around. Rogers delights in comparing Lloyd's to George Edmund Street's Law Courts in the Strand, which also achieves a romantic skyline by putting its staircases on the outside of the building – though Street used Gothic turrets to hide them rather than stainless steel.

Unlike the revivalists, Rogers believes that a contemporary vocabulary of materials and forms can still be an appropriate way of building within the city. Rogers and other latter-day modernists, such as his one-time collaborators Renzo Piano and Norman Foster, view urbanism as a species of surgery. Schemes such as Rogers's National Gallery proposal for Trafalgar Square, and his Royal Academy scheme for remodelling the Thames embankment, depend on selective demolition and rebuilding to reveal connections and relationships between existing spaces and buildings, in the way that an art editor will ruthlessly crop a familiar picture to give it new life, or that I.M. Pei used the glass pyramid at the Louvre to frame historic buildings to allow them to be seen in a fresh, different way.

Rogers attempts to render new buildings transparent by putting their contents on display. In this way he hopes to bring them alive and to make them play a part in the life of the street, rather than to present a closed, anonymous exterior. Terry's project on the other hand, despite the apparently familiar qualities of its facades, is actually the product of a highly contemporary brief, to design speculative offices on an out-of-town site for an unknown tenant. Ready-to-wear, rather than made-to-measure. Architects of all kinds have struggled to find appropriate clues to design such buildings. Some, like Rogers, attempt to do it by concentrating on the structure, looking for meaning in the often over-muscular display of the means by which the building lives and breathes. Terry, equally arbitrarily, uses Palladian themes. Frank Gehry, working in the same sort of territory as Claes Oldenburg, makes his buildings look like fish.

The Richmond building has a lovingly made skin of rubbed brick, slate and stucco, but that is hardly enough to cancel out the anti-urban demands of the brief. Terry, despite sharing Leon Krier's rejection of industrial society, albeit from the perspective of a high Tory, has been asked to design a variety of highly commercial projects. Yet he professes the most radical of programmes, the elimination of industrial society itself.

It is an absurd proposition, but no more absurd than the revolutionary impulses of the early modernists, with their dreams of replacing existing cities with sunlit sixty-storey glass towers rising out of lush green parks. And, absurd or not, in time they duly came to pass.

Leon Krier, with his faltering conviction that to build anything in the present climate is to collaborate in the destruction of the most precious of man's creations, the European city, and Terry, with his radical conservatism, represent the most extreme position of those who see the traditional city as the ideal urban model. But there are many more who are prepared to attempt some kind of accommodation with present realities. Under the direction of Josef Kleihues, West Berlin's building exhibition of the 1980s was an attempt to direct the talents of a wide range of different architects, from Peter Eisenman to Aldo Rossi, to explore ways of recreating the nineteenth-century Berlin tenement block in a contemporary idiom.

With its high density layout of blocks built around courtyards, the edges of the blocks form the perimeter street fronts handling the traffic, and the inner courtyards remain the preserve of the pedestrian, shops and cafés at ground level, apartments above. Similar forms are to be found in most of the nineteeth-century developments of Europe, from Barcelona to Glasgow. Wartime destruction and post-war reconstruction represented a decisive break with the past in Berlin as everywhere else. Kleihues's intention, lavishly funded by West Berlin's government, was to repair the city's shattered fabric with new blocks that took up the old pattern. The experiment was a serious-minded, painstaking, partial success.

In America, contextualism was seized on, somewhat implausibly, by the generation of architects who have been the most active in offering their developer clients flamboyant alternatives to the discretion and reductivist aesthetics of modernism that had by the start of the 1970s become the conventional building type for large corporations. Context for them meant recycling the motifs of the skyscrapers of the 1920s and 1930s, inflated to enormous scale, while abdicating all responsibility for any wider issues.

The New York-based practice of Kohn Pedersen Fox is among the most conspicuous in its use of this approach. Design partner Bill Pedersen claims 'The idea that a building stands as an object in space has decimated almost all our American cities. Presently urban buildings as representative of the private realm are visually dominant over the spaces that represent the public realm. I consider that condition to be antiurban. The tall building must begin at its lower levels by acting as a facade that can join with the other facades to create the urban walls that define a street. Once it meets that need the tall building can rise as a free-standing object to fulfill the demands of its own programme'. These sentiments have not stopped Kohn Pedersen Fox from applying the same Art Deco-on-steroids solutions everywhere from Singapore to Chicago, and Versailles to London. It's a seductively simple, undemanding formula, one that doesn't ask that developers stop building the 75-storey behemoths that are blotting out what little sunshine New York City has left and doesn't require them to treat the content of their buildings any differently, or even spend any more money on them.

It is misleading to call their activities 'historicist'. What does it mean to call a 800 feet-high skyscraper 'neo-classical'? It is a contradiction in terms. Either you build such things or you do not; their meaning is in their bulk, not in their facades. What Kohn Pedersen Fox and scores of less accomplished imitators try to offer is the impression of building things that are not new. Perhaps this really will provide some sense of the continuity which the ever more rapid pace of change is threatening to destroy. But it does not seem likely.

Fashionable acceptance for this kind of post-modernism coincided with the building boom of the Reagan years, and had an immediate impact on the skyline of the major American cities. In the sunbelt in particular, where civic pride and economic health are still measured by the height of the buildings, towers got up in every kind of period dress from Art Deco to Gothic sprouted like weeds. In five years the stubby, gridded towers of Houston, one barely distinguishable from the next, were overtaken by a new crop of corporate ego trips, each shouting for attention.

The conventional view of the recent history of architecture is that modernism, the prevailing mode of architectural expression since the founding of the Bauhaus, which in some sense represented a radical break with the historical tradition of architecture, has been displaced by a more sympathetic view of the past. But it is already clear that post-modernism, the much heralded replacement for modernism, has shown a distinct lack of visual staying power.

Post-modernism has been subsumed into *fin de siècle* overexcitement, as fad has followed fad. Even the very recent past is now seen as material fit for recycling into some new synthesis, which then itself is discarded as old hat and overplayed for the second time in two decades.

The 1960s, for example, are seen as dreary but also as the inspiration for a group of younger architects. Simultaneously they are too modern, and too old-fashioned.

It is a pace of change that has already made us view the very recent past with fond nostalgia, which is seeing us resurrect the forms of the naive 1960s with an edge of irony. The projects of Rem Koolhaas, particularly his unsuccessful design for the masterplan of the Parisian new town of Melun-Senart, and his Hague Dutch Dance Theatre, try to learn lessons from the recent past, to create plans for buildings that would connect the central city with the looser urban structure of the edge city.

For the greater part of the 1980s, Koolhaas, and those who shared his views, were in a lonely minority. Then came the fashionable success of the American firm Arquitectonica, which produced a highly decorative version of the *sputnik moderne* of the 1960s. And at the very end of the decade, even Philip Johnson, as ever a weathercock, jettisoned his mansarded skyscrapers for the bitterly controversial redevelopment of New York's Times Square – in favour of sixties revivalism.

A younger generation, both in New York and Los Angeles, and often with the encouragement of the European academics, started looking to tougher, blunter means of architectural expression. Some were interested in the literary theories of the French structuralists, others in the enigmatic drawings of the Russian constructivists. To this group, Frank Gehry, perhaps the most considerable architectural talent to emerge from Los Angeles since Charles Eames, served as a mentor.

Gehry's early works, such as the Loyola law school, the Los Angeles aerospace museum with a jet fighter pinned like a gnat to the facade, and his own house in Santa Monica, were inventive and original. His rejection of picturesque urbanism is as decisive as Le Corbusier's diatribes against the diseased arteries of the old Paris. But instead of planning to clear everything away to start again and to impose a sense of unity, like Le Corbusier, Gehry, taking his cue from the artistic currents around him, is prepared to embrace the influences of the unformed, unself-conscious litter that constitutes the contemporary American city. Los Angeles is a city of free-floating images and superimposed views, and Gehry's work echoes that unsettled transience. Like Oldenburg, Gehry is prepared to use found objects in his work. His architecture accepts its context with its seemingly random collisions of shapes, formless disturbing silhouettes, and odd juxtapositions. The carefully considered artlessness of his work gives it its directness, as does his acceptance of the nature of the materials. He employs sheet rock, cardboard and aluminium siding as he finds them, rather than making them into something else. The biggest question facing him is whether he can maintain his creative integrity in the face of ever larger commissions. And indeed, whether projects that have a vitality and integrity as insertions in the tide of urban flotsam simply become mannered formulas when they take on more of a foreground role. Building a corporate headquarters for a smart advertising agency in Los Angeles that incorporates a five-storey-high pair of binoculars is one thing, but when Gehry's proposals for redeveloping Cleveland's downtown include a 64-storey-high skyscraper reading a copy of the *Cleveland Plain Dealer*, you start to wonder.

Gehry's acceptance of the American city is by no means uncritical, but he attempts to work with it, not against it. He knows the formless, mundane reality of the endlessly mobile city of Los Angeles, and accepts it for what it is, rather than trying to idealise or monumentalise it.

The idea that the city is a work of art is deeply ingrained in the architectural pysche of the West, but it has had little influence in Japan. Perversely enough, in view of the way in which its architects have tended towards the slavish imitation of Western ideas, it is Japan that most accurately conveys the true flavour of architecture in the closing years of the twentieth century. It is a country that sheds no crocodile tears about the demolition of the recent past. Nor does it labour under neurotic delusions about the morality of one architectural style against another. It is prepared to engage any architect of interest from outside Japan, no matter how apparently impractical his drawings may seem.

In the process, Japan has turned into a kind of laboratory of ideas, a microcosm of the increasingly global nature of architecture. There is now an international flying circus which travels the world leaving signature buildings in its wake. The major cities of the world share a need to collect them, in the same way that art galleries from Osaka to Liège need Henry Moore, David Hockney and Julian Schnabel. So Richard Meier builds essentially the same building in Frankfurt and in The Hague, and Michael Graves builds apartment towers in Yokohama and offices in Atlanta.

The frenetic pace of development through the second half of the 1980s gave London a taste of the New York way of doing things. Of course Tokyo, a city destroyed twice in the past seventy years, has a pace of change that is even more rapid. Architecture there has lost any sense of permanence, and buildings are written off in ten years or less, a pattern that is spreading. Land values have the final word in most discussions of architectural longevity.

Paradoxically, this escalating transience has been accompanied by the reopening of long abandoned stone quarries in the USA to cope with the

London's railway stations disappeared under a series of new developments to accommodate the banks liberated from the grip of the old square mile. Developers had begun to see self-interest as extending beyond the maximising of square footage, and were including fragments of urbanity. Broadgate even has a faint echo of the Rockefeller Center's ice rink

demand for the raw material for stone facades that give many of the new structures a sense of solidity.

Yet the new office, with its ever-increasing technological content, has contributed to the marginalisation of architecture. Often all that occupies the attention of the architect designing a new commercial building is the creation of the skin. The very depth of the new buildings, with floors the size of a football pitch, reduces architecture to the slender zone around the windows, and even that is often selected off the peg from a manufacturer's catalogue.

The buildings of Broadgate in London, of the World Financial Center in New York, and the office towers of Tokyo's Shinjuku district spend an ever-diminishing percentage of their gross cost on 'architecture' set against the computer-controlled air conditioning, cabling, and all the other technology now seen as an essential part of the accoutrements of a modern office building. In this context, the architect sees his role steadily reduced.

Of course no architect, despite the recurring attacks of a messianic sense of mission which the profession is given to, can transform society. Rather he is a messenger boy, carrying the news of the often unpalatable realities of the changing nature of life to people who do not want to hear it. In a very few cases, he has the ability to transform that reality into poetry.

Unwisely, architects have tried to present themselves as much more, and in the popular reaction against architecture in the 1980s, they paid the price. Critics took their messianic pronouncements at face value, and proceeded to blame architecture for everything from broken marriages to street crime.

This has been dangerous both for society and the architect. When architecture provides a convenient scapegoat, there is no need to scrutinise the mechanisms that are really behind social disintegration.

Yet simple expediency from the architectural profession will not be any improvement either. The role of the architect can still be a visionary one, offering a critical commentary on the state of society at large. But when he is too insistent, then he presents an easy target for those who believe in shooting messenger boys.

The uses of power

4

In the sweltering calm of an August morning in 1983, François Mitterrand, President of the French Republic, stepped out into the garden of the Elysée Palace. With two aides he walked down towards the Avenue Gabriel. Straining his eyes against the glare, he gazed towards the Arc de Triomphe and the office towers of La Défense in the distance. Through the haze, he could make out the outline of the tallest crane in France, driven here from Bordeaux on his orders – a week-long journey for the 263-ton exceptional load and its police escort. Teams of engineers had worked in secret all weekend to set the monster up on the six-lane motorway that loops around the pear-shaped La Défense complex, closed to traffic especially for the purpose. From its enormous boom dangled a steel-reinforced slab, sixty feet long, hoisted 370 feet up off the ground, braced by guy ropes to stop it spinning in the wind, and painted white to look like marble.

Mitterrand's purpose in this remarkable demonstration of the far-reaching powers of an imperial presidency was to weigh the consequences of building a monumental thirty-storey-high open cube, a giant high-tech riposte to the Arc de Triomphe. It would be the crowning landmark of the axis that defines the heart of Paris. From the courtyard of the Louvre, where Mitterrand had already started building his notorious glass pyramid, it runs through the Tuileries, across l'Etoile, along the Champs Elysées, and through the Arc de Triomphe. It culminates at La Défense, site of the memorial to the defiant resistance of the Parisians to the invading Prussians in 1870 and now the biggest office complex in France.

Mitterrand wanted to judge for himself the impact that the height and bulk of the arch would have on some of the most historic views of Paris. After going back later that same day to see how the curious object looked at sunset, and taking a drive along the Champs Elysées the following morning, Mitterrand made up his mind to go ahead, and six years later the arch was completed.

It is a curious episode, not the least of whose lessons is that, as far as decision making about development is concerned, Paris is still closer to Louis XIV and Napoleon III than the milk and water expediency that passes for modern planning elsewhere. Mitterrand was attempting to impose some kind of individual order on the chaotic and impersonal forces

More than anything, the arch at La Défense is a memorial to an imperial presidency, the questionable result of François Mitterrand's attempt to impose his will on the apparently chaotic forces that shape the modern city. Mitterrand selected the design, went to enormous lengths to judge the impact of the arch on the Paris skyline for himself, and saw that it was built. Its actual purpose was a secondary issue. What had been touted as a Beaubourg of the media, a focus for international communciations, ended up as an eccentrically-shaped office block, with a vertiginous lift dangling beneath the arch that shape the modern city. Sitting at the head of a double file of crude mirror-glass towers, the arch, designed by the Danish architect Otto von Spreckelsen, has the authentic smack of the empty monumentalism of despotism. Perhaps that's not so surprising, given that Mitterrand spent a great deal less time worrying about what his monument was for than how it should look. Entrants in the architectural competition staged to select the design were asked only to accommodate a highly nebulous Beaubourg for communications, outlined in the vaguest terms. But even under Mitterrand, the French treasury could not come up with all the cash needed for such an obvious indulgence. Once construction was under way the project was commercialised, and most of its floors modified to form offices. The British publisher Robert Maxwell, eager to ingratiate himself with the French president, bought a slice, and the rest was allocated to ministerial departments.

It was not simply the height and form of a single building, albeit a particularly conspicuous one, that was determined for Paris in this dictatorial fashion. Mitterrand's no less imperial predecessors at the Elysée, from General de Gaulle to Giscard d'Estaing, between them created the La Défense complex, with its potential for up to twenty-five million square feet of office space, by decree, and administered it like some particularly well favoured colonial possession. More than four hundred derelict acres were designated for office use in a conscious attempt to build a European Manhattan, in many ways the forerunner of the World Financial Center in New York, or Canary Wharf in London. And the not inconsiderable powers of the French state were mobilised to ensure that the plan duly came to pass. In 1958 the Etablissement Public d'Aménagement de La Défense, or EPAD as the French with their fondness for acronyms christened the undertaking, was inaugurated to build the project. EPAD was, and is, a government corporation controlled by the presidency. Just as in the days of the Second Empire, when the Parisian city council was appointed directly and not, as Haussmann put it, 'subject to the accident of the vote', so the French capital was still being shaped by a body that had neither shareholders nor direct public accountability.

While EPAD was responsible for planning the form of La Défense, a central government department, the Délégation à l'Aménagement du Territoire et à l'Action Régionale – DATAR – used its draconian powers to coerce tenants into the La Défense compound. For those who complied, DATAR held out a wide range of financial inducements. Those that didn't were denied office permits to move elsewhere in Paris.

Through good times and bad, and through every change of political administration, the French government maintained its enthusiasm for La

The uses of power

Défense. At the depths of the property slump of the 1970s when, with one million square feet of offices empty for five years and accumulated debts of seven hundred million francs, the whole enterprise faced bankruptcy, Mitterrand's predecessor Valéry Giscard d'Estaing ordered compliant state-owned savings banks to shore up the failing project. Even after the private developer Christian Pellerin took a fifty per cent stake, the state continued to nurture La Défense.

How it looked was at every stage a crucial issue for the French government. The politicians endlessly asked architects and designers to tinker with the masterplan, moving from formal symmetry to Alphaville mirror glass. I.M. Pei came and went, producing a bizarre design for a building that looked like a giant tuning fork on what was to become the site of Mitterrand's arch. At EPAD's offices there is a whole storeroom crammed with plaster models of ill-fated attempts to design La Défense. Should the axis finally be closed by a landmark? Or left open with some sort of window on the world? Nothing, it seemed, appealed to French cabinet ministers more than the chance to pore over one proposal after another, rendered at the scale of toys.

The rebuilding of the old Parisian food market at Les Halles was another product of an imperial presidency. In 1959 De Gaulle made up his mind to close Les Halles and move the market out of the city. He planned to flatten not just Baltard's iron and glass pavilions but a large part of the surrounding city as well. Though the size of the project was subsequently scaled back, Les Halles was duly demolished and replaced by a troglodytic warren of shops.

In 1977, when Paris finally elected Jacques Chirac as its mayor after more than a century without one, he took just as egocentric a role in the detailed planning of Les Halles as De Gaulle, Giscard d'Estaing and Mitterrand had before him. 'L'architect en chef à Les Halles, c'est moi,' he exclaimed, using the fifty-one per cent stake in the project owned by the City of Paris to dismiss Ricardo Bofill, commissioned to design the complex by Chirac's political rival Giscard d'Estaing. Bofill's quasi-classical development was already under way, but it carried the wrong message for Chirac, and had to go. Bofill's part-built arcades were demolished, and Chirac oversaw the establishment of what he called a French garden in their place.

Nothing, however, was to prepare Paris for the scale of what was to come when Mitterrand took over the presidency. After a brief pause for reflection, he adopted a few of the projects started by Giscard d'Estaing – the building of a new finance ministry, the conversion of the Orsay station into a museum, and the transformation of the never-completed abattoir at La Villette into a science museum – and added a whole stream of his own

ideas. He moved the planned Arab Institute to a site on the Seine, hired I.M. Pei for the Louvre pyramid, commissioned the arch at La Défense, set about building a music conservatoire and park at La Villette, as well as a new opera house at La Bastille, and presented them all as a single package, the Grands Projets, to be completed in time for the celebrations marking the bicentennial of the French revolution in 1989.

The Grands Projets add up to a highly self-conscious attempt to remodel the fundamental character of Paris, a mixture of hubris and cultural ambition that could only be French. 'Visitors will come to see the Paris of architecture, the Paris of sculpture, the Paris of museums, the Paris of gardens, a city open to imagination, ideas and youth,' enthused Mitterrand in his foreword to the official guide to the projects, *Architectures Capitales*. 'Disturbed, and often devastated by industrial change, economic crises, demographics and immigration, the city must rediscover its unity, the centre must be put in touch with the periphery, and the marginal neighbourhoods. The science city, the Villette park, the music city will eliminate the barriers between the centre and Seine St Denis. The La Défense arch will become a common meeting point not just for the citizens of Paris, but also of Courbevoie, Puteaux, Nanterre, and even Saint Germain-en-Laye.

'This new generation of institutions must address a wider public, and offer them access to the diversities of culture left us by generations of architects, artists, craftsmen and scientists. Only in this way can we all grasp the continuous movement of invention and thought and be prepared for technological, cultural and social change.'

Yet the quality of the new Parisian developments hardly lives up to the portentousness with which Mitterrand approached them. While Napoleon III created an aesthetically unified city characterised by the architectural restraint that made sceptical contemporaries call Haussmann the Attila of the straight line, Paris in the 1980s became a city of slick, vapid monuments. The banality of the arch at La Défense is echoed by the daunting new finance ministry at Bercy which presumes to step into the Seine and the paunchy Bastille opera house crammed inelegantly onto a site manifestly too small for it.

Nevertheless, all these projects add up to an extraordinary demonstration of the direct control that the state, in the person of a single individual, can have on the shape of a modern city. Not even the Prince of Wales, with his well-publicised fondness for meddling in questions of architectural taste, nor Ed Koch, who did his best to leave Manhattan with the tallest building in the world as a memento of his final term of office as mayor of New York, presumed so much. But the example of Paris certainly inspired other European cities to try to follow suit with ambitious building pro-

The uses of power

grammes of their own: Barcelona in the run up to the Olympics of 1992; Seville preparing for the international exposition in the same year; Frankfurt with its museum programme; Berlin struggling to reflect a newly reunited city in physical form. All of them put development to work in one way or another for political ends.

Most western societies are now too squeamish to allow quite the same free rein that the French have given their presidents. It wasn't always that way. Patrick Abercrombie's plan for the post-war redevelopment of London, prepared for the London County Council in 1944 and still conventionally presented as the height of enlightenment, makes uncomfortably authoritarian reading today. Abercrombie drew up a list of what he saw as London's defects: traffic congestion and depressed housing, due 'not as in some other great cities to high density, but to general drabness and dreariness', an impression that he no doubt formed from a glimpse of the brick-covered plains of East London from the window of his first class compartment on the way to Cambridge from Liverpool Street.

Abercrombie singled out inadequate and maldistributed open space, and indiscriminate mixed development as chief among the capital's evils. By the standards of the multiple deprivation that London's inner boroughs suffered in the 1980s, they seem trifling enough problems, the product more of Abercrombie's prejudices than any objective criteria. But he judged them serious enough to call for draconian remedies. As Abercrombie saw it, the population of inner London had to be urgently and drastically reduced. He calculated that more than one million people would have to be moved, whether they liked it or not. 'The anonymous slightly over one million people involved, must be selected, *with as little restriction on their freedom as possible,*' he wrote (my italics), apparently fully prepared to use compulsion should the need arise. And he was equally ruthless on the question of where the displaced should go. The flats versus houses controversy was important, he conceded. 'Wherever a choice can be made without harm to the community at large, personal preferences should be taken into account, but these should not be allowed to conflict with the need for accepting standards dictated by the practicalities of the problem.'

Abercrombie came up with one chilling concept that not even the French considered, 'the Population Advisor', who would 'adjust, and arrange population movements'. And, in his view, 'the location of industry will, within certain limits, be spelled out for the industrialist'. To this end, constant surveillance would be required by the regional planning board's industrial section, 'which should be responsible for studying the types of industry most suitable for a town at any stage of its growth – including the balance of male female jobs, and a proper diversification'. Abercrombie went so far as to draw a map of London, showing where additional industry should be banned, areas he claimed where 'there can be little justification for the introduction of further industry employing male labour, as it would only lead to interference with the existing industry's labour supply'.

Abercrombie's version of the corporate state cannot be explained away simply by the particular circumstances of the war in which it was formulated. Its theoretical underpinning came from Ebenezer Howard, while the Committee of Inquiry into Unhealthy Areas, presided over by Neville Chamberlain, reported as early as 1921 'that nothing satisfactory can be achieved unless the reconstruction of London is studied and planned as a whole'. And the Barlow Commission had already advised a policy of population redistribution from London, in preference to vertical expansion into multi-storey buildings.

Despite a paternalism which came close to downright Stalinism, Abercrombie's conceptual model of the city was a sophisticated one and formed the model for forty years of planning policy for London. He cut the city into four concentric rings, and advocated transplanting people from the centre to the outermost ring, leapfrogging the third 'green belt' ring. This and many of his other prescriptions were followed to the letter. Covent Garden market, he suggested, 'is now the source of great congestion, and its position cannot be justified'. It took thirty years, but the market duly moved out of the centre. He selected Heathrow as the site of London's main airport, and suggested a high-speed rail link from the city centre. The airport opened in 1947, but the link to Paddington, due to start running in 1994, was longer in coming. Abercrombie even earmarked the South Bank of the Thames for a major new theatre.

But the legacy of paternalist planning on the Abercrombie model has left both Britain and America with a marked reluctance to pursue such solutions. Urban issues rallied a new alliance of local activists and ordinary citizens not usually involved in politics. And their temporary coalitions achieved important successes.

In New York, where blazing ghettos provided a menacing background to urban politics in the 1960s, Robert Moses's plan for a West Side highway was defeated and the streets of what later came to be called SoHo were saved from redevelopment, even though the tragic legacy of his expressway building schemes lingers in the burnt-out slums of the Bronx. In Covent Garden, the bulldozers were kept at bay, though the preservation of its existing community proved impossible once the vegetable market closed. In London, activism reached its height at the start of the 1980s, when the

Coin Street development was opposed by a highly organised group, generously funded by the Greater London Council, which succeeded in defeating an attempt to develop offices next to the South Bank cultural centre, and instead designed and built its own low-rent housing scheme. This was an unusual case in that the outcome was eventually clear cut, arguments more often ending inconclusively.

The popular consent on which democratic government and its legal system depends was stretched to breaking point by a series of enormously protracted planning battles in New York and London. In Britain, costly but ultimately futile judicial inquiries into the major schemes for London produced only a stalemate. The system, it seemed, offered neither democratic control nor a satisfactory mechanism for managing change.

The utopias had turned sour, and attempts at consensus were no more fruitful. Hence the marked reluctance in the 1980s to attempt anything more ambitious than expediency. Rather than allow politicians to dictate by personal decree in the manner of Mitterrand, the British and the Americans formulate legalistic mechanisms, and quietly manipulate them to the ends which they seek. Control is left in civil service hands, but this can bring just as arbitrary and wilful an approach to city planning.

'The job of the city planner,' wrote the American academic Alan A. Altshuler, 'is to propose courses of action, not to execute them.' Despite this comforting picture of planning as a measured process of research and reflection, the supposedly disinterested expert's view of the city is often based more on subjective emotions than objective necessities.

Faced with the apparent impossibility of managing change through the supposedly democratic political process of local government, the Conservatives put the most problematic city areas in Britain under the control of development corporations. This was actually a revival of a mechanism used by the post-war Labour government to implement Abercrombie's plans for building the new towns. Government-nominated boards, not answerable to any electorate, were expected to prime the pump for private investment. But even the largest and most powerful of these corporations, the London Docklands Development Corporation, concedes that it had no guiding vision for the eight square miles of its empire beyond bumbling pragmatism.

Reg Ward, the corporation's first chief executive, admitted with startling candour and even more startling complacency in 1987 that 'No masterplan or detailed framework has been produced, no coherent development thesis has been elaborated'. In March 1990, the LDDC approved plans to spend £368 million, a substantial sum that, according to Ward, was being disposed of as 'the result of a whole series of random, certainly ad hoc initiatives, which only seem to have coherence in retrospect'.

He spoke with apparent pride about a series of decisions which, while they certainly led to a great deal of construction, contributed to such fiascos as the £77 million light railway system which had to be rebuilt as soon as it was completed because it was inadequate to cope with the demand. Under Ward's direction, London's dockland produced the glummest collection of architecture that could be imagined. But such is the extent of British nervousness with the idea of positive planning in any form that this short-sighted approach – Ward calls it organic – could be presented as sensible.

In the 1980s, Britain blundered completely unprepared into the age of the giant development. The country suffered a curious inability to grasp the scale of the transformation that was overtaking it, finding it much easier to focus its highly selective outrage on individual pieces of architecture, in the manner of the Prince of Wales, than to frame an adequate response to the impact of the pressure from a more affluent population, leading a car-borne life, on the wider quality of life.

When the channel tunnel threatens a Kentish village, or commercial housebuilders try to put up a new town on the green belt in the Tory heartland, the articulate are moved to fury. But their fury only worsens the problems to which they object. Protesters rise to peaks of moral fervour in their denunciations of the new towns, or of the channel rail links, but it is the new towns that could stop sprawl all over the home counties, and it is the channel tunnel that represents the best hope of heading off the building of a fourth London airport. No politician dare advocate either policy. Yet by avoiding making tough decisions in the short term, more trouble is being stored up for the future. The planning system which might once have hoped to resolve these conflicts in a rational way is incapable of meeting the problem.

Despite the red in tooth and claw image of the American city, shaped by unrestrained skyscraper building, limitless suburban sprawl and rip-roaring neon, most are actually very highly regulated. And the basis of that regulation, despite the welter of scientific jargon that surrounds it, is just as wilful and arbitrary as the French way of doing things. When it is not high-minded paternalism that is setting the agenda it is the big city businessmen playing Monopoly for real.

Though the fundamentals of the American planning system were ostensibly conceived with the most limited of ambitions, to regulate such apparently uncontentious issues as daylight and drainage, they ended up deliberately rigged to favour certain kinds of city. That at least was the intention, but so complex and unpredictable are the effects of zoning powers, particularly in New York, that they have degenerated into arbitrary mechanisms, breached in the spirit even when they are followed to the letter, exploited by developers to extract the maximum financial advantage.

Zoning came to New York as early as 1916, bringing with it the setback system, introduced in response to the outcry which greeted the eruption of the Equitable Building, forty-two storeys sheer up from the pavements of Broadway and Nassau Street. To stop skyscrapers casting the city's streets into permanent darkness, New York was divided into commercial and residential zones, each of them with a specified maximum parapet height that limited the level to which a building could rise straight up from the pavement. Anything higher had to be stepped back, to follow a line drawn from the centre of the street, intersecting with the top of the parapet, and extended upward as high as necessary. It was still possible to build towers rising sheer as high as a developer could afford, provided that they covered no more than twenty-five per cent of their sites.

These simple regulations created the wedding-cake style, which became the archetype for the skyscraper reproduced around the world even when no such restrictions applied, simply because it produced buildings that looked the way skyscrapers were meant to look. The system remained in force until 1961, when the setback law was abolished. By this time, the charms of the wedding-cake style were fading. Gordon Bunshaft's Lever building and Mies van der Rohe's Seagram tower, both slim and sheer structures rising from public plazas on Park Avenue, had set a glamorous new precedent for the skyscraper, following in the urbane footsteps of the Rockefeller Center.

Under the old setback rules, the provision of open space in front of a tower required an owner to forego a substantial part of his allowable floor area, so the plaza was presented by its partisans as a munificent piece of private generosity. Accordingly, those developers prepared to build plazas were to be compensated for their public spiritedness with bonuses allowing them extra floor space, and a new system was drawn up to control densities. It was based on the introduction of floor area ratios. Every site was assigned a fixed FAR which specified the maximum floor area permissible expressed as a simple multiple of the site area that the developer had amassed. An FAR of 12 for example, calculated on a plot 300 feet square, allowed for a building with a total floor area of 1 080 000 square feet. Under the new rules, a developer could cover forty per cent of the plot with a tower, which allowed a building with a maximum of thirty floors. If he wanted a taller building, it would have to have a smaller footprint. But if he created a public plaza, the city allowed him a twenty per cent increase in the size of the tower. That made the 30-floor, 1 080 000 square foot building into a 36-floor, 1 296 000 square foot building. So attractive was this option that, between 1961 and 1973, 1.1 million square feet of plazas were created in New York. It has been calculated that for every dollar the developers spent on creating plazas, they made a return of $43 on the extra office space they were allowed to build. It was, in effect, a massive public subsidy for modernism, whose principal effect was to recast the look of Manhattan. Rising above the old ornate skyscrapers of the 1930s came a new, more anaemic crop of glass boxes, floating above their plazas.

Thanks not least to William H. Whyte, who set up time-lapse cameras to map the way New York's public spaces were actually used throughout the day, it soon became clear that some of the new plazas were far from the civilised, urbane spaces their enthusiasts had promised. Downdraughts made many too uncomfortable even to cross, let alone to linger in. There was often nowhere to sit. Some owners even breached the terms of their zoning bonuses by fencing off their plazas.

Having tasted the power to shape the city through zoning, the planners were reluctant to let go. Rather than simply abandon incentive zoning, they looked for other uses for it. Just as Mies van der Rohe's plaza and slab formula had captured the planners' imaginations in the 1960s, so the atrium hotels of John Portman, with their inevitable glass-walled lifts and relentless indoor palms, seemed to be the last word in urbanity in the 1970s. Having discarded the plaza, New York seized on another, equally short-lived whim with the same enthusiasm. To encourage developers to build atria into their towers, even more substantial zoning bonuses were offered. A developer could pick up a twenty per cent FAR bonus, and a further twenty per cent if the ground and two other floors of his building were secured for retail use – not, on the face of it, an obvious hardship. So that 1 080 000 square foot building became a 1 512 000 square foot building, and it rose to 42 floors. Yet more bonuses were offered to developers who included subway entrances, and it eventually became possible to buy and sell unutilised air rights from historic landmark structures.

The result was not, as had been hoped, to direct investment to the less desirable parts of the city, but the massive, publicly subsidised over-building of the highly desirable East Side. The once civilized stretch of Madison Avenue in the East 50s in particular, with its busy pavements, and handsome architecture, was overwhelmed by a wave of new buildings, including Johnson's AT&T Tower, the IBM Tower opposite it and the Museum Tower next to the Museum of Modern Art. The notorious Trump Tower attracted so many subsidies and bonuses that it eventually won a FAR of 21.6, almost twice as much as the figure of 12 originally considered the maximum appropriate for the area.

The uses of power

The results were widely acknowledged to be just as undesirable as the wedding cakes and plazas before them. The excitement of Manhattan's syncopated skyline dissipated into monotony as solid walls of office towers shut out the sky in regimented, claustrophobic rows.

But even in the 1980s, the city failed to draw the obvious conclusion about the use of such a blunt instrument as zoning for the delicate fine tuning required to shape the detail as well as the broad outlines of development. At the urging of Mayor Koch, the city planners set about using incentive zoning to try to create two giant new landmarks. When the New York Coliseum, an auditorium built by Robert Moses at Columbus Circle, became redundant with the opening of the I.M. Pei-designed convention centre on the West Side in 1985, the city put the site up for sale. Koch had two interlinked objectives, to extract every last cent of potential profit that he could, and to give New York the doubtful kudos of building the world's tallest skyscraper.

The city threw in all the zoning bonuses it had to offer, and a few more besides, theoretically to allow for the building of a 2.68 million square foot structure 130 floors high, then invited developers to submit designs and bids. 'This', said Koch, 'is a once in a lifetime opportunity to make an indelible mark on the city's skyline.'

For six months Koch basked in the reflected glory that this primitive reassertion of the city's virility brought him. Donald Trump could not resist the bait and actually submitted two different bids – neither successful. Perhaps the city's financial advisors were perceptive enough even then to see how much of Trump's empire depended on hot air and mountains of debt.

In the event, Koch picked a behemoth designed by Moshe Safdie for Mort Zuckerman's Boston Properties, not as tall as the regulations permitted, but massive by any standards. Safdie proposed two granite-faced origami towers, respectively 57 and 72 storeys high, containing offices, a hotel and condominiums, sweetened by Zuckerman's bid of $455 million that would go straight into the coffers of the city's Metropolitan Transit Authority. Doubts quickly set in when it became clear that such a giant structure would cast large areas of Central Park in shadow on winter afternoons. The Municipal Arts Society went to court to stop the project. And in response to that pressure, as well as the softening of the New York property market, Safdie was replaced by David Childs of Skidmore, Owings and Merrill, who marginally reduced the size of the structure, though not its shadow over the park.

Twenty blocks away at Times Square, Koch pursued his other long-cherished dream of driving out the sex cinemas, and evicting the hustlers from 42nd Street. At the same time, the planners wanted to shift the pressure for office development away from the East Side. The two objectives were brought together with the most intricate piece of zoning juggling yet attempted in the shape of the midtown development project. With the concentration of theatres in the area, blanket demolition was out of the question. So the city's plan, drawn up in 1982, divided midtown in three. It created a growth zone west of the Avenue of the Americas, with an FAR of 18, for buildings started before the end of 1988. The theatres themselves were protected by much lower FAR, while to the east, in the area in which the planners wanted to damp down the pace of rebuilding, avenue sites were allocated an FAR of 15, and mid-block sites were 12, a level deliberately set so as to make tower developments uneconomic. The Museum Tower and several others would certainly have been blocked under these restrictions.

A total of sixteen office buildings went up under the new rules – accounting for more than nine million square feet of rentable space – but the rebuilding of the 42nd Street/Times Square areas bogged down in recriminations and money difficulties. The city claimed that its plans would allow private developers to tackle the clean up of Times Square, but the utter dullness of Johnson and Burgee's proposals for four overscaled towers with a total of 4.1 million square feet of office space around the square failed to convince anyone, either in their first, mansarded incarnation, or in the revised, Miami Vice style they eventually came up with. The developer was Park Tower Realty with Prudential Insurance, Park Tower incongruously enough being the firm that presents itself as the saviour of Paternoster Square in London, with its promise of a classical development around St Paul's Cathedral.

In effect, New York's legalistic zoning formulas are an attempt to provide an apparently rational means of enforcing an aesthetic prejudice. London's planners, while they claim to have no powers to control overall aesthetic issues, are actually prepared to consider each approach, case by case. New York, on the other hand, tries to come up with general rules.

San Francisco's current zoning regulations are if anything even more specific in their attempt to produce a particular kind of development than those in New York. In the city which produced the very first restrictive zoning laws in the United States when it put three hundred Chinese laundries out of business by banning them from residential neighbourhoods in 1895, buildings which conform to the aesthetic prejudices of the planners have a much better chance of being built than those that don't.

The burst of growth that the city went through in the early 1980s provoked an articulate community into bitter opposition in defence of San Francisco's older pattern of urbanism, to save its natural topography from the tide of undifferentiated high rise building. In 1985 the voters astonished everyone when they approved a bill to limit new office development in the city's downtown to an annual ceiling of 950 000 square feet, amounting to one substantial new building a year. Bigness and growth had hitherto been essential parts of the American dream as far as it applied to the city. Restrictions like these seemed positively un-American. Since that figure is considerably below the potential demand, permissions have been allocated by an aesthetic review panel, in effect an annual beauty contest. To qualify for consideration, developers must follow a detailed set of rules that aim to make high rises appear more slender on the city skyline, and to accentuate distinctive building caps. Building heights are also varied in relation to each other, to avoid what San Francisco planners call 'benching', and to create a softer skyline that reflects the hilly form of the city rather than fights against it. The city's controls divide towers into four zones – base, lower tower, upper tower and top. The base has to follow the lines of the street walls, and must include a cornice line or equivalent projection to harmonise with the surrounding city streetscape. But direct mimicry or replication of historical detail is discouraged. Hipped roofs, domes, stepped parapets, cornices and sculptural treatments are all possible for the tops of towers. It is a policy that has prompted Philip Johnson to top one tower with castellated turrets, dormers and neo-classical statuary, and another tower by Cesar Pelli has an exploded top, designed in collaboration with the sculptor Siah Armajani.

It is all part of an attempt to shape the city both physically and socially. The city's agenda was made explicit when it attempted to ban fast food restaurants to encourage neighbourhood delicatessens. Its lawyers advised that it was unconstitutional to discriminate against McDonald's and Burger King. So instead, San Francisco zoned all restaurants out of some residential areas, and then chose not to take enforcement action against existing businesses.

The planners also tried to use their powers to create more public open space. San Francisco insists on one square foot of open space as the price for every fifty square feet of commercial development, and wrote tight guidelines in an attempt to make the resulting spaces accessible and attractive. They did not have to be directly attached to the building which was financing them, but could be in other locations, or aggregated as a contribution to the new downtown park. They could be made up of several small terraces, or simple corners for office workers to be able to eat a sandwich lunch in the sun.

For all the city's good intentions, the immediate effect of the restrictions was to increase the pressures on the city's periphery. What had been quiet suburban communities such as Walnut Creek saw the construction of millions of square feet of offices in their backyards during the 1980s, where previously there had been none, and despite having a rapid transit link to downtown, Walnut Creek's roads quickly filled up with constant jams.

San Francisco's other weapon, one which is used in other large American cities, is exaction, or what the British call planning gain. It is the practice of demanding benefits in cash or kind from developers in return for permission to allow them to build commercial schemes. San Francisco has a five dollar per square foot levy in return for planning permissions on new construction, benefiting the mass transit system, as well as a trust fund for affordable housing which in the course of the 1980s raised nearly $30 million and built 5532 homes.

With exactions running at an estimated $1 billion a year nationally, the American courts require a 'reasonable relationship' to be demonstrated by the city between development and the projects for which cash is levied, but they have been prepared to accept a very flexible definition of what constitutes such a relationship.

In London, similar demands that developers provide low-cost housing as part of office developments, build sports halls and theatres, even make direct cash payments, have been made by local authorities. This last practice is so close to outright blackmail that the government has tried to stop it. The policy stems from the notion that 'mixed' developments are more desirable than single use projects. And while exactions have become the only means of financing public housing in many places, the idea of doing so is as much an aesthetic one as it is a social policy.

The dangers of using planning powers to encourage aesthetic ends can clearly be seen in London, where one of the major amusements for developers has been the demolition of the visually unified set pieces of the 1960s to make way for supposedly better, certainly larger new buildings. The most striking example is London Wall, the closest that London ever got to Le Corbusier's *La Ville Radieuse*. Six identical slabs were placed, parallel to each other on either side of a dual carriageway, like dominoes hiked twenty feet up off the ground, as a deliberate counterpoint to the residential area of the Barbican being planned at the same time. The City's planning department drew up a rigid pattern for the assorted group of developers who actually built the project to follow. Each new slab had to be 58 feet wide, 142 feet long and 220 feet high, and be set on a two-storey-high podium building.

Astonishingly, the rules remained in force for more than a decade. A troupe of architects, ranging from anonymous commercial hacks to once-celebrated firms, designed the slabs at intervals from 1963 to 1972. It is the kind of exercise that would once have had the optimists enthusing about a new architectural language, a discipline that allowed new buildings from different hands to relate to each other. In truth, the range of expression was limited in the extreme. With the exception of Powell and Moya's suave bronze and smoked-glass slab, perched awkwardly above the Museum of London, the curtain walling is crude and makeshift when set against the polish of North American and Japanese technology.

But there was nevertheless a certain sullen drama to the conception as a whole. London Wall is – or was – an identifiable London landmark, instantly recognisable if not exactly winsome, just as are the Avenue of the Americas in New York and the Europa Platz in Berlin.

Now it is all vanishing. In the struggle to find new sites for development within the square mile of the City of London, the planners gave the green light for the demolition of just about all of the 1960s buildings that had changed its face so much. They sealed the fate not only of London Wall, but Paternoster Square around St Paul's, and a dozen other unloved 1960s buildings.

There was a lot of talk about an aesthetic second chance. But for the developers the attraction was the chance of securing better plot ratios. So Lee House was demolished just twenty-five years after its completion to make way for Terry Farrell's replacement, almost twice its size.

Despite a government which insists that local authorities have no legal powers to judge planning applications on matters of aesthetics, the capital's network of local planners in the boroughs and in the cities of London and Westminster continually demand that new developments respect the character of buildings around them. That apparently innocuous instruction has created a school of buildings whose aircraft hangar-proportioned interiors are hardly concealed by pitched roofs, gimcrack pilasters and cynical decorative flourishes.

The approach was typified by Stuart Murphy, one-time chief architect to the City of London, the successor to the men who were responsible for building the old London Wall. When Murphy was discussing the design of Richard Rogers's first project in the City of London after the completion of the Lloyd's building, one of his officers saw fit to produce a photocopy of a Victorian building in Glasgow and suggest that this was just the kind of thing that Rogers would be well advised to imitate if he was interested in getting planning permission for his building.

The Japanese, their fascination for learning from the West in full flood, drew up their own version of the Abercrombie plan for Tokyo in 1956, in the shape of the National Capital Region Metropolitan Development Law. It defined the twenty-three wards of metropolitan Tokyo, together with the cities of Yokohama, Kawasaki and Kawaguchi, stretching in a ten-mile radius around Tokyo's central station, as the city's inner ring. It planned a seven-mile-wide green belt beyond that, and the construction of a ring of satellite towns to take the surplus population in the outer zone up to forty-five miles from the centre of Tokyo.

It was an instant, and spectacular failure. The pressure of Tokyo's surging economy brushed aside the feeble constraints of the plan. Even though the building of major new factories, universities and colleges was banned within the central ring, 80 000 new jobs were being created every year from the growth of smaller plants. With two million people moving into the so-called green belt between 1955 and 1965, the whole plan was abandoned. In the 1970s, Tokyo followed a rather more pragmatic policy. A thirty-mile area around the capital was divided between urban control zones where development was discouraged, and urban promotion zones where the Tokyo metropolitan government hoped to concentrate new jobs and homes.

To try to take the pressure off the city's financial centre, where 1.5 million commuters converge daily, placing a pressure on the transport system that would be intolerable in any society less disciplined than Japan, Tokyo's city government began to use its own land holdings to try to create alternative focuses. The old water treatment plant at Shinjuku was reclaimed to provide 240 acres of development land, used for a crop of high-rise towers shooting up out of the shacks of the old bar district. Tokyo City Hall moved here in 1991, leaving its original site clear for the building of a massive conference centre. The old city prison at Ikebukuro provided twenty acres for another skyscraper complex. Both sites are on the Yamanote loop line that circuits the city. The one hundred feet height limit, imposed since the earthquake of 1923, was abolished and Tokyo's National Planning Agency has rezoned the densities for Marunouchi, which will allow for the building of scores of fifty-storey skyscrapers.

With its chaotic patchwork of local governments, the powers of the City of Los Angeles extend only to a fraction of the metropolis. If you take the widest definition of all, that is the Los Angeles water district, it shares powers with 125 other city authorities. Moreover, large parts of the city are currently controlled by an institution that, in its lack of public accountability and the resentments that it has aroused, harks back to the days of

The uses of power

Robert Moses in New York and a way of doing things that went out of favour in London and New York in the 1960s.

Los Angeles established the Community Redevelopment Authority (CRA) in 1948. It was born of the federally sponsored drive for urban renewal, but it was from the beginning the chosen instrument of the coalition of business and organised labour that represented the two key constituents at City Hall in those days. Authority members are appointed by the mayor, and are not subject to recall. Their decisions need no ratification from city or electorate. Its critics, and there are many, see the CRA as unaccountable, using public money to help its friends in the development and construction industries make fortunes from the eviction of the poor from the city centre.

The CRA works on projects for specific areas, designated as blighted, in which it has sweeping powers to commandeer land, raise funds and force its plans through. The CRA does not initiate developments however. Designation is a quasi-political process set in train by the mayor or a city councilman, but once a redevelopment area has been designated, the CRA has the right of eminent domain to acquire any property it sees fit. The property tax base is frozen, and any increases in tax revenues which come from new developments go not to the city but to the CRA, which raises money to pay for land accumulation infrastructure work by issuing bonds against the expectations of its tax increment revenues. California insists that twenty per cent must go to affordable housing, but given the prejudice of Los Angeles home-owners against any kind of social housing, it is getting harder and harder to find anywhere to put it.

So powerful and wealthy has the CRA become, that it now takes 3.5 per cent of all property taxes in Los Angeles. The CRA also earns revenues from retaining a direct commercial stake in the developments it plans. At California Plaza, for example, the CRA takes fifteen per cent of the profits.

The CRA has eighteen redevelopment areas, which account for more than six per cent of the city. The biggest, and the most notorious, is the Bunker Hill area on the edge of downtown. At the turn of the century this was an area of large, ornate timber houses, not unlike the florid gingerbread houses which are now the pride and joy of San Francisco. It had the Angel's Flight funicular railway as a reminder of the LA of Raymond Chandler. But the rapid spread of Los Angeles spelled decay for the centre and turned Bunker Hill into a slum, at least into a slum as it was defined in those days. The freeway network tied a knot around downtown and cut it off from the rest of the city. But the old city core, a traditional North American city built on a trolley transport system overlaid on a nineteenth-

After sixty years of neglect, Los Angeles finally rediscovered a recognisable downtown in the 1990s. Asian and east coast development money poured into the city, transforming its skyline. The Bunker Hill project, built on principles at least two decades out of date, started to fill up, while I.M. Pei's cylindrical tower, the tallest in the city, provided downtown with a new focal point

century grid, though dusty and down at heel, remained intact if fossilised. In the 1970s, the Mellon family developed Century City, far to the west, whose high rises are now the most expensive offices in the city, leaving only the banks, City Hall and skid row in downtown.

Even as downtown atrophied, Los Angeles began to make ambitious plans for its future. In the 1940s, large areas of land occupied by tract houses and orange groves were zoned for enough apartment blocks and high rise offices to accommodate a city of ten million people. It was exactly the opposite of the conventional image of LA, and it was only in the 1980s, as developers began to tear down houses to make way for bulky condominiums, that the reality of the old plans became clear. After much campaigning the zoning laws were repealed, and densities reduced. But it was too late for Bunker Hill, where clearances started at the end of the 1950s, even if nothing was built for three decades. The CRA says that perhaps 6500 people were removed from Bunker Hill, others claim as many as 9000 were pushed out. In any case there were still disputes about compensation dragging on in the courts thirty years later.

But it was only in late 1979 that the CRA was in a position to ask developers to bid for the sites, and to put forward their proposals for meeting the CRA's brief for a mixture of offices and apartment towers.

The slick mirror-glass towers of the winning scheme, designed by the Canadian Arthur Erickson, represent an architectural dinosaur, a bout of old-fashioned 1960s urban renewal that will not be completed until the end of the 1990s, three decades late with no more than cosmetic adjustments to its mirror-glass facades. But the CRA is showing no signs of faltering. With California Plaza well under way, and the rest of downtown booming thanks to the influx of Japanese money in the 1980s, it turned its attention westward. Its draft plan for Hollywood was published in 1990.

While the form of Los Angeles as a whole is shaped by the authoritarian powers of the CRA, at the other end of the scale the detailed appearance of many of its neighbourhoods is the subject of very stringent control, through a network of design review panels that take their powers from restrictive covenants. Beverleywood, for example, has residential areas where there are three approved styles: Mediterranean, that is terracotta tiles; Chateau, with casements; and Tudor, that is to say timber-framed.

On a far larger scale, Don Bren of the Irvine Corporation has design controls for the whole of his holdings on the 144 square miles of the Irvine ranch, the largest private new town in the USA, masterplanned by William Pereira, six times larger than Manhattan, with jobs for 115 000 and homes for 80 000 people. At Bren's insistence, houses must have tiled roofs and stucco walls, and all offices must be white, with flat roofs.

Like a lighthouse rising from the Houston swampland, Johnson's Transco Tower is a landmark to navigate your car by. The fountain – parking provided – is a strong enough lure in the heat of the Texan summer to get you out of it

Even cities like Los Angeles and Houston must eventually come up against intimations of their own mortality. Unfettered capitalism, when it meets the absolutes of photochemical smog and water shortages, finds itself having from necessity to think about its future just like any social-democratic, Northwest European utopia.

Houston, supposedly the most unplanned Western city of all, is in fact nothing of the kind. It is perfectly true that Houston has no zoning legislation, unlike every other major city in the United States. The voters of Houston rejected the idea as recently as 1962, but though they might change their minds one day, the city is certainly not without planning, and it has an armoury of regulations that achieve very much the same ends. What makes Houston – the Third Coast as it presumptuously calls itself – different is the extent to which development control is in the hands of the private landowners and developers who have made fortunes out of the city's explosive growth.

Right up until the 1960s, Houston was run from regular meetings at a suite in the Lamar Hotel by a clique that made the decisions, formed the committees and fired the mayors. Taxes and services were kept at survival level, with infrastructure investment put off until crisis point was reached. They used tax money to bail out their flooded suburbs and to provide water and sewers for private developments. Hints of the skulduggery that accompanied the city's foundation in 1836, when a couple of carpetbaggers from New York, Augustus and John Kirby Allen, bought the swamps on which Houston is built sight unseen, continue to surface.

Land use in Houston is controlled by restrictive covenants in the title deeds that cover most of the city's developed land. There are ten thousand such covenants dealing with use, size, cost and height, administered by 630 civic clubs which function exactly like private zoning boards, backed up by the city itself, which has acquired the power to enforce private covenants.

The point about Houston is that it provides a snapshot of how Los Angeles was forty years ago as it embarked on its surge of growth, and before the bungalows in their orange groves began to be swamped by giant condominiums popping up in their neighbourhoods like beached Queen Marys. It too spread endlessly onward. It too seemed to have grown without much serious thought about its future. Yet, almost without knowing it, it had established an underlying structure that was to shape its future. Looking at Houston at the start of the 1990s provides an insight into that process of city growth in its early stages. It tells us something about Los Angeles, just as Los Angeles tells us something about Houston.

With its shimmering, sculptured and faceted skyscrapers, Houston's downtown, seen at a distance rising above the trees of Post Oak, is extra-

Downtown Houston is only the city's centre in a purely abstract sense. The bankers and the lawyers may congregate in the cluster of high-rises, but just a few yards away the city starts to unravel and the lots revert to scrub, while a dozen other centres, scattered almost at random over the city's vast expanse of land have just as much claim to call themselves its focus

ordinarily beautiful, half San Gimignano, half Brasilia. But this being America, we already know that when we get close up we will find an unravelling carpet. The Republic Bank with its sandstone Dutch gables, and its long-empty mirror-glass neighbour topped by what looks like Grant's tomb, stare down on the shotgun and welfare housing of Allen Parkway Village. Two blocks from the tallest of the high rises, among a tangle of derelict rail tracks where migrant labourers feed at open-air soup kitchens, Houston is reverting to scrub. Even the Salvation Army has left town for a strip mall, housed in what looks exactly like a shopping centre.

It is misleading to see these spires and towers, linked by underground malls that allow pedestrians to take refuge from the intolerable humidity of the climate, as the city's centre. The banks and attorneys are here, so is the concert hall, the public library and city hall. But the city doesn't depend on it for anything much more than a visual signal. There are half a dozen other alternative centres, including the Texas Medical Center, the Rice University Campus, Post Oak Galleria and Green Bay Plaza. What structure that the city has is the loop 610 road, circling downtown at a distance of ten miles. And if the downtown towers are the keep, the loop is like a medieval wall: either you are inside it, or you are not. The loop functions as a main street, forty-four miles long. To get from anywhere to anywhere else in the city, if you don't actually drive on 610, you will use it to orientate yourself.

The city has yet to create any other sense of itself. There is perhaps an axis of a kind that runs from downtown to the Galleria, and it's this axis that the city contemplated formalising by building a rail link. It could one day be the westside corridor of Los Angeles. But you feel an emptiness everywhere.

The sense of people looking for what seems like a public place, as opposed to the privacy of their homes and workplaces, is palpable nowhere more than at Philip Johnson's Transco Tower, with its pleated mirror-glass tower rising up like a lighthouse 850 feet high in the midst of vivid greenery. Driving around you find a sign which points out 'Visitor Parking for the Fountain'. In front of the tower, Johnson has designed a free-standing pediment with three linked arches opening onto a massive stone horseshoe, down which water comes flooding at the rate of 110 000 gallons a minute, courtesy of Gerald Hines Interests, as another sign helpfully informs you. There are permanent knots of people standing in the clouds of spray which offer a respite from the excruciating summer heat, or lounging on the nearby lawns. In this centreless city, the fountain is a gesture to an older kind of urbanism. People drive here from miles around simply to walk and to sit, to experience a sense of place in the midst of placelessness.

they have been consulted, Houston's voters have decisively turned down any attempt to impose zoning controls on the city. Nevertheless, the city's spectacularly beautiful downtown skyline is hardly the product of development with no planning controls. A system of private covenants, legally enforceable by the city's lawyers, comes very close to a planning system

In a European city, you could walk somewhere afterwards; here, you just get back in your car.

Planning, as it is practised in Houston, has no remedies for this isolation. True, the planners say that introducing zoning would protect older areas of housing, making them safe for gentrifiers who want their investments shielded from the threat of mushrooming commercial strips, trailer parks and business parks, but the appeal of Houston is in the planning testbed it provides as a city without official zoning. There is the idea that there is nothing and nobody to stop you building a skyscraper in your back garden, or opening up a cinema on your front lawn. It's a quality that has been legislated out of existence in most Western cities. But what planning does try to do in Houston is to instil the sense of parade-ground neatness so beloved of middle America.

What Houston's planners think of as good planning is the landscaping of parking lots, to insist on trees, and earth berms along their frontages, and small discreet business signs. Though there are still traces of the exhilarating, giddying sense of disorientation that comes from finding a $50 000 shack next to a tower full of $500 000 condos in River Oaks, it's slipping away. It hasn't all gone yet: the producers of *Robocop*, filmed in Dallas, found enough urban dystopia in Houston to use it as the backdrop for the sequel in 1990.

Zoning, as it is used in most big American cities, allows the city government to determine the form and nature of development. It can specify height and density. It can create streets in residential areas in which the poor – or even the middle class – are excluded by provisions for minimum plot sizes. It can insist on minimum set backs from the street, and floor area ratios for offices which determine the height of downtown.

All of these powers have been replicated in Houston. The city itself has drawn up a comprehensive plan which uses sewerage and water provision to direct new housing towards areas that the city planners – or the business community – want to see it go. A sewerage moratorium in large areas of the city – circumvented by a busy black market in sewer connection permits – provided a serious check on development in the early 1980s.

The city is passing laws that specify strict off-street parking requirements for businesses in residential areas. Houston sets minimum building setbacks outside the central business district of between ten and twenty-five feet from the street line. It mandates a maximum block length of 1400 to 1800 feet to prevent traffic congestion such as that at the Galleria. And in 1980 the city banned all new billboards, and set size and height standards for what was already there. It established a minimum distance of a

The uses of power

thousand feet between sex-orientated businesses, which are prohibited from mainly residential areas of the city – where presumably they would be allowed only discreet business signs and would be required to provide plenty of off-street parking.

What Houston has, and Los Angeles had, is the sense of constant urban change that is now almost impossible to comprehend in a European city. The idea that a city is going to double in size in a lifetime is a daunting as well as an exhilarating prospect. It brings a quite different psychology from living in a static or a declining city. Houston is a place that has yet to get sentimental about its past, as the unceremonious destruction of the eighteen-storey Shamrock Hotel, erected in 1949, painted green from top to bottom, and the scene of the oil men's wild days, demonstrated.

The bookshops and cafés of Montrose, the Museum of Fine Art with its Mies van der Rohe extension, Renzo Piano's De Menil, a fine museum in a leafy suburb, all suggest that if the Los Angeles model is anything to go by Houston will one day begin to solidify around these coordinates. The key to planning then must be to ensure that options are not foreclosed. What it needs is somebody with the vision of a Mitterrand to make it happen, but at the moment all that is coming out of Houston is parade-ground neatness.

It is dangerous to be dogmatic about the positive power of planning. Too often the plan is a Canute-like fiasco of changing objectives and futile helplessness in the face of irresistible forces. Yet there are constraints that planners set which do have the most striking results, though not always those intended by those who frame them. The city that faces up to the future must have some sense of its destiny, some sense of looking beyond expediency. Yet it is hard to reconcile these qualities with the everyday realities. What marks out the successful city is a sense of the possible.

The world of work

5

Thirty years after Walt Disney mourned the passing of small town America by building a sanitised simulacrum of Main Street at the entrance to Disneyland in Anaheim, the corporation started thinking about a similar epitaph to the factory age. Disney's imagineers drew up plans to build a theme park based on the idea of work. They looked at ways of bringing together a string of industrial processes – steel-making, car-building, and textiles possibly – and turning them into what in Disneyspeak are known as 'gated attractions'.

To judge by Main Street, with its horseless carriages, nickelodeons and ice cream parlours, circa 1910 going on 2000, patrons would fly in for a two-day stay at the Coketown Marriott to file through Steam Age World, watching muscular navvies stripped to the waist, gleaming with the sweat of honest toil as they wrestle with molten metal at open furnaces. Or they could wander through a pre-Japanese car factory, making quaint old Thunderbirds on manual production lines, lost in the baffled wonder of a suburbanised child introduced to the cow as the source of milk for the first time. So cars *don't* just arrive on freighters from the East of their own volition.

It's hard to believe that Workworld would have quite the same charm for the hundreds of Mexicans, Guatemalans and Salvadorians who line up before dawn at Los Angeles gas stations not so far from Disney's Burbank studios, waiting for potential employers to drive by in pick-up trucks and hire them for a day's labouring. They belong to a culture which has yet to savour the ironies of post-modernism.

Of course there is already an assortment of museums and heritage centres which share Disney's brutally honest view of manufacturing as little more than a picturesque crowd-puller, but they have less courage about saying it quite so openly. In Britain, you can pay to watch redundant coal miners dressed as caricatures of nineteenth-century pit men, going through the motions of mining using the very techniques that their fathers fought to abolish.

If Britain can no longer make money out of making ships, it can at least sell tickets to show how it used to do it. The shipyard that built the Falklands veteran *HMS Invincible* won a £1.5 million grant from the

The daily ritual of going to and from work plays a decisive part in shaping a city. In Tokyo, which has gone in for a massive subway expansion programme, the Salaryman faces long commutes whose rigours are tempered by the reliability of the service. The gap between the office worker and the factory worker has been all but obliterated. The office and the factory in Japan as in America and Europe look indistinguishable, with their VDU screens, and their five-wheeled chairs

English Tourist Board to turn a derelict Victorian repair dock at Barrow-in-Furness into a museum of steel shipbuilding. Brennan and Whalley, the designers responsible, got the job on the strength of their work for the commercial vehicles section at the National Motor Museum, where elderly trucks and vans are displayed in the midst of a thicket of flimsy replicas of contemporary street life. There is a butcher's shop, a pub, bakery and railway station. Allegedly in the interests of authenticity, visitors have their senses assaulted by the noise of factory sirens, steam trains, and the smells of baking bread, brewer's malt, soot and oil. The shops are stocked with replica food, and the whiskery, cloth-capped figures in unconvincing period dress that inevitably infest such places are sealed with a specially formulated resin to withstand even the most determined mauling from visitors.

For sheer spectacle, work as it is presently organised can hardly compete with the age of steam. Clanking steel pistons, brass connecting rods and mechanical levers have given way to anaemic plastic and the bland bleep of touch-sensitive electronics. But even if it doesn't look like much, new or newish technology has driven a transformation of the world economy that has had an enormous impact on the city. With bewildering speed, the location and nature of the workplace has changed out of all recognition, and with it the form and structure of the city. It is usually the impact of the motorcar that urban historians concentrate on when they try to assess the impact of technology on the city. But a whole string of other, often obscure and inconspicuous developments, most of them to do with work and the way it is organised, have played an equally important role in reshaping the city.

When the first shipping container, a steel box eight feet high by twenty feet long, was deployed on the run between Puerto Rico and the US in 1955, it was not on the face of it the most radical of technological innovations. But the success of the container doomed traditional enclosed docks the world over. In London, eight square miles of wharves, stretching all the way from the Georgian brick splendour of St Katharine's Dock, next to Tower Bridge in the west, to the reinforced concrete of the Royals in the east, were immediately obsolete. When any manufacturer could load a container in the security of his own factory, and ship it around the world with nothing more than an occasional gantry crane to shift it from truck to boat and back again, the teeming gangs of dockers, organised with all the intricacy of a medieval craft guild to pack each bale and barrel into the hold, became redundant. Even the warehouses in which goods in transit used to be stored were now useless: steel boxes keep the rain out well enough by themselves. All that is needed for a modern container port is a deep-water berth, enough empty space for platoons of fork-lift trucks, and

The world of work

giant travelling cranes to marshal boxes between ships and lorries. It is a formula that is efficient, but which hardly offers much scope in urbanistic terms. However, there is little reason to get too sentimental about the old docks that the modern container port has replaced. St Katharine, built during the third decade of the nineteenth century, involved the destruction of hundreds of houses, a medieval church, and the enforced eviction of thousands of people.

The Thames is simply too shallow and too awkward a river for deep-water container ships to come any further upstream than Tilbury, where the once mighty Port of London Authority maintains its last surviving enclave.

Nevertheless, after the container ship's maiden voyage, it took more than a decade for the first upstream London dock to close. Only after St Katharine was shut down in 1967 did the pace of closures begin to escalate until the last of the upstream docks finally closed in 1981. What had once been the busiest port in the world was reduced to rows of rusting cranes hunched over empty berths, and an expanse of mirror-calm water disturbed only by the occasional scrap dealer's barge. It was a disturbing, eerie sight; powerful and sombre witness to cataclysmic social change.

The 25 000 London dockers' jobs of 1960 had gone. And another 75 000 that depended on them went too. London had lost one of its primary functions, one which had helped it to grow into a world city in the first place. All that remained were miles upon miles of rotting warehouse hulks, their ranks decimated by arson, the survivors fenced off by corrugated iron curtains. Virtually the same story was repeated in every port city from Sydney to Yokohama. In Hamburg and Rotterdam and Copenhagen, there are the same blackened brick warehouses, and the same efforts are made to turn them into studios and apartments.

London had already turned its back not just on Docklands, but on the East End as a whole. For a generation the city had moved steadily west towards Heathrow and the corridor of growth focused on the motorway to the rapidly growing satellite towns of Slough, Reading and Swindon. Because the docks were cut off from the rest of the city, barricaded by high walls, well away from the main thoroughfares, few outsiders were aware of the sheer scale of what was happening. But to those who did know what was going on, the prospect of another five thousand empty acres in what was already one of the capital's poorest areas, looked more like a disaster than an opportunity. Some property companies had bought up a few of the wharves, but made little headway redeveloping them.

But as we have seen, under the control of the London Docklands Development Corporation, set up in 1981, the area began to emerge as an important secondary office location, slowly at first but with rapidly growing momentum as generous tax incentives and zoning concessions took effect. To the dismay of local politicians who bitterly resented the electorally unaccountable LDDC, few of the new jobs coming into the area were within reach of the manual and unskilled workers who made up the bulk of Dockland's existing population. The LDDC's critics argued that the job losses would best be overcome by building factories and workshops, a view dismissed as unrealistic by the government. Technological change had destroyed the traditional working class. The skills needed for ship building, steel making, car production and electronics had been appropriated by South Korea, Taiwan and the other Asian powers emerging from behind Japan. London's future was in services, tourism and what are called the information industries — remedies recited with increasing desperation by cities from Turin to Portland, all of them attempting to grapple with the bewildering rate at which the industries that had fuelled their prosperity and growth a generation earlier were now wasting away. With Japanese corporations moving their factories to Thailand, Malaysia and Korea for their lower wage costs, even Japan was beginning to chase the vital command and control and service jobs.

Undaunted by the competition, the Docklands were duly recast in the image of the information economy. In 1990, the London property consultancy Hillier Parker calculated that, while no less than thirty-six million square feet of offices were planned for Docklands, considerably more than twice the office space in the whole of downtown Detroit, just three million square feet of industrial space were contemplated for the area. It was an imbalance that reflected Britain's shifting employment base and the increasingly marginal role occupied by manufacturing. Jobs in the information industries on the other hand, which had accounted for ten per cent of London's workforce in 1900, had reached fifty per cent by 1980. The fact that big metropolitan cities such as London and New York were never major centres for heavy industry probably served them in good stead in the post-industrial age. They were not as severely hit by overseas competition as Manchester or Pittsburgh. And indeed, printing and fashion, major industrial employers in New York and London, are also important to the economy of Tokyo, suggesting that they provide an economic base with more longevity than low-margin metal-bashing.

The rapidly changing pattern of the world of work in recent years is by no means confined to rustbelt industries overtaken by Asian competitors. The effects of technological change have been just as far-reaching in the office, and almost as conspicuous, as they have in the heavy industries. As the heirs to the printers and booksellers who had clustered around St Paul's

Cathedral for three centuries, Britain's national newspapers concentrated along Fleet Street for more than a hundred years. By the end of the 1970s, newspapers represented central London's last remaining large industrial employer. Hemmed in by the law courts, smart restaurants and advertising agencies, with massive machine rooms shaking through the night and gleaming delivery trucks lining up outside their offices ready to speed early editions away, newspapers were effectively a heavy industry in the very centre of the city.

Poisonous labour relations and dilatory management kept new technology at bay for a generation. Long after photocomposition and computer typesetting had become commonplace in far less sophisticated printing plants, Fleet Street remained a museum ruled by trade unions who, with their arcane organisation run by fathers of chapel, seemed closer to the middle ages than the twentieth century. Change, when it finally came, was brutal and swift. Rupert Murdoch presented his workforce at *The Times* and his three other British newspapers with an ultimatum: accept new machines, and the working methods and job cuts that came with them, or be sacked. The printers went on strike rather than agree. Murdoch responded by springing the trap he had set for them. Over a single weekend he abandoned three Fleet Street buildings and moved all his newspapers to a new plant in Wapping, readied in secret. He had brought 1500 jobs to Docklands, but fired 3500 people to get them there.

For more than a year the fortified News International plant saw running street battles as the sacked printers struggled to shut the plant down. Perhaps they didn't know it, but it was a battle that was as much about the shape of the city as it was about trade union negotiating rights and technology. It was an unequal struggle between the old centralised city and the new diffuse one. Long before Murdoch's former employees gave up the fight, the Fleet Street newspaper precinct was as dead as the old dockland. Within four years of Murdoch's ultimatum, every major newspaper had transferred its printing operations out of central London.

The old newspaper palaces, with their journalists in offices piled up on top of printing halls, fronted by grandiloquent facades and lobbies, symbolised the civic role that the press has in a metropolitan city. They did more than give Fleet Street its distinct architectural character; they kept alive the working-class suburbs in Essex where printers lived.

Fleet Street was not just a collection of highly specialised buildings. The dense grain of the area, with its restaurants and bars in which journalists worked just as diligently as they did at their desks, the greasy spoon cafés and pubs that catered to the night shift, the specialist libraries, the newsstands selling esoteric professional journals and international magazines, the bookshops, stationery stores, typewriter repair workshops and picture agencies, even the dinner jacket hire shops, were all part of the mechanism that allowed the press to do its job. So was the mixture of scruffy low-rent offices for freelances and out-of-town papers, cheek by jowl with the palaces of the grander papers. The pedestrian scale of the area and its proximity to the law courts, the City and Westminster allowed for chance meetings, informal contact and gossip. This was where news was manufactured, and without it journalists were just as lost as landless farmers. This was not a community in the mawkishly sentimental sense. It was a piece of highly functional machinery, like a university town geared up to cater for each successive generation of students who then graduate and move on.

Now that the area has been stripped of all those meanings, the old newspaper offices have been rebuilt behind their carefully preserved facades as trading floors and offices for accountants, bankers and solicitors. The press meanwhile has been translated to a series of stockades, strung out for ten miles from *The Daily Telegraph* in the east, under the shadow of the towers of Canary Wharf, to which it eventually intends to move, to *The Daily Mail* in the west, its offices carved out of an old department store in Kensington. This last at least is decently urbane in its intentions, but its brutal Docklands counterparts hide behind blank walls, security fences and surveillance cameras.

Newspaper buildings lost their distinctive qualities and their individuality when they separated out their distinct functions. The presses are based on low rent industrial estates, while the journalists work in mundane slabs on slightly less remote sites indistinguishable from any other office building, bland at best, mean and shoddy at worst. They have given up any attempt at addressing the public world, retreating instead into introversion and anonymity. It is a transformation that was symptomatic of the 1980s, one which had as much to do with the culture of industry as with economic necessity or architectural ambition.

The arguments over the civic role of the workplace crystallised in Britain when the BBC started thinking about replacing its central London headquarters at about the same time that Murdoch was planning his move to Wapping. Having outgrown the original Broadcasting House, the corporation's first plan was to construct a new headquarters across the street from its Portland Place building. It would have stood on the site of the Langham Hotel, closing the vista down Portland Place at the centre of the Adam brothers' monumental set piece. Sir Norman Foster was appointed as its architect, and designed a building which would have eloquently expressed the BBC's significance as a national institution, as well as dealing with its complex technical demands. Significantly, a key feature of his design was to make a number of broadcasting studios transparent, putting them on show to passers-by through glass walls like hothouse flowers. It is a measure of just how far the contemporary workplace has sunk into bland anonymity that those rare survivors which do still have a recognisable character are treated as exotica.

In the event, the BBC's governors, struggling with an unsympathetic government over the funding of the corporation's budget deficit, changed their minds about making such an overt demonstration of their public role, dropped Foster's design, sold the site, and built a banal aluminium-faced box close to the BBC's Shepherd's Bush television centre in a gloomy inner suburb. Set over the whole life of the structure, the savings involved in moving to the edge of town rather than building in the centre were marginal. But antipathy towards making the assertive gesture that such a major central London building would have represented allowed the decision to be presented as the act of a sober, responsible management, rather than a cultural abdication.

For central London to lose such a significant institution was a step towards the North American pattern of single function centres. London still has a long way to go before it becomes a Houston or a Dallas, where the central business district is no more than a symbolic focus of civic life and work is carried out in isolated, fortified compounds, but it is moving in that direction.

New York has suffered far more than London from institutional flight from its centre. The drain has been a conspicuous fact of life since the 1960s, and the city has poured millions of dollars into largely futile attempts to bribe high-profile companies to stay. It's an uphill struggle when such a significant company as J.C. Penney can move from the middle of New York to the edge of Dallas and save $60 million a year.

Even the future of the city's remaining anchors is in doubt. While *The New York Times* clings to Times Square, paying the price for its difficult location with heavy security, both *The Daily News* and *The New York Post* have fought to move to suburban printing plants for very much the same combination of labour and cost savings that prompted Rupert Murdoch to make the move to Wapping.

The daily rituals of going to and from work, of supplying the necessary raw materials, and social interaction at the workplace define the geography and character of a city. They give the city its sense of cohesion and shared purpose. In Paris, London and Tokyo, the architecture of the ministries and legislatures makes manifest the role of each city as a seat of government. In Los Angeles, the film studios, the oil derricks and the citrus

groves make it quite clear what sort of city it is – as do the factories in its industrial suburbs, painted two tones of avocado, that provide 900 000 manufacturing jobs. In London, New York and Tokyo, the skyscrapers testify to their role as international financial centres. They are all symbols of the way that a city earns its living, as well as functional buildings underpinning its prosperity.

The last decade has seen the explosion of these physical aspects of the city. The Bank of England used to insist that the major financial institutions remained within a few hundred yards of its headquarters opposite the Mansion House, so that settlements could be made by the direct transfer of financial instruments carried by bank messengers who still walked from one bank to another. At the end of the 1970s those restraints were relaxed, and the banks embarked on a diaspora all over the city. Many had already moved their back offices to the outer suburban ring. Now developments on top of Victoria Station, redundant department stores in the West End, and the sprouting towers of Canary Wharf have all become office locations. So have the so-called City fringes – Broadgate, Spitalfields Market and King's Cross. Exactly the same pattern marked the development of Paris and New York, where more and more organisations that had no need to be in the centre of town moved to cheaper suburban sites.

The pace of technological change shows no signs of slackening. The old stock market floor became redundant once computer screen-based trading was introduced. The next step is the computerised international trading of stocks, a move that could have far-reaching effects on the centralisation of the financial markets, and for junior stock market jobs.

Between 1981 and 1984, London lost 97 000 manufacturing jobs while in the same period banking, insurance and finance put on 45 000. But London cannot afford to take its financial services jobs for granted. The City has seen a continuous growth in the amount of office space available ever since 1955, but the number of people employed in the City peaked in the early 1960s, and between 1971 and 1981, it actually declined by twelve per cent. By some measures, the exports balance of payments surplus in services, so-called invisible earnings, was reckoned to have gone into deficit in 1990 for the first time since the Napoleonic wars. And the recession of the early 1990s hit the 'modern' industries of finance and information much harder than manufacturing firms.

Meanwhile, the rush to suburbia by the big corporations has been no guarantee of prosperity. The highest rate of vacant office space in the New York area in 1989 was not in midtown or downtown, where the effects of the shake-out in the financial markets was still being felt, but was actually in Fairfax County out in leafy Connecticut. Stamford, according to

Rostenberg-Doern, real estate agents from the Connecticut town thirty miles from midtown Manhattan which, though its night-time population is only 100 000, is at the centre of one of the largest concentrations of multinational corporate HQs in the world, had an office vacancy rate of 27.6 per cent in 1989. This was far from being made up of time-expired industrial slums, or newly completed over-ambitious speculation. Many of the buildings were less than ten years old, and had been purpose built by large companies moving out of New York.

One giant building for which no takers could be found was the former headquarters of the American Can Corporation, built in 1970 and empty for the last three years. The company had moved 2200 employees out from its Park Avenue tower into Gordon Bunshaft's elegant lakeside building, with its carefully landscaped, beautifully wooded 175-acre setting, and its invisible underground car park, then abruptly changed direction. The company sold off its manufacturing business and metamorphosed into a much smaller organisation, specialising in financial services, finally changing its name to Primerica and deciding to quit the building altogether. A company that in 1970 had employed 54 000 people had simply ceased to exist.

Not far away in Danbury, the award-winning glass and steel headquarters of Union Carbide designed by Kevin Roche and only completed in 1982 was also going begging. Union Carbide sold its 53-floor, Park Avenue, Skidmore, Owings and Merrill skyscraper to a bank for $110 million, and spent $190 million on Roche's new building designed to accommodate no less than 3200 employees. Then came the disaster at the company's Bhopal plant in India, a subsequent downturn in the company's fortunes, redundancies for headquarters staff, and finally an attempt to lease off large blocks of space in the building in the teeth of a buyer's market.

With parking for 4000 cars, lush landscaping, mature stands of trees, and lakes, Kevin Roche clearly saw his building as setting a new standard for the workplace, creating an archetype for the modern office. He claimed that the front door for Union Carbide 'is the act of arrival by automobile. You drive from home on a highway system, you get off the public highway onto a private highway system, which goes straight into the garage'.

Roche began the design process by interviewing the staff. It seems that they disliked waiting for the elevator; they felt cramped and compartmentalised in high rises; they didn't like the status games about windows with views and office sizes that make up the daily round of skyscraper life. What they wanted was an office environment much like their living rooms.

Union Carbide and American Can are by no means the only examples of corporations which have failed to prosper in suburban surroundings.

William H. Whyte in *City*, his tract on the virtues of downtown over suburbia, acidly reports the results of tracking the lacklustre performance of corporations that left New York in the 1970s against those that stayed. Isolating their executives behind a gatehouse and moat has proved disastrous, he claims, concluding that 'a firm that is tired of New York, is tired'. Judging by the carpet slippers ethos of Union Carbide's headquarters, he has a point.

Yet there is no doubt that the move out of the big American cities, especially from New York, is continuing, despite the short-lived turn around in its fortunes in the course of the 1980s.

According to US Bureau of Labor statistics in 1989 (*NYT* 22 October 1989), Manhattan had lost 23 000 white-collar jobs in the previous five years – which translates to 5 750 000 square feet of office space coming vacant, or five of the large new buildings just completed in midtown Manhattan. And at the end of 1989, the Bank Leumi Trust surveyed six hundred executives of medium-sized companies – those with annual sales of between $10 million and $250 million – then located in New York, and found that twenty-three per cent planned to move their companies out of the region in five years. The most frequently cited reasons were drugs, crime, taxes and high housing costs.

Many jobs were lost in what used to be seen as the bright hopes of the New York economy. While there had been sharp upturns in some of the financial and services sectors in the 1980s, they were down from their peaks. Security and commodity brokers, though well up on the 85 000 of a decade earlier at 150 000 in 1989, had come down from the peak of 160 000 two years earlier. Banking employed 162 000 people, up from less than 150 000 in 1979, but again down from the peak figure of 172 600. Only legal services, which employed 75 000 people in 1989 – up by 30 000 in the decade – remained strong. Even the advertising industry at just below 40 000 was in decline.

Where were all these jobs going? The shake-out in post-big bang banking and the sluggish state of the financial markets had killed off many of them for good. Others were lost to New York's rivals as international banking centres. London put on jobs at just the same time as New York in the 1980s, and was losing them at the same time. But Los Angeles had also begun to make its presence felt as a financial market, forming a focus for the emerging Pacific Rim economies. It was a development that could be seen in the rapidly changing Los Angeles skyline with its forest of new high rises.

Yet other jobs were draining to the edge cities that were the major discovery of American planning in the 1980s. Early in the decade, the high-tech start up firms had made the running, mushrooming on Route 128 orbiting Boston, and along New Jersey's Route 1. Both locations were tied to university science parks, with Harvard, MIT and Princeton as the important draws. Along Princeton's periphery, defined by a five-mile strip of Route 1, there were twenty-five million square feet of offices in 1987. It was more than software wizards and high-tech manufacturers out there by now. Even market makers were beginning to leave Wall Street for New Jersey. Merrill Lynch, for example, had a fifty-strong dealing room for its managed fund accounts out on Route 1.

Tyson's Corner, the fastest growing office concentration on the East Coast, represents the new edge city at its starkest. Twenty years ago it was still a tract of undeveloped Virginia countryside. Half an hour's drive from Washington's Dulles airport, through thickly wooded forests where you can still smell the leaves and hear the birds as the sun goes down, 1-7 suddenly jolts you into another world. There is a high-rise hotel with a conical pointed roof protruding through the trees. Then you see a Nieman-Marcus store, housed in a brick palazzo – windowless, but with a passable cornice. In front is the parking structure, four storeys high, beautified with the liberal addition of pastel stripes, the most universal symbol of the area. This is a place which grew in parcels of little private estates, their individual presence marked by vestigial gates bearing names such as Tysons 2. From the humblest beginnings – distribution depots, start up software companies, professional buildings to house lawyers and dentists – the scale has ballooned. Suddenly, here in the middle of nowhere is Bloomingdale's, and Taco Bell, and Holiday Inn, next to Woolworth's and Nordstrom.

The low rise business parks and the brick boxes have started to give way to high rise towers. But there is nothing at ground level, no street fronts, no public transport, and no attempt to relate one building to another. This is the kind of place that respectable architects get very coy about. In one sense they would rather not think about it, yet it exercises a powerful hold on them. They enjoy the frisson of anxiety that comes from looking into the abyss, fascinated yet repelled by what is by any economic standard a thriving city, but one which has a complete absence of any of the urban characteristics that normally define such an entity.

Philip Johnson was not too proud to turn his attention to a thirty-storey office tower here. In the context of Tyson's Corner, Johnson and Burgee's banal design, with its detached columns rising the whole height of the building and its venetian window motif, provides some sort of sense of identity to a placeless address that is otherwise defined only by work and mobility. He has at least built a corner.

Las Colinas, once a ranch near Dallas/Fort Worth Airport and now

Tyson's Corner, the fastest growing office centre on America's east coast was open country two decades ago. It was the rise of such 'exurbs' that pulled the majority of office space out of downtowns during the course of the 1980s. Though Tyson's has its skyscrapers – including one by Philip Johnson – there is no pavement, no centre, and certainly no corner, just an amorphous outcrop of stores, malls, tract houses, and towers. Under the noses of the urbanists and the activists, Tyson's Corner, along with scores of places like it, has become the new incarnation of the city

boasting a collection of towers that rivals that of the self-styled Metroplex itself, is another, more premeditated version of the same phenomenon. It is built around carefully landscaped grounds, artificial lakes and canals, with clock towers that self-consciously suggest European antecedents, and with even a transit system of its own that clearly gives it a competitive edge over other less elaborate office parks.

These new threats to the old downtowns typically employ as many as 100 000 people. And despite the attempts of local planners to insist that they are cast in the image of suburban campuses, their developers are going higher and higher, with thirty-floor buildings increasingly common. The spread of the edge city is underlined by research from the Office Network of Houston, quoted in *Planning*, which found that while in 1981 fifty-seven per cent of all office space in the United States was located in downtown areas, in 1986 it was down to forty-three per cent. Downtown Detroit had fifteen million square feet of office space, while the Southfield Office Park in its suburbs had twenty-one million square feet.

With a shift that pronounced, how long is it before an office heritage building becomes a gated attraction, and Disney's imagineers have groups shuffling around lost in nostalgic wonder at the photocopier and the desk?

While corporations left to themselves have been seeking out these edge-of-town sites, the big cities have started to compete increasingly bitterly in the scramble to attract jobs which are in short supply. To this end straightforward financial inducements are not always the most effective. Grants that may persuade Japanese car makers to set up branch plants in Europe are seldom effective in attracting the kind of jobs that the big cities need most. These tend to be divided at one end into the managerial high technology service jobs, and at the other the low-skilled, blue-collar manufacturing jobs such as textiles. Enterprise zones of the sort adopted by the London Docklands Development Corporation, in which normal development controls are suspended and tax holidays are offered, may have a role to play. But equally important have been the glut of image-building campaigns, designed to present a positive impression. Hand in hand with this is the assiduous cultivation of the kind of cultural, social and communications amenities that not only create jobs in their own right, but which also attract employers.

Allied to this move are deliberate attempts to diversify the employment base of cities such as Houston with the Texas Medical Center. It was originally established in 1942 with a $20 million endowment from Monroe Anderson, a local cotton magnate who saw the idea of a medical campus as both a charitable endeavour and an employment generator. Building on the base of two large hospitals, and a medical school – coaxed away from

Dallas, Houston's long-standing rival — there are now forty-two separate institutions on the site, including thirteen hospitals, research laboratories, two medical schools, health organisations, as well as doctors' offices and hotels. More than 52 000 people work on the complex, which sprawls far beyond the original 134-acre site. Helicopters clatter constantly in the air, with three different landing pads. More open-heart surgery is performed here than anywhere else in the world. This is by any reasonable definition as much of a city as you will find anywhere in Houston, with several hundred buildings, scores of high rises, from hotels to office towers, all of them reliant on medicine.

The theorists and the planners have been stranded, struggling to catch up with the shape of the new city brought on by these shifts. The most conspicuous change has been the convergence of different kinds of workplace. The early days of industrialisation saw the construction of highly specialised building types. Textile mills, forges, foundries and ship-building works were more or less giant machines, in which form quite literally followed function. Each of them looked distinctively different, and immediately communicated their individuality. Their location had to be equally specialised, sited close to transport or to the raw materials.

In the late twentieth century, that degree of specialisation has given way to an increasing convergence in the surroundings in which work is housed. High investment manufacturing has come to resemble what was once seen as white-collar employment increasingly closely. Production lines and dealing rooms both involve workbenches to support costly equipment and large open-plan spaces.

The new disciplines of space planning have rearranged offices around flow chart diagrams just like production lines, so the share dealing room, the travel agency, or the sales department of a clothing company look increasingly the same.

The up-to-date corporate headquarters of the 1970s would have had an elaborate computer room, air-conditioned to surgical standards, in which the computer itself occupied the space of an entire room. Now that computer power is distributed throughout an entire building, no special air handling is required, and the machinery itself, far from being treated with the awe of a totem, is taken for granted.

Equally, the distinctions between the location of industrial and office buildings has become hopelessly blurred. The out-of-town industrial park, with low-rent, simple shed-like buildings used for distribution or warehousing, has now been invaded by the workplaces of an increasing number of highly skilled workers too.

Typical of the new genre is Stockley Park in London — built on a

The world of work

reclaimed rubbish tip ten minutes away from Heathrow airport. The model is the campus, with 1.5 million square feet of space on one hundred acres, including an artificial lake, lawns, 100 000 trees, and a central services building. It houses Apple Computers' British headquarters, the Marks and Spencer Computer Centre, Toshiba, Fujitsu and Quotron. There are service roads, but no streets and no pedestrians. A bus service does skirt the edges of the scheme, to bring in cleaners and the occasional secretary and canteen worker, but as much as possible the individual buildings are kept away from the roads. Rather they are focused on the landscaping, and hidden one from another. It is an image that Ebenezer Howard would certainly have recognised. Apart from the road layout, it is exactly the same kind of place as the factory estate of the 1970s, except that more money has been spent on the cladding systems, and the place is not dominated by up and over garage doors and turning circles for articulated lorries.

It's done decently, and tastefully. A variety of different architects have been used by the developers, and the place will undoubtedly be a showcase of its kind. But a slice of city it certainly is not.

It is in places like this that the central core of the city faces its greatest challenge. They offer space that is less than half the cost of prime city centre space, and provide a whole new way of working – where it is impossible to walk out at lunch time to the pub or the café, where going to buy an aspirin means a ten-minute car ride.

Even more threatening to the old definition of the boundaries of a city is EuroLille, the massive eight million square feet development of offices planned on top of the TGV station at Lille. Once an industrial desert, Lille now sees itself as being able to profit from the building of the channel tunnel, and TGV lines to Brussels, Paris and Calais to make itself a major office location. When the trains start running in the mid-1990s, Lille will be within one hour of a catchment area of thirty million people. Where better to build low-rent offices? It's the same kind of logic that saw the building of the giant out-of-town shopping centres, and one which the project's master planner Rem Koolhaas has seized on. 'The train will destroy the idea of an address. People will just say their office is fifty minutes from Disneyland, or one hour from London,' he claims.

Meanwhile, the shape of the workplace in the city centre itself is also moving away from the individual landmark. The corporate headquarters is giving way to the very large, uninflected space in the wake of a series of market research-driven studies at the beginning of the 1980s that revolutionised commercial space within the city.

The Orbit study, as it was called, concluded that the technology already available at the start of the 1980s would have an enormous impact on the shape of the workplace, never mind what was being developed. Information technology is not easy to absorb into existing buildings – it produces many miles of cables and ranks of equipment in general office areas, and generates large amounts of heat.

To deal with the changing nature of work, there would also be much greater cellularisation, a need for meeting rooms and places for visitors to work, and the realisation that the workplace has to function as a club. The average size of the workplace is increasing too – each employee is reckoned to need as much as 250 square feet now. Technology requires raised floors and a minimum depth of 1.7 metres to allow for cellularisation. That means that many buildings are in danger of premature obsolescence. A mean floor to floor height of less than 3.7 metres does not allow for high capacity air conditioning or extra trunking for central air conditioning services embedded in the shell. The logic of all this has led to the demolition of a large number of comparitively recent buildings. Industrial sheds are more appropriate to office requirements than sub-standard office shells.

Architecture does still have a role in establishing an identity for a corporation. Witness the Hongkong and Shanghai Bank, AT&T's broken pediment in New York and the Transamerica pyramid in San Francisco, all of which used architecture to convey a message about their owners. The Hongkong and Shanghai Bank, for example, was a signal, albeit a not entirely sincere one, that the bank was committing itself to the future of the colony. In Los Angeles, meanwhile, I.M. Pei's building for Creative Artists Agency celebrated with its understated elegance the shifting balance of power in Hollywood away from studios to agents.

And in San Francisco, the Esprit fashion company, a retailer that depends more on the manufacturing of image than of clothes, has its headquarters in an old timber-frame warehouse with sandblasted brick walls. The restaurant-quality staff canteen, the strict rules against high heels in the office and smoking or eating at your desk, and the physical jerks that start the day, are both an obvious sign that Esprit wants to be taken as a progressive company and a curious throwback to the paternalism of the enlightened nineteenth-century employer.

In terms of communications technology, most of the attention on its impact on the workplace has focused on the notion of the electronic cottage – the possibility that more and more people will soon be able to work from home, linked to their head office by fax machine and modem. By the end of the 1980s, twenty-five per cent of British households owned a computer of some kind, and the facsimile machine was beginning to escape out of the office too, affecting a lot more people than the motorcycle dispatch

The world of work

riders whom it is already unsaddling. With rapidly falling prices, the domestic fax machine threatens to make the postman redundant, and even the newsagent in the longer run, when publishers start to push their magazines through electronic letter boxes every week, at off-peak rates.

While this invasion of technology may well change the working habits of academics, journalists, consultants of one kind and another, and also some categories of outworkers – the printing industry for example, which has been transformed by the migration of typesetting to low-wage areas outside the big cities – it is unlikely ever to affect more than a minority. But what is happening is that more and more jobs are being transformed by the introduction of the telephone service to such functions as catalogue sales, and ticket reservations. An increasingly common building type is that in which people work with telephones and computers taking customer orders. It can be American retail stores setting up a mail order division in Salt Lake City, or British Airways putting their telephone sales in Newcastle. But the decisions that lead to the location of such buildings, and the jobs that go with them, are quite different from those which have traditionally applied. A city's strongest sales point will be the availability of a motivated and educated pool of potential employees.

Work in the widest sense is what shapes the city. In the eighteenth century, before factories and offices became widespread, many people worked in their own homes, or at the homes of their employers. It made for very dense cities. Now the city is still reshaped by the changing pattern of employment, which more than anything else is behind the dispersion of the city and its ever larger geographical spread. We are still in the middle of a period of massive change in the pattern of working habits. Workplaces are simultaneously moving closer and further away from people's homes. Some people are commuting longer and longer distances, while others have the chance to live in outer suburbia and still be in reach of business parks.

The effect in the long run has yet to be seen, but already it is helping to turn the city into an amorphous blanket, dotted with high-intensity points of activity that function as quite different kinds of city centre.

The museum as landmark

6

The day in 1979 that the Los Angeles Museum of Contemporary Art was born is commemorated by a small rectangular plaque. It is bolted to the red sandstone skin of Arata Isozaki's building, perched on top of five levels of car parking, and under the shadow of the slick and streamlined mirror-glass towers of California Plaza, Los Angeles's much belated born-again downtown.

It bears witness to what the infinitely narcissistic community of California's great and good chooses to describe as the museum's birth. But in fact MoCA, as it calls itself, self-consciously attempting to upstage New York's MoMA, came into being through an altogether more tortuous and long-drawn-out route than the pious rhetoric of the plaque would suggest, one in which battling egos and naked self-interest played as much of a role as the pursuit of high culture.

It speaks only of 'a group of citizens who shared their vision with Mayor Tom Bradley'. Next to it, with all the painstaking unsubtlety with which North America approaches charity, is a stainless-steel scoreboard that carefully grades these vision-sharing citizens into distinct categories. Immediately to the right of the plaque are the charter sustaining founders, a group not to be confused with mere sustaining founders who are acknowledged a little further away. There are enough of them to fill a whole wall. Then, as the scoreboard moves around the corner, it turns its attention to the distinguished benefactors, the major benefactors, and the supporting benefactors. A helpful footnote explains that the triangle against certain of the names denotes charter status.

And what names. For the purposes of the scoreboard, the citizens of Los Angeles appear to number not merely the English hairdresser Vidal Sassoon, a charter sustaining founder, but the Italian fashion designer Giorgio Armani, a sustaining founder, and Louis Vuitton who, though himself long since deceased, makes an appearance thanks to being coupled with the managing director and his wife, Charles and Elizabeth Rocamur, of the luggage company that still bears his name.

It is a collection that says a lot about the nature of modern Los Angeles – and not a little about the underpinning of social anxiety that sustains this, and many other cultural institutions. Los Angeles is the fastest grow-

Every museum and gallery worth its salt embarked on an expansion programme in the 1980s. Museums had become a major economic force, and to run them a new breed of cultural entrepreneurs came into being, to whom attendance figures and donations were all important, and who found new buildings the most effective way of getting them

ing big city in the developed world. Where the major metropolises of the rest of the western world are engaged in redistributing their populations in ever widening circles, Los Angeles, according to some estimates, will reach a population of twenty-two million by the end of the century. That growth is being achieved partly by spreading tract houses further and further into the California desert. But it is also causing population density in certain areas of the city to increase, as bungalows and courtyard apartment blocks give way to condominiums. Los Angeles has become the same focus for the ambitious and the dispossessed that New York once was. With an eye to posterity, the most successful of its citizens are funding a burst of civic improvement, not quite of the kind that transformed the Victorian cities of Britain at the height of the industrial revolution, but one which has many parallels with it. Los Angeles isn't getting many new parks or churches, Philip Johnson's drive-in Crystal Cathedral excepted. Its universities are for the wealthy. And while endowments for hospitals are part of the agenda – witness the Max Factor pavilion at Cedars Sinai – they mostly take the form of practical but invisible utilities. Cedars Sinai, across from the Beverly Center, actually has to resort to a massive ground-level timber structure that might easily be mistaken for a sculpture, to draw the attention of the short-sighted to the munificence of the benefactor who installed the hospital's rooftop helipad. So conspicuous culture is soaking up the lion's share of the attention.

Plans to build the Frank Gehry-designed Disney Hall for the Performing Arts on a downtown site not far from the Museum of Contemporary Art are well advanced. Far across the city to the south, Renzo Piano's idea for an underground museum came to nothing, but at La Brea the Los Angeles County Museum of Art has completed its kitsch addition, a posthumous execution of a design by Bruce Goff, and the Getty has Richard Meier's vast new museum underway.

It was the mill-owners and ship-builders of Victorian Britain who paid for the municipal monuments of their era. In Los Angeles, as the scoreboard demonstrates, the money comes from oil, entertainment, fashion and aerospace. For a couple of generations, Los Angelenos sweated it out in a remote overgrown cowtown that had a sunny climate, but otherwise had precious little to recommend it, a view that is underscored by the paucity of big corporations who made their headquarters there.

The early comers were happy to go on making money, and living the kind of restricted civic life that is still the norm in cities like Houston. But what's the point of being rich if you have to do it in a place that the rest of the world refuses to take seriously? In the most simple-minded terms, being taken seriously as a city means an abundance of restaurants and museums. For Los Angeles's affluent whites, for whom waiting in line for a valet-parked car to come back outside a Rodeo Drive boutique is the nearest they come to experiencing street life, museums and restaurants represent the only socially acceptable kind of public realm.

The vainglorious presumption of the scoreboard display betrays the unvarnished realities that lie behind the project. Here, buried among the benefactors, is Cadillac Fairview – the Canadian-owned development company that back in 1979 won the Los Angeles Community Redevelopment Agency-organised competition to build California Plaza. The competition came at the same moment that Mayor Bradley – the city's first black mayor, and a former policeman – was talking to the aforementioned concerned citizens about the idea of a museum. So the CRA came up with a scheme that would see the citizens got their museum for nothing. Local laws insist that 1.5 per cent of the construction budget of redevelopment projects such as California Plaza goes on commissioning works of art. The CRA's plan was to spend the whole $20 million on building a museum – in effect a tax on the development. The completed museum would then be handed over to the MoCA trustees to be maintained and run privately.

Cadillac Fairview went along with the idea, and its architect, Arthur Erickson, came up with a design for the museum that the MoCA board turned down flat. They wanted to choose their own architect. In the event Cadillac found that it couldn't raise the funds for the office scheme, sold the project on and bowed out, leaving behind little more than its name on the scoreboard and Erickson's much-amended masterplan. Just a few columns away from Cadillac Fairview on the scoreboard is the name of Metropolitan Structures, the development arm of Metropolitan Life, the Chicago insurance company which took over California Plaza when Cadillac faltered. Alongside is the architect Arata Isozaki, who designed the museum, a commission that took him to the brink of resignation as he found himself caught in the midst of a bitter war of egos between curatorial staff and benefactors. The trustees spent a pleasurable few months touring the world looking at other museums, now the prelude to every major and quite a lot of minor museum-building projects, and came back with a shopping list for Isozaki, just like an over-enthusiastic couple discussing their ideal bathroom with their decorator over a box file full of clippings torn from *Architectural Digest*. At the same time Metropolitan Structures, which paid for the project, had an even more onerous list of non-negotiable demands for the design. It had to be incorporated into the parking structure for California Plaza's as yet unbuilt shopping centre. Furthermore, its column structure had to repeat that of the parking levels below for the sake of economy, and symbolically most important of all, it must not block pedestrian access to, or views of the shopping precinct that Metropolitan Structures will eventually build when the project is complete. A clearer statement of priorities would be hard to imagine, and it is small wonder that Isozaki disowned his first attempt at designing the museum, winning a breathing space to have another go without quite so many interested parties breathing over his drawing board.

To Los Angeles, a relatively young city, these issues have a special resonance. MoCA's painfully self-conscious gestation period marked the end of the city's long cultural inferiority complex. The choice of architect for the museum was indicative. Hiring a Japanese designer was seen at the time as the height of exoticism, a nod to Los Angeles's Pacific Rim status and its blend of cultures, a signal of the city's determination to take a leading role in setting the cultural agenda. Before Isozaki's appointment it was all but inconceivable for a major American museum to consider a Japanese architect. Now it is commonplace.

Los Angeles already has a stunning collection of cultural artefacts from all over the world housed up at Malibu in the Getty's reconstruction of a Roman villa. Even in Los Angeles, the initial scorn this piece of seemingly wilful kitsch attracted coloured the perception of the museum for years after its opening. It took quite some time before the realisation dawned that Getty is not a robber baron's freak show, but one of the world's most formidable museums. The Getty Foundation is now busying itself with the construction of a second museum, a sprawling complex of a dozen buildings spreading over twenty-four acres, designed by Richard Meier. All the Getty collections bar the Greek and Roman will be moved out of Malibu and into the new buildings.

The fact that visiting the Getty Villa in Malibu depends on pre-booking a parking space brings home starkly just how different life is in a motorised metropolis from the two-hour pedestrian precinct view of most European cities. Meier's new complex will have a rapid transit link with the six-level, 1200-car underground parking structure. Two automated electric trams carrying ninety passengers each will take four minutes to do the 3/4-mile trip.

Despite its underground car park, MoCA does, on the other hand, underline the city's attempt to build itself a 'real', that is to say European, museum, a place which you can walk into for a quick look at the masterpieces and, above all, gives a chance to take part in the shared life of the city, the essence of the new civic role of the museum.

It is the creation of a generation which has confused ideas about just what constitutes museum art, the creature of a society which is used to

The museum as landmark

buying its art from New York lofts and barricaded former dairies in Venice, California. Hardly surprisingly then, MoCA has a ghostly reflection of this view of art in the shape of the Temporary Contemporary, a converted transport depot on the edge of downtown's Little Tokyo, one of the two or three ethnic ghettos that alone give Los Angeles's rotting downtown some semblance of life. 'I just swept the floor,' says Frank Gehry of his conversion of the building for the now permanent Temporary Contemporary.

The habit of tattooing names all over museums is a deeply ingrained part of the American way of doing things. At the Museum of Modern Art in New York, it is done in serif letters cut deep into polished travertine, celebrating the city's rich and image-conscious citizens from the 1930s, who have now safely turned into old money. In Houston, you can wander through downtown, look down, and suddenly find that every brick on the plaza floor beneath your feet has had the name of a benefactor inset into its surface in tiny brass letters.

Here in Los Angeles, there are so many names to deal with that they look more like the kind of graffiti that used to be sprayed all over the subway cars in Manhattan. Many of them could of course have picked up the whole tab for the museum's construction all by themselves. But that would have been merely to build another rival to the Getty or the mooted Hammer collection. And the Getty, though it casts a huge shadow, is a magnificent train set whose owner never had anybody to play with. It failed to provide that sense of municipal pride that comes from getting together with your peers that Los Angeles lacked.

Unlike Dallas, which has gone to the length of naming the city's new symphony concert hall the Morton H. Meyerson Auditorium, MoCA at least has a name of its own. Yet for all that is riding on it, the museum has a curiously insubstantial quality. Moored on top of the parking garages of California Plaza like the funnel of an ocean liner, MoCA contrives to suggest that it is more a work of art than a building.

MoCA opens its doors every day with the same precise, neat ritual. Six blue-blazered Hispanic warders march out, like a colour party, to set up the sandwich board at pavement level that proclaims the museum open. In fact there is not that much to see up here. There is a modest little water garden, a few large-scale pieces of outdoor sculpture, a ticket booth, and the museum store, which offers the usual range of merchandise branded with the museum logotype.

To hint at the subterranean nature of the museum, Isozaki has burrowed out a courtyard beneath the pavement but open to the sky. It's the site of the MoCA café, with its outdoor tables sheltered by Italian marketplace umbrellas. Authentic-tasting cappuccino is on offer, along with an enterprising fax lunch takeaway service for the financial district workers in their offices all around. There is even an own label MoCA mineral water.

Once inside the cool white interior, everything comes with a name tag. Everything is somebody's turf. Collectors are celebrated for their discernment, their taste, their generosity, while artists, unconsciously no doubt, are made to seem like incidentals. Large-scale abstract works of art merge into the background, more like pieces of design than art. Meanwhile the commentary on the walls concentrates on their acquisition and provenance, at the expense of their content and meaning. MoCA's exhibition in the summer of 1989, for example, was accompanied by an announcement which claimed that 'the recent gift of eighteen masterworks from the renowned Rita and Taft Schreiber collection marks an extraordinary event for both the museum and the art-viewing public of Los Angeles'. It took several paragraphs in which 'the Schreiber family's commitment to the cultural life of this city' was chronicled and the suggestion made that their pictures were 'a lasting tribute to Los Angeles, whose gift to the museum guarantees the continuous and permanent enjoyment of these important works for future generations', before a single artist was so much as mentioned.

There is even a space in MoCA that is officially described as 'Nancy Epstein's Grandchildren's Gallery' – which, as it happens, does not come decked out in Nancy Epstein's wallpaper.

The Metropolitan in New York has no such qualms. It has been only too happy to accept bequests that stipulate that the benefactor's collection is displayed within the museum after their death exactly as it was in their living rooms, a custom that is uncomfortably close to the funeral rites of the wealthier type of ancient Egyptian. If the Alexandria Mouseion, originally built to house painters and artists for the glorification of the Ptolemaic kings of Egypt, really is the forerunner of the modern museum, perhaps it's not an entirely inappropriate development.

Clearly the emotions at work behind the worldwide epidemic of museum building in the 1990s – and the closely associated crop of assorted cultural buildings: opera houses, concert halls and the like – run deep. The museum has become the focus of a quasi-religious cult, one that promises immortality of a sort for its subscribers. For the newly wealthy, benefactions for the right museum are now the price of entry to polite society. The art museum in particular has become the only sacred building that the modern world is still capable of building. A persistent emphasis on architectural exhibitionism and technical virtuosity serves to underscore its status as a place dedicated to ritual, set apart from the everyday world.

But the modern museum has also had a public and a political role – a potent blend of vanity, and economic and national policy – ever since Napoleon determined to make Paris Europe's cultural capital. He planned to loot his conquered subjects of their art treasures and bring them back to France in triumph. The bronze horses from St Mark's, which were, temporarily at least, among the early highlights of the Louvre's collection, were high on his shopping list. It's hard not to see the twentieth-century Japanese enthusiasm for acquiring works by Picasso and Van Gogh in similar terms, a means of demonstrating national prestige and economic ascendancy.

Museums have an increasingly explicit role as instruments of economic policy. In Britain, the arts in the widest sense were calculated as employing 430 000 people in the mid 1980s. When factors such as travel, hotels and catering connected with museum-, theatre- and concert-going is taken into account, the arts in the UK had a turnover approaching £2500 million.

Disneyland, sprawling over hundreds of acres in California, gets twenty million visitors a year. Comparing visitors per square foot, the British Museum, the single most popular tourist attraction in the UK, which gets less than four million a year, is actually far more heavily visited. It's a traffic that provides the basis for a thriving industry, one that takes in the manufacturing and retailing of merchandise, stationery and books, along with mail order and catering businesses.

The British Museum is in fact among the most conservative of institutions. Its display techniques have conceded little to the showmanship that is now seen as an essential part of a museum's repertoire. London's Natural History Museum, on the other hand, has had no such restraint. It attracted ridicule when its director and a dozen of his senior staff invested in the price of a Disney-organised course on visitor care.

Museums have acquired an economic role on two quite distinct levels. They are involved in commercial activities of a straightforwardly opportunistic kind. The extent of what is at stake was demonstrated in one of Sir Roy Strong's more than usually quixotic pronouncements, made shortly before he resigned as the director of the Victoria and Albert Museum. He announced his belief that the V&A should seek to become the Laura Ashley of the 1990s. Sure enough, the museum has indeed established a subsidiary known as V&A Enterprises, which collects royalties from companies such as Habitat for the sale of textiles and other items based on designs in the V&A's archives. And Saatchi and Saatchi, the advertising company headed by Maurice Saatchi, a trustee of the Tate, was behind a tasteless publicity campaign, calculated to reverse the decline in visitor numbers in the wake of the introduction of admission charges, which relied heavily on posters blithely describing the V&A as an 'Ace caff with museum attached'.

Meanwhile, at the Museum of Modern Art in New York, there are actually two large retail outlets. One is an always crowded, two-level space immediately next to the museum's main entrance, where elegant blond-wood shelves sag under the weight of merchandise. Across the street another, even more prominent retail outpost, opened in time for the 1989 Christmas season, sells items far removed from the postcards and catalogues that used to be the staple of museum stores. Drawing on the wide range of consumer goods on show in MoMA's industrial design gallery, the museum store sells high ticket merchandise that is anything but an impulse buy. There is furniture from Aalto to Le Corbusier, clocks, cutlery, lights and consumer electronics.

In the Les Halles shopping centre in Paris, France's national museums have grouped together to open their own shop, to sell Babar dolls and reproduction Bastille keys. Nor have they neglected the retailing possibilities of their own premises. The Beaubourg has a kiosk selling tape measures and kettles as the most prominent element of its entrance floor. At the Louvre, one of the primary results of I.M. Pei's pyramid has been to create an elegant means of providing natural light for an underground shopping centre.

But all these museums are dwarfed by the Smithsonian Institute in Washington, which runs a retail empire fifteen shops strong with a turnover of $24 million in 1987. Sam Greenberg, director of the Smithsonian's shops, has raised turnover by fifty per cent each year since he was appointed, adopting such hard-headed commercial techniques as setting up exhibit shops with merchandise related to special exhibitions, building a 38 000 square feet warehouse to store all his books, records, posters, postcards, calendars, toys, models, kites, ethnic crafts, foods and reproduction jewellery, and instituting computerised bi-weekly reports on the best sellers.

All this has been the subject of considerable scepticism from those who see the museum as abdicating its responsibilities in the face of rampant trivialisation and hucksterism. But the division between culture and commerce has never been as clear cut as some critics maintain. It is the narrow line that divided the Victorian museum builders from the showmen of their day that may partly account for the sensitivity some scholars have to the present-day popularisation of the museum.

While museums have been busy trying to turn themselves into smooth-running, cash-generating machines, using all the blandishments and guile of the retail industry, they also offer special possibilities within the wider urban context. They are seen, rightly or wrongly, as being outside the com-

The museum as landmark

mercial nexus, and are therefore looked on with special favour by zoning authorities, planners and governments. The museum has become an important bargaining counter in the development business. In New York, MoMA sold its air rights for $17 million to Charles Shaw, who built the 52-storey Museum Tower next door. It will also net an extra $4 million in property taxes levied on residents of the tower, that will go to the museum's trust fund, not the city. Air rights have also been important issues at Carnegie Hall, the Whitney, and in the 42nd Street/Times Square theatre district. In urbanistic terms, the city has had to pay a heavy price. Cesar Pelli's Museum Tower in West 54th Street, elegant though it is, overshadows MoMA's old sculpture garden, and has opened the way to all kinds of less attractive additions to historic cultural buildings.

In London, cultural institutions blundered disastrously into the business of development on their own account. The National Gallery, denied the use of public funds to develop the long vacant Hampton site adjoining its Trafalgar Square building, was pressed into attempting a commercial office development on part of the site to raise the funds to build more gallery space. The contortions that a bevy of architects went through to accommodate these two radically different elements into a single building – though not beyond the talents of Louis Kahn with the Mellon Center for British Art in New Haven – provoked the entry of the Prince of Wales into the public debate on architecture, and turned the redevelopment into a long-drawn-out saga. In Covent Garden, the Royal Opera House embarked on a similar course, with results perhaps more architecturally convincing than the National Gallery, but just as long-winded.

Museums are pump primers, their presence can be compared to the opening of a subway station, or even an airport: an investment which has the effect of raising property values. They have the ability to raise the profile of a development, bringing life into an area. At Canary Wharf, Olympia and York offered space to a variety of museums, including the National Portrait Gallery, which in the event declined, in order to increase the attractiveness of the development.

In New York, the Whitney Museum has cooperated with at least one developer to establish downtown branches – that is to say putting on displays from its collection within the public areas of new office blocks. The developer benefits from zoning advantages and the kudos of an association with a museum. The museum increases its exposure.

Not surprisingly then, the museum industry is being coopted into playing a substantial role in the attempt to breathe new life into sinking cities, and to give ascendant ones more of an edge over their competitors. Urban basket cases from Lowell, Massachusetts to Liverpool look to museums for economic salvation. Dallas is busy trying to build a cultural equivalent to the Texas Medical Center, Houston's astonishing would-be alternative downtown.

Locked in mortal combat with Houston, Dallas sees every scrap of cultural prestige as a prop for its economy. Houston has its opera, and its De Menil Museum. Dallas needed to hit back with a concert hall. The $81 million Meyerson Center has allowed the Dallas Symphony Orchestra, with its presumptuously titled 'maestro' Eduard Mata, to move out of its old and less than dignified home at the State Fair Ground, and is now the focus of the sixty-acre arts district established by the city in 1983. The city restricts the types of development permitted here, and controls the design of frontages and heights. Half the land is in not-for-profit or public ownership. Ed Larrabee Barnes's Dallas Museum of Arts and the Arts District Theater are already complete, and the next stage is the Lone Star Project, which includes a fifty-storey office tower. The planners for the development, Sasaki Associates, forecast thirty thousand jobs will eventually be created by the $1.6 billion complex.

Revealingly, Dallas chose I.M. Pei as the architect for its concert hall, the designer of choice for the patron who has made some money and is now keen to demonstrate his taste and discrimination. Pei's purist geometry unambiguously suggests an aspiration to classicism rather than the vulgarity of obvious display. Better still in the Dallas context, it is at the opposite end of the architectural spectrum from the post-modernism of Philip Johnson which has played such an important role in establishing the Houston skyline.

More dependent on public funds, there have been projects such as the Massachusetts Museum of Contemporary Art – Mass MoCA – the highpoint of Governor Dukakis's now tarnished-looking Massachusetts economic turnaround. Thomas Krens, a hugely ambitious museum impresario from New York, in a hurry to make his mark and with an education that concentrated as much on business administration as on fine art, chanced upon the derelict mills of the small industrial town of North Adams, already engaged in a vigorous campaign to raise itself out of dereliction. Creating a large-scale, new museum in North Adams – sprawling over 400 000 square feet in a twenty-eight-building complex – offered the hope of helping to reverse the town's declining fortunes, and creating at least a few new jobs. Dukakis, just as he was beginning his hopeless run for the presidency, and eager to look statesmanlike, used the Massachusetts state budget to fuel that ambition. Krens, before taking off to assume the directorship of the Guggenheim Museum in New York, recruited a team of architectural stars including Frank Gehry and Robert Venturi to help his absurdly over-optimistic $72 million fund-raising campaign for the project. No sooner than he had secured the New York job, Krens was again touring the world, indulging his edifice complex with plans to build satellite Guggenheims.

Some of the same impulses were at work in the decision of Britain's Tate Gallery to take space in the Albert Dock development in Liverpool. The Tate's presence was enough to give the fragile project some of the critical mass needed for success. The gallery's northern outpost acts as a magnet for people, and it bestows a degree of credibility on the entire development. The reaction has not been uniformly positive. Militant Liverpudlians profess to see money spent on museums rather than on improving a rotting social infrastructure as an affront.

Despite such doubts, the museum has developed a new role. Once it was a place that had instruction and the propagation of a particular view of the world as its underpinning. Now it has come to be seen as an urban landmark – a replacement for the missing agora, a place devoted to spectacle.

Piano and Rogers's design for the Beaubourg in Paris brought home just how far the museum could be pushed in the direction of becoming a public space. It was conceived by two architects intoxicated with the rhetoric of impermanence and flexibility. Explicit in the design was the idea that the museum was a focus for people and spectacle, as much as it was a place for instruction or enlightenment. It was seen from the outset as a magnet for the social life of a city, and has been designed as a crowd-pleaser, attracting countless thousands of visitors who never have any intention of looking at the art contained within its walls.

At the opposite extreme from the privately funded magnificence of the American museums is the wave of new public museums in Europe. Nowhere is it more in evidence than in President Mitterrand's Paris, which saw an avalanche of new museum buildings in the 1980s, part of the conscious move to reassert Paris's cultural importance internationally.

In the course of the decade, the city opened a whole string of massively subsidised museums, from the museum of science and technology in the remodelled city abattoir La Villette, commenced but never completed during the era of Gaullist giant projects, to the surrealist conversion of the old Gare d'Orsay, the Seine-side railway terminal built in a fit of grandiloquence to bring visitors to an early twentieth-century grand exposition and never of much practical consequence thereafter, into a museum of nineteenth-century art. Following in the footsteps of the Beaubourg, itself one of the largest museums in the world, with its permanent modern collection, its library, music performance space, and cavernous football-pitch sized office floor full of arts bureaucrats, Paris has built an architecture museum, a strip cartoon museum, a Picasso museum, an Arab Institute, and has remodelled the Louvre – all in the course of a single decade.

To Mitterrand, it is the duty of the French state to build museums, for a variety of reasons, only one of which is the enlightenment of its citizens. An even stronger, and by no means silent factor is the recurring French mission of making Paris the unchallenged centre of European culture.

Museum-going has become a major part of visiting Paris, just as it has in London, Washington or New York. Paris's breakneck construction of new museums has introduced an element of fashion and novelty into the process. Thus the opening of I.M. Pei's aesthetically questionable pyramid at the Louvre had the effect of siphoning off the crowds who used to flock to the equally sensational, though by the end of the 1980s somewhat jaded-looking Beaubourg. This rush to put the Louvre back at the top of the list of most visited museums had endless queues shuffling round and round the pyramid waiting for admission. Yet it was the elimination of just such delays that Mitterrand had used to justify the project in the first place.

Gae Aulenti's remodelling of the Orsay raises even more questions. The finest works within the new museum are the impressionist paintings that come from the old Jeu de Paume, yet these, hanging under the cast-iron roof of the old station against modish sandstone, have been crushed into visual insignificance. They look like postage stamps, past which endless crowds of visitors shuffle in search of the more obvious thrills of a building that has been constructed like·a giant urban adventure playground, full of glass lifts and bridges. You shoot from Aulenti's restoration of the first class waiting room, now a restaurant, with its gilt mirrors and plaster splendour, out into the museum, then plunge down to the enormous retail space in the old booking hall.

The collection has clearly taken second place to the idea of the museum as a place to be. The Musée d'Orsay is conceived as a series of streets and piazzas, with its shops and places for refreshment, its quietly contemplative corners, and its bustling crowds. It is a place in which for an hour, with its citizens drawn from all over the world, there is a fleeting sense of community, one which vanishes again as you pass the security checkpoints on your way out.

The sheer scale of the Paris projects has left the curators struggling to fill them. The idea of establishing a museum of science and technology at La Villette betrays the scent of desperation. It was a white elephant of a building, twice the size of the Beaubourg, in the middle of a bleak desert of mud, which nobody knew how to handle. The science museum scheme soaked up an awful lot of the endless acres on the site but, bereft of a real collection, the museum relies on a large number of interactive video displays, providing neither the sense of spectacle that comes from the presence of 'real' objects, nor the otherness that museum visiting relies on. Apart from all its flashing neon, intersecting escalators, and its showy approaches, the visitor is left with the memory of an experience not so different from what he could have had at home with a personal computer.

Frankfurt has been no less ambitious than Paris in its programme of cultural building. Here it is the city authorities who have been responsible for the creation of a museum quarter on the Schumankai. Frankfurt's cultural building programme began with the renovation of the city's opera house in 1977. The city's social democrat cultural commissioner proposed concentrating all the city's new museums on the river. It is a scaled-down version of the museums on Washington's Mall, or of the museums of South Kensington, densely packed together, positioned so as to allow cross-visiting. Museums now line the Main, embracing everything from the post office to the cinema. One by one, big old villas have been taken over and put to new uses as museums. And in between them are completely new buildings on a larger or smaller scale. They face the sprouting towers of the city's banks across the river. This is where Richard Meier built the first of his white refrigerators, for the Museum of Crafts and Applied Art. Together with its twin, the Atlanta High Museum, it set Meier on course to become the most ubiquitous museum builder of the 1990s, with commissions from the city councils of Ulm and Bonn, for a second museum on the Frankfurt riverfront, and of course the Getty in Los Angeles.

The Frankfurt museums have been designed by a selection of German and international architects chosen in a series of invited architectural competitions staged by the city over the years. The strategy has been to use architects from a strictly limited group, whose approach could loosely be described as cool rationalism, and to keep the more flamboyantly expressive designers away from the river. Hence the prominence of Meier on the waterfront, and the more discreet positioning of Hans Hollein's highly idiosyncratic Museum of Modern Art two streets behind. But the city's tidy strategy has been disrupted by the federally funded Post Office Museum, erupting in the midst of the cool riverfront museums.

Meier's first building, commissioned in 1980, was completed in 1984. His second, the Anthropology Museum, should be completed in 1994. Paradoxically, it has what is widely acknowledged to be the best of Frankfurt's collection, even though it has taken the longest to get a new building.

In fact the Anthropology Museum has been the subject of two architectural competitions. The result of the first was overturned just before build-

ing work was about to start, when Frankfurt was taken over by a Green-SDP coalition, because it would have meant the loss of sixty-eight trees. A second competition was staged, and Meier's design duly won.

In the German context, the museum has a particular significance. While Berlin was a divided city, the federal republic's cities battled it out with each other for leadership. And in that battle museums assumed crucial importance. Cologne, Mönchengladbach and Stuttgart – where James Stirling's extension to the Staatsgalerie propelled a little-visited collection into the international first rank – all have major new museums, but it is Frankfurt that has made most of the running. With reunification, its planners hope that the investment will not have been in vain.

When the Red Army reached Berlin in 1945, it seized the symbolic heart of the city, the city palace, the opera house, the university, the grand public spaces, and the museums – the very museums that Schinkel built for the Prussian kings in the early nineteenth century in the struggle to make their provincial capital a city to be reckoned with, and with which he defined the museum in its modern form.

Partition left the Allies with little more than the city's western suburbs. West Berlin had to build its institutions from scratch, though it had the pick of all the most portable items from the old national museums in the Soviet sector, spirited away by fleeing curators. For forty years, Berlin had two rival national galleries and two competing museums of archaeology, each clinging on to their half of the old collection.

So far it is New York which has set the pace for the cultural impresario who operates from the museum base. Thomas Hoving's now much questioned tenure at the Metropolitan Museum saw the emergence of curatorship as a serious career alternative to merchant banking or industry for the ambitious entrepreneur. Budgets soared, buildings multiplied, and the blockbuster exhibit ushered in an era of bread and circuses. The museum has become a central part of the way of life of the modern city, less a storehouse of scholarship and treasures than a place in which many of the conventional parts of civic life can take place, public spaces in which families and individuals can promenade to meet each other and to encounter strangers. A place to eat out, and in which to go shopping, or to browse in a bookshop. It's a change which is reflected in the way that museums are designed. You can see the priorities clearly at work in I.M. Pei's extension to Washington's imperial National Gallery. Pei's building functions as an almost self-contained pavilion, which has as its centrepiece a vast empty space. It is, as museum curators never cease to point out, hardly the best place to show art, which is in fact banished to the cellular spaces at each apex of Pei's prism. The purpose of the new building, acknowledged or not, is to lift the experience of museum visiting out of the ordinary, to signal that this is a special place, one which in some senses puts the visitor on show. It has become a surrogate for civic life.

The airport as city square

7

Forty years ago, the terminal buildings of what is now the world's biggest international airport consisted of row upon row of olive-drab tents, furnished with a few chintz-covered armchairs and an incongruous rank of cast-iron telephone boxes. Inside the largest of the tents was a W.H. Smith kiosk selling *Picture Post*, and a folding card table on which stood a vase full of cut flowers. You could dictate a telegram sitting at the table, while keeping an eye on the blackboard in the corner on which arrivals and departures were chalked up.

Hurriedly converted from military use, London Airport, as Heathrow was called until the city's second and third airports at Gatwick and Stansted matured, took shape in the closing years of World War Two as a runway for the Royal Air Force's heavy bombers. It was born as the Great West Aerodrome, a grass landing strip first laid out in the 1930s. Sir Peter Masefield, one-time chairman of the British Airports Authority, remembers cycling down a leafy lane, past the Magpie Inn, and finding a runway tucked among the market gardens for which the area had been famous since Oliver Cromwell's trained bands fought off Charles I.

Today, its perimeter fence encloses five square miles, and Heathrow is the focus for a massive industrial and commercial complex stretching far beyond the airport's gates, one whose importance to the British economy approaches that of the City of London. Yet its presence is signalled to the outside world in the most anonymous fashion by the Forte Crest Hotel (formerly the Post House), which sits in an angle of left-over land formed by the M4 motorway and the airport spur road. It is an undistinguished structure, dating back to the hotel building boom of the 1960s and the rush to qualify for the subsidies the government offered for every hotel bedroom completed before the end of the financial year.

In international terms, Heathrow is a vital part of what makes London a major city. It is one of the capital's last employment generators with a substantial demand for unskilled labour, offering 58 000 direct jobs. The baggage loader may not have the same touchy pride in his job that the docker once did, but he does at least have a job.

With 39 million international passengers annually, more than Paris and Frankfurt, its nearest two rivals, put together, Heathrow is so far ahead as

Norman Foster claims his third London airport at Stansted is a return to a simpler age of air travel, when you turned up and took off. In fact it is already generating the complexities of airports that function as shopping-centres, employment-providers, and social focuses to be out of sight. The airport gives Britain a head start when international business considers where to locate. And it gives London, and in particular its western suburbs, a massive economic boost over the rest of the country. Of course it also pollutes a large area of West London with jet noise and the fallout from aviation spirit, jettisoned by aircraft as they manoeuvre to land.

An airport can make otherwise worthless land highly desirable. Around Heathrow the asbestos cement sheds of the early days are giving way to more elaborate developments, reflecting the increased value of the land. Like universities which spawn commercial science parks, airports have developed a significant economic role that goes far beyond the engineering, catering and cargo that one would expect. As well as the airport's own payroll, more than 300 000 jobs depend on the runways, from managers and skilled computer operators to truck drivers.

Without Heathrow, London's place in the pecking order of European capitals would take a precipitate tumble. The airport generates business, it attracts industry, and it creates jobs. But its significance goes beyond its contribution to the balance of payments statistics. It creates a sense of London being at the heart of things, in both a symbolic and a practical way. The other big European cities are well aware of it. Pressure from Heathrow helped France to take the hugely expensive decision to build a brand new airport at Roissy in 1964. It had become clear that first Le Bourget, and then Orly, had reached the limits of their capacities. To compete in the European context, the French government decided that it had to start from scratch. A decade in the making, Charles de Gaulle opened in 1974. In the autocratic French way, traffic was switched from Orly by decree to make the new airport the country's main international gateway overnight. Now the French are planning a five-fold expansion.

Frankfurt is equally ambitious. Running neck and neck with Paris in passenger numbers, it is already the city's second largest employer, building exhibition centres, offices and conference halls within walking distance of the terminal buildings.

Frankfurt is a classic hub airport, which is to say that one in every two passengers changes planes here, so it is filled with attractions aiming to tempt the transit passenger into spending money. The terminal area is organised like a small city, with more than a hundred shops selling everything from mink coats to hi-fis, twenty-six restaurants, three cinemas, a chapel which offers wedding ceremonies, a medical centre with five doctors equipped to handle child birth and heart attacks, and a battery of resident social workers. Even the sex cinema is signalled with the usual teutonic attention to detail, by a pictogram drawn from the same catalogue as the

The airport as city square

fire exit and the bureau de change signs.

Both Frankfurt and CDG, unlike Heathrow, are linked to mainline as well as metro railways, and motorways. The next stage in Frankfurt's plans is a magnetically levitated transit system for movement around the airport. Like Heathrow, Frankfurt is run by a privately owned company, a sign that the big airport is no longer seen as a piece of state-controlled infrastructure, but has become a business. Heathrow's owner, BAA, has eight other airports under its control. With its massive revenues from landing charges and duty-free sales, it has the resources to buy up property companies, develop hotel chains, and go into retailing. It even contemplated taking a stake in the development of New York's Kennedy Airport by bidding to buy the Pan Am terminal there.

Along with a handful of other international airports, Heathrow has reached the critical mass that makes it much more than simply an interchange between passengers, aircraft and cargo. If not actually a city in its own right, it has become a vital constituent of the city as a whole. Despite the fact that large areas of the airport are restricted to people who have tickets, it has authentically urban qualities that self-consciously fabricated tourist traps such as New York's South Street Seaport or London's Covent Garden do not. It is a place which attracts tourists and plane spotters, job hunters and salesmen, criminals, retailers and caterers. Businessmen come here for conferences. Punjabi women from nearby Southall find work as cleaners and kitchen staff. Entrepreneurs, fresh from their business school MBA courses, come to put their marketing theories into practice with new ideas for retail franchise chains. Its immigration halls have become the setting for political demonstrations: Tamil refugees have stripped naked here rather than quietly submit to deportation. Libyans have bombed the baggage hall and, along with those at Gatwick, the airport's approach roads are the only place in mainland Britain on which the Army regularly deploys armoured vehicles. The Wapping paparazzi keep the place permanently staked out on watch for passing celebrities. Clearly this is as highly charged a part of the public realm as Trafalgar Square. By most reasonable definitions it is as urban an environment as you can get, a forum as well as a gateway.

All Heathrow lacks to qualify as a conventional town is a housing area: if you discount the hotels. The transience of the airport embodies contemporary urbanism in a real, as well as a metaphorical sense. The number of times in the course of a year that a citizen of London, or New York, actually visits their city's main airport is likely to be rather greater than the trips they make to the National Gallery or the Metropolitan Museum. The poor and the very rich come into closer contact at an airport than

Previous page: In the late 1940s, Heathrow Airport was a row of tents, pitched along the edge of an old military runway. Today, the busiest international airport in the world is the centre of a sprawling city, employing directly and indirectly many thousands of people, in its own factories, shops, and hotels

almost anywhere else, despite the elaborate hierarchy of classes and facilities for them.

Croydon, Le Bourget and Tempelhof, and the other early airports, represented an era in which flying was a gentlemanly recreation. The buildings, designed with gentlemanly polish, were modest. There might be a small terminal that tried to provide a comfortable retreat. But from its windows, you could see the oily-fingered mechanics across the grass runway. What followed them was the baroque phase of airport building, characterised by the outward show of luxury. The amateurs and enthusiasts of the early days had given way to the professional traveller. While air travel was still reserved for an elite, and ticket prices were high, passengers expected more than what Reyner Banham once called the yacht basin look of the early aerodromes. So when Sir Frederick Gibberd rebuilt Heathrow in time for the Queen to open it in December 1955 – flights were transferred to another ex-military airstrip at Northolt while construction was underway – he filled the single passenger terminal with exotic finishes. There was black marble and weathered sycamore, terrazzo and hessian. With its massive clear spans and lofty, wide-open interiors, Heathrow was built to impress, even if its brick exterior served to take the edge off the impact of the vast extent of plate glass that characterised much of its facades. And it was built to provide reassurance in the middle of what was for many a landscape of stress.

This was the modern world in its *Dolce Vita* incarnation: Cuban heels, Dacron, midnight-blue suits, and silver metal aircraft waiting to whisk the masters of the universe away. London in the 1950s, like most of the major metropolises, was still a city much as the Victorians had left it. There were steamships tied up in the Pool of London below Tower Bridge, just as there were passenger liners all along the piers of Manhattan's Lower West Side, and at Sydney Harbour's Ocean Terminal. The railways still ran on steam, while not a yard of motorway had been built in Britain. Soot-streaked, and poorly maintained during the war and in the post-war austerity that followed, the buildings of the recent past looked not just grubby, but embarrassingly outmoded. They seemed to represent a bleak and difficult episode, from which the country was desperate to escape. Victoriana seemed not so much priceless heritage, but the cause for national shame, a constant reminder that much of the country's creaking industrial infrastructure was already a century old.

In the dowdy London of the fifties, there was nothing that was quite so thoroughly modern as Heathrow. It was a place to escape from the messy world outside and bask in the sleek gloss of its wide-open spaces, the sheen

The airport as city square

of costly materials, voluptuous modern furniture, and carefully coordinated lower case typography. The railways went green with envy. British Rail was goaded into demolishing Hardwick's splendid building at Euston to make way for a vapid glass and marble hall in an attempt to match the glamour of the jet age. And throughout the system, makeshift attempts were made to mask the quaint detail of the Victorians with simple modern materials, just as hardboard was being nailed over the nation's panelled Victorian doors to give them the look of up-to-date flush panels.

Yet, as Reyner Banham perceptively pointed out, airports were inevitably out of date before they were completed. Writing in 1962, the year that Heathrow handled 6.5 million passengers and built its first multi-storey car park, Banham saw that 'airports are permanently obsolete'. Looking at Idlewild, as Kennedy used to be called, where a flock of terminals is drawn up like a wagon train in a defensive horseshoe, around a pointless Beaux Arts reflecting pool in the manner of Versailles, Banham noted that it had been designed for Lockheed Constellations, but by the time it was ready had filled up with Comets and Boeing 707s, requiring the terminal's airside to be encrusted with jet blast deflectors. Driven by technological and social change, the world's successful airports have been permanent building sites since they were first opened. In fact, this is the condition of all dynamic cities. Paradoxically, airports are already acquiring the rarefied status of heritage sites. Saarinen's Dulles airport outside Washington, with its ski jump roof and its mobile lounges, is functionally redundant. But it is being updated with satellite terminals, linked by an underground railway, that carefully defer to the original design.

Heathrow was originally designed by Gibberd in 1953, at a time when air travel was being reshaped by the Constellation, the world's first pressurised cabin airliner. In Britain, the Tudor vainly attempted to compete, while flying boats were still seriously being contemplated for intercontinental routes as late as 1950.

Heathrow's runways intersected to form a misty, diamond-shaped patch of meadow at the centre of the airport. Gibberd was given a 158-acre plot of what looked to be dead land as the spot to which to move the terminal buildings away from the airport's perimeter, where a clutter of temporary sheds and shacks straggled along the Bath Road back towards central London. On the face of it, it seemed a tidy and economical way to use land that would otherwise have been wasted. But it depended on punching a 2000-feet-long road tunnel into the central area from the perimeter, a choke point that was to cause trouble almost immediately. What nobody foresaw in the 1950s was that such an apparently generous site would prove hopelessly inadequate in the face of the explosive growth of air traffic, less than twenty-five years after the first terminal was completed. By the end of the 1980s, Sir Richard Rogers was drawing up plans for a fifth terminal, bigger than the first three put together, located on the site of a reclaimed sewage plant adjoining the airport, in an attempt once and for all to shake off the tyranny of the access tunnel.

Gibberd's first stage for what was then the most complex and sophisticated airport in the world included a control tower, a crew building, and a single passenger terminal with eight gates, now, much modified, known as Terminal Two. It was designed for just 1200 passengers an hour in both directions. Chicago's O'Hare, by contrast, had 778 aircraft movements an hour at peak periods in the 1980s. When it opened, Heathrow still wasn't equipped with airbridges, invented only at the start of the fifties. Instead, passengers had to walk along jetties and down steps onto the tarmac, then up mobile stairways to board their planes.

With its segregated arrival and departure levels – check-in on ground level, passengers moving upstairs and progressing by stages to the departure lounge – Heathrow set a pattern that was followed all over the world. Idlewild was first mooted by the New York and New Jersey Port Authority as early as 1947, and still stands out for the way in which each major airline operates from its own separate terminal, ranged around an oval road system. But the consolidated international arrivals building, opened in 1958, is on the Heathrow model. Frankfurt was first planned in 1950. Los Angeles International was built between 1957 and 1961. Dulles at Washington was the first airport planned specifically for the jet, though without much long-term success.

Heathrow's strategists thought that there was room for four more buildings in the central diamond, after the first terminal opened. Heavily remodelled in fibre glass, it was renamed Terminal Two; then came a second long haul terminal, eventually designated Terminal Three and a cargo building. Finally, what was called Terminal One opened in 1967. It was the largest of the three terminals and included an integral car park. But it had long since been clear that a second major airport was needed for London. Less than a decade after Heathrow came into being, a search was started for a second site, a pattern repeated in New York, Paris, Los Angeles and Tokyo. The result was Gatwick, whose first stage opened in June 1958 when it was welcomed by *The Architectural Review* as, at last, 'a real machine age design with airport, road, rail and aircraft brought together'. The main London to Brighton road ran underneath the terminal, which was itself linked to a British Rail station by footbridge.

Despite the building of Gatwick, passenger numbers at Heathrow came close to doubling between 1970 and 1980, stretching the inner circle to

　　　　　　　　　　　　　　　　The airport as city square

breaking point despite ever more desperate attempts to make more space. A fourth terminal eventually opened on the opposite side of the airport.

The government was ambivalent about Heathrow from the start. Protests about noise from aircraft had yet to start in earnest – in the 1970s formal complaints were running at 3000 a year – but in the 1950s the airport was already seen as a land-hungry monster which threatened to turn the market gardens of Middlesex into an endless tarmac prairie. It was a development that foreshadowed the endless battles over the siting of London's third airport in the 1960s and 1970s that left a deep scar on the British planning system. Despite funding the airport's buildings to the tune of £500 million at 1980 prices, the government did all it could to keep its creation in check. Hotels were strictly limited: provision at the airport was restricted to overnight beds for aircrew and transit passengers, while the town terminal was seen as the most promising way to cope with traffic growth into the foreseeable future.

The norm in the early days was for passengers to check in at a town terminal, and to be bussed out to the airfield in an airline coach. British European Airways was building itself its fourth successive London terminal as late as 1964, which turned out to be redundant before it even opened. In New York, the East Side terminal attempted to fill a similar function, but enthusiasm for the idea faded as traffic grew and the novelty of air travel evaporated. In highly regimented Japan, Tokyo's Narita airport, driven seventy miles from the city by the lack of flat land, still has a functioning town terminal. But the West London Air Terminal is a block of apartments now, and its baggage hall is a supermarket.

By the start of the 1960s, the world's major airports had already grown into reasonably convincing two-dimensional facsimiles of authentic cities, each with its multi-denominational chapel, its bank, its hotel, its fire station, security force and industrial estate. At Heathrow there were signs indicating the way to such novel attractions as the hairdressers' shops, and the 'waving base'. You could find a municipal masonry clocktower here too, impaled on a traffic roundabout, haunting the hangars of the maintenance area like the ghost of a traditional town centre. In many cases it was these backwaters of the airport that had the most interesting architecture. Sir Owen Williams built BOAC's hangars in monumental concrete. Myron Goldsmith did the same for the United Airlines hangar at San Francisco.

In the early days it was possible to consider these and the terminal buildings as isolated landmarks set in what, despite the concrete of the runways, was virtually a rural landscape. The flat prairie of the apron was relieved by the distinctive geometry of the intersecting tailplanes of the big jets. But as the complexity and scale of the airport has increased, and the city beyond has decentralised, so the gap between the airport and its surroundings has diminished.

From the moment that you step on the robot train which insists on clearing its throat and making a short welcoming speech on behalf of 'Gatwick Airport in association with Canadian Club Whisky', as it takes you to the new North Terminal, you realise that airports have moved into an era in which travel is hardly the main issue.

Gatwick's new terminal has given up all pretence that the modern airport is anything other than a shopping centre. It has gone far beyond the duty-free state which turns the departure lounge into an assault course littered with perfume and gin. This is very heaven for the niche marketeer. Tie Rack stands next to Knickerbox, which is next to Sock Shop. There are Skyshops and Bodyshops, Gift Shops and Olympus sportswear shops, W.H. Smith and Teddy, 'your dedicated soft toy store'.

Here you find a fully fledged shopping mall that makes no apologies for itself. Dorothy Perkins and Burton glower at each other, all twinkling spotlights and blond wood, just as Bloomingdale's has turned up at Pan Am's terminal at JFK, Marks and Spencer has plans to open a store at Heathrow, and Harrods is at Heathrow, Frankfurt and Madrid.

BAA, Gatwick's owner, sees shifting people as a secondary objective to its primary responsibility to its shareholders of making as much money as possible by letting every available square foot to people peddling silk underwear and cheese-filled croissants. It is not alone. With a more than averagely affluent captive audience, already in a state of suspended animation, airports are the perfect place to persuade people to spend more money. Anchorage offers perhaps the strangest luxury shopping arcade in the world. Caught in the Alaskan wastes, the airport is the refuelling stop for polar route flights to Tokyo. Few ever leave the airport, they just rush to stock up on Cartier wristwatches and airbrush-free pornography aimed at the Japanese market.

There are precedents for the role that the airport has adopted. The railway terminus was an essential part of the Victorian metropolis. It was a new kind of civic space, and called for the creation of a new building type to accommodate it. The magnificence of the architectural expression of railway buildings made them among the most prominent of nineteenth-century landmarks – competing with the town halls and the museums for attention. London's King's Cross, and the now demolished Euston were among the earliest examples. Milan's Stazione Centrale was a late, and perhaps as a result a particularly grandiloquent specimen. In New York there were two prominent stations: Grand Central and Pennsylvania –

both now sadly mutilated. Even Los Angeles has its Union Station, still imposing despite shrivelling into insignificance as a transport centre, and Tokyo has its exotic, European-styled main station.

Discovering the original Heathrow buildings under the continuous succession of accretions, extensions, new buildings, adaptations and demolitions is a task for an archaeologist. Massive increases in passenger numbers have changed the way that airports operate. For a while it seemed as if the coming of wide-bodied jets might keep the need for ever more passenger capacity at bay. At Kennedy, for example, aircraft movements in the 1970s dropped to sixty per cent of their 1968 total after the deployment of the new, big jets. But the slack was quickly taken up.

Banham would not have been at all surprised to find that the extended-range Boeing 747 – 400 that took to the skies at the end of the 1980s had a wingspan too large to negotiate all but a handful of the world's airports. And in the 1990s a fresh scramble of airport building is going on all over the world to cope with the 900-seater double-deckers that Boeing is promising, and expected traffic increases.

Just like the old railway companies, airlines went through a phase of using architecture to assert corporate pride. You can see it in the way Eero Saarinen created a swooping, soaring terminal for TWA at Idlewild (now Kennedy), and also in Pan Am's equally distinctive circular building at the same airport. Between them they set the tone for the airports of the early 1960s. By comparison with those innocent, far-off days of Constellations and 707s, Helmut Jahn's gaudy United Airlines terminal at Chicago's O'Hare – which in sheer passenger numbers is larger even than Heathrow, thanks to its domestic flights – seems like hubris. Its self-conscious evocation of the railway stations of the past, with its jazzy neon-decorated interiors and ostentatiously decorative structure, belies the cramped and less than opulent standards of late twentieth-century air travel. The real spectacle takes place away from passengers' eyes: United has a 250 000 square foot baggage make up hall to cope with the complexities of moving a thousand bags per flight. Even with bar codes and laser readers, it is still a process on an industrial scale, with a workforce to match.

Nevertheless, new airports have become the focus for national and civic prestige, just as railway stations once were. Paul Andreu's first terminal at Paris Charles de Gaulle, with its science-fiction, blank-walled beehive building, criss-crossed by transparent tubes carrying moving walkways in tribute to Fritz Lang's *Metropolis*, was a deliberate assertion of the modernity of the French state. Similarly, a decade later, Skidmore, Owings and Merrill's Hadjh Terminal at Riyadh, with its Teflon-coated fabric tent roofs, testified if not to Islam then to the new wealth of the Arabs.

The airport as city square

Architecturally, airports have been an exception to the headlong rush towards historical revivalism of the 1970s. A Palladian air terminal, while it might yet be attempted, would still lack the air of technocratic reassurance that most people still need to be persuaded to venture into an aircraft with confidence.

But the modernism of the first airports has been abandoned for the interiors at least. The waiting areas at Gatwick have been turned into what is called 'Gatwick Village', a place in which the only signs of the English countryside are the swallows and red admirals let into the ceramic wall tiles. Here the cafeteria, within scent of aviation spirit exhaust fumes, is called 'The Country Table'. And the 'Gatwick Village Inn' has an oak-effect panelled fireplace and ceramic spaniels on its mantelpiece. Only the fact that there is no mud on the wheels of the luggage trolleys parked between tables suggests that patrons haven't had to negotiate ploughed fields and five-bar gates to get here.

Heathrow turned out to be an unstoppable force. Its geographical position, range of airlines, and transport connections made it perhaps the most important focus of international airline travel in the world. Its effect on the pattern of development in the Southeast was equally dramatic. The presence of the airport, and its position just off the main motorway to the west accelerated London's headlong rush westwards that had started centuries earlier. At one point, just about all new growth in Britain was concentrated on the Heathrow/M4 corridor, with towns such as Reading, Swindon and Bracknell getting the lion's share.

In the late 1960s and the 1970s, the prospect of all this rampant development gave Britain a bad fright. The search for a third site for an airport for London turned into a decade-long fiasco. Every one of the seventy or so sites considered in the Home Counties seemed to throw up its defenders, desperate to ensure that no such development took place in their backyard. Stansted, like Heathrow another military creation, was an early contender. Cublington, close to Aylesbury, was another. At the long-drawn-out and enormously costly public inquiry, the poet laureate Sir John Betjeman was an eloquent witness. 'This is not, I realise, a matter of economics,' he told the inquiry. 'One cannot assess in terms of cash or exports an imponderable thing like the turn of a lane, or an inn, or a church tower, or a familiar skyline. Only the choice of Stansted could be worse…'

For a while, following the decision of the veteran planner Sir Colin Buchanan to join the protesters' cause from his vantage point on the committee of inquiry set up to review the case, the government panicked. It knew it had to do something to cope with the ever increasing demand for

The airport as city square

more air traffic capacity, but it could not build it anywhere in Southeast England without offending some of its electorate. It opted in desperation for Foulness – a reclaimed mud flat in the Thames estuary. No matter that costs would be far higher, and that it would require the construction of fifty miles of motorway and rail links. A similar protest wave hit America, where consumer advocate Ralph Nader and his supporters introduced limits to night flights and noise abatement measures, as well as Germany and, not to be left out, Japan. Tokyo's second airport was met with a sustained barrage of guerilla warfare. Student radicals battled with molotov cocktails, mortar bombs and staves against a Samurai army of riot police for the best part of a decade. The airport still has the atmosphere of an armed camp, surrounded permanently by water cannon, barricades and militia.

But Foulness was quietly dropped in 1974, when it became brutally clear that Britain could not afford to risk building an airport that nobody would use. And equally quietly, the government started to divert traffic to Stansted. When Stansted was eventually named the third London airport in 1985, and Norman Foster appointed its architect, hardly anything was said. A moment in history had passed, and a generation grown accustomed to its package holidays in Spain and its cheap flights to America decided that it could perfectly well measure the value of the twist of a lane.

In more squeamish times, the British government attempted to counteract the immense attractions of Heathrow, vainly trying to tempt new airport investment into other parts of the country with a mixture of bribes and exhortation, partly in the name of regional balance, partly to placate affluent voters who lived around Heathrow. Now that the old state-controlled British Airports Authority has been recast as the privately owned corporation BAA, there are no such qualms. BAA makes no secret of its plans to squeeze every drop of revenue-earning potential from its property assets. It intends to make itself a major hotel operator, and plans to build them beyond its own airports.

The BAA terminals have more than 600 000 square feet of retail space between them. The space is auctioned off to retailers in parcels every three or five years, with a fixed percentage of the profits going to BAA. Concessionaires get a monopoly within each terminal, so it's hard for them not to make money. As aircraft get larger and larger, so it takes longer to board them, and so passengers have more time to spend in the airport shops – in the jargon, dwell time. To tempt them to spend more, BAA is pushing retailers up market: Heathrow has four caviar shops, and is Britain's largest single outlet for Havana cigars.

BAA is also moving into retailing on its own account, with soft toy shops aiming presumably for the custom of guilty fathers. Such strategies are essential for the continued profitability of the enterprise once the EEC abolishes the customs barriers within Europe that have made duty-free sales such a lucrative business. Airports are now developing an unexpected role as regional road-transport interchanges. Heathrow and Gatwick have become informal bus stations as opportunistic coach operators use the airport terminals as pick-up and drop-off points. According to BAA, one in five bus passengers who arrive at its terminals never goes near an aircraft. At Gatwick they switch to British Rail and to other buses. At Heathrow there is the connection with the Underground system. BAA professes to see this phenomenon as parasitic, and is trying to charge operators for the privilege of using its terminal bus stands. Of course they could also provide more potential customers for its retailers and caterers.

Not everyone is pleased by the magnetism of Heathrow. Provincial British airports have clamoured for a slice of the infrastructure investment that has been directed to Heathrow. Leeds, Manchester, Birmingham and Glasgow have all argued for Heathrow traffic to be diverted in their direction. The most powerful voice against these arguments has been British Airways, which sees anything that weakens its grip on the traffic that pours into Heathrow from around the world as disastrous. And the Thatcher government clearly believed the most effective way of using infrastructure investment was to concentrate, rather than to decentralise it. Thus, despite the protests of both those who live in the Southeast, and the major provincial interests, air traffic growth remains concentrated to a unique degree on London.

The American pattern is different, as it must be given the size of the country. But it too has adopted the hub and spoke system. Airlines channel their operations to hub airports, where as many as fifty per cent of passengers pass through in transit for other flights. It makes most efficient use of the airline's resources, and it underscores the economic position of the hub airport at the expense of less central parts of the system.

The modern airport goes far beyond the multiplicity of uses of the railway terminus. The sheer number and variety of different buildings gives the airport the potential to become a real part of the city, despite the scale of the runways and the impact of aircraft noise.

The airport is by no means as segregated from what goes on around it as the haphazard nature of its growth would suggest. In fact most airports are laid out by engineers who believe that they are pursuing a pragmatic course towards the most efficient movement of aircraft and passengers. Actually, their work has far more implications for the urban world and, consciously or not, very often addresses them.

In the European sense, as a densely built-up area and an intricate network of pedestrian streets and civic squares, there may not be much to recommend the airport city. But the airport has become not just a gateway, but a destination in its own right. The world's airports are entering their fourth generation.

Through the 1960s, they went through a hectic expansion programme. Traffic targets were exceeded almost as soon as they had been set, aircraft grew larger and faster. This was the period of the airport as never finished building site. The airport, as much as the university building programme, made a generation of architects and planners question the idea of the finite architectural statement more than anything else. Experience taught them that every prediction simply became obsolete, that every inch of excess capacity would be soaked up by economic growth and technological change.

In the 1970s, airports decentralised. They extruded endlessly to each horizon, like Dallas/Fort Worth, where such was the awareness of the need to plan for growth that an 18 000-acre prairie was set aside for the project, and a string of circular satellite terminals now stretches out along a motorway spine.

Each satellite at Dallas has its own parking garage, the idea being that passengers drive as close to their departure gate as they can, park, and walk the short distance across the thickness of the terminal to their aircraft. In fact this decentralised layout has given way in the 1980s to a denser format. The decentralised airport has fallen foul of air traffic delays which may require passengers to switch from gate to gate, and also the need for more security consciousness. In classic strategic terms, the more extended the perimeter, the more difficult it is to defend.

The airports being planned for the 1990s form part of a clearly defined hierarchy: the smaller regional airports are comparatively modest, the metropolitan hubs – Heathrow's Terminal Five, Japan's Kansai, being built on an artificial island off the coast of Osaka, and Frankfurt – are enormous. They include not just substantial shopping centres, aimed at both local workers and passengers, but also hotels, offices, massive car parks, often a trade mart and a conference centre, all in buildings constructed immediately next to the main terminal building, within the airport perimeter. There becomes less and less need to go into town at all.

The balance of power shifts to and fro between the airport operator and the airline. Once airlines took long leases on terminal space, and insisted on having them designed in their own image. Now airlines tend to take shorter leases, and themselves have a shorter longevity. Yet they still sometimes fight the airport for control. At London, Terminal Four was the cause of a bitter struggle between BAA and British Airways. The airline wanted to take on the whole terminal, as a highly visible flagship. BAA didn't want to give such a powerful position to any one airline. As a result the terminal stayed empty for six months after it was completed while the argument was resolved.

Especially in the USA, airports are beginning to earn as much revenue from parking charges as from landing dues, which is also affecting the form of the layout of the airport radically. In Britain, BAA has earned enormous sums from franchising duty-free sales areas. It learned the habit of seeing things in retailing terms, and it started to replan its terminal buildings not for optimum passenger flow, but to ensure the most prominent position for the duty-free shop. Now it has put the expertise learned in this way to good use, and is constructing fully fledged shopping malls on both sides of the passport control desk. In so doing, the line separating the airport from what surrounds it is growing ever more blurred.

Most accounts of airports consider them entirely from the landside. That is, as they are experienced by the occasional passenger passing through. Their buildings are seen only in terms of the face they present to the world outside. Once through the security and passport controls, there is a deliberately fostered sense of being cocooned in an environment where normal rules of everyday caution and self-preservation do not apply. Just follow the signs and all will be well. It is a sense that is only reluctantly relinquished on arrival at the final destination. Beyond this is a third spatial system, one which the passenger rarely penetrates, involving enormous areas of open space, the aprons, the maintenance bays, the baggage handling, operations rooms, radar sites, and computers for air traffic control and hangars. Then there is a fourth level on the airport, the ground movements of the aircraft themselves.

These four domains are one of the most intricately interwoven spatial hierarchies to be found anywhere in the modern city – as complex as the Forbidden City of Beijing. Small wonder the dislocation and unease that passengers can experience. Picking up a telephone in the arrivals wing of Tampa's modestly scaled airport, a young woman calls a friend in town. 'How do I get out of here?' she asks. It's not directions from the airport into town that she is looking for, but for help in finding a route out from the gate where she is standing to the baggage claim, and on to the car rental desks that mark the back door of the modern airport, by way of a mass transit shuttle.

Despite the practice of successful airports reproducing themselves abroad by exporting the professional services of their managements, in the

The airport as city square

way that the French and the British have, there have been a remarkable variety of different approaches adopted, from the centralised beehive with satellite gates reached by underground moving walkways as at CDG's Terminal One, to the mobile lounges of Washington's Dulles.

The American model, now adopted at Gatwick by the British, is to use a tracked, robot-operated train to move people back and forth between terminals and the more distant gates, an undertaking of considerable complexity not helped by the decision to design these transports to deny the idea of their involving movement. Instead of platforms there are lift doors that open on a concourse, no gap, no sign of the tracks.

The airport is the closest many cities come to a public realm, in some cases hardly limited to travellers. At Chicago's O'Hare, you can find political groups exercising their constitutional rights and handing out leaflets to incoming passengers about issues ranging from nuclear power to whales. Religious sects patrol the arrival halls in search of the confused and the vulnerable.

The airport is an extraordinary mixture of the planned and the unplanned. Built on the scale of the largest new towns, and representing a massive investment, it is free of the usual zoning constraints. You find hotels cheek by jowl with engineering plants.

In American mid-western airports, where even the taxi is a disappearing species, the courtesy bus taking travellers to the perimeter hotel or the car hire compound and back is very often the only form of public transport. America has all but lost the art of building buses, and these are often strange, customised vehicles, deliberately styled to look like limousines to avoid the stigma of riding a bus that many Americans feel.

The complexity of transportation systems at busy airports is remarkable. It can combine conventional railways, moving pavements, robot-controlled trams, and an array of buses. Houston Intercontinental, with its series of island terminals, has a continuous figure of eight underground tram that looks and feels very much like a ghost train. While the massively busy hub Atlanta links its gates with a network of robot trains that gives the place some of the feeling of a railway terminal.

As the twentieth century comes to a close, the airport is becoming an ever more complex problem, one which it is not sufficient to consider simply as a building, no matter how elegant. Norman Foster's crystalline box at Stansted, with its forest of steel columns holding up the roof, attempts to do this. Foster maintains that his intention was to restore the simplicity of the early days of air travel when passengers simply walked across a field to their waiting aircraft. The reality is less clear. Foster's diagram is

The airport as city square

At Gatwick the automatic trains that take passengers from the main terminal building to the departure gates clear their throats to welcome passengers on behalf of BAA and a whiskey company, a clear sign that there is more to the business of running airports than getting travellers from A to B

compromised by practicalities and threatened by a management committed to filling its airports with shops. There are plans for a full-size branch of Marks and Spencer at Heathrow, and for a lot more shops at Stansted, which not only point to shifting architectural priorities, but underline the reality of air travel.

The usual strategy of the architect has been an attempt to stamp a sense of urban normality on the landside of an airport, to create a fragile illusion that this is a familiar environment: that the terminal is just another concert hall, or university library, rather than a transition between the ground and the air. As the complexities involved in moving people in and around aircraft on the ground grow more difficult, the fiction that landside is a normal part of the environment in which conventional urban design rules apply becomes harder and harder to maintain. In fact the airport is a hybrid kind of space, one for which there are next to no conceptual frameworks, just the pragmatic expediencies of keeping traffic moving.

These are high-stress landscapes, full of anxious people on unfamiliar territory. Airports represent the costliest investment in building and engineering we see in the city. Yet the buildings themselves hardly address these implications. It's only by default that Los Angeles International has become a surrogate downtown. The main distributor road, actually an extension of Century Boulevard, is one of the busiest pedestrian streets in the city, with a constant press of crowds moving back and forth from terminals to the parking structures, and both sides of the runway are lined with a continuous wall of ten- and twelve-storey office towers and hotels.

America's only purpose-built major new airport in the 1990s, the replacement for Denver's Stapleton, is at last acknowledging the relationship of the airport to the city fabric. It is planned on a grid that matches the scale of downtown Denver city blocks. The next stage of the development of the major airport looks as if it will be its most interesting.

Living in the past

8

The attitudes of a city towards its own past are as much as anything the product of the way that it views its prospects. When London and New York were at their peak, the idea that redundant buildings had a role to play in defining their futures never occurred to more than a handful of their citizens. Certainly not to the politicians or developers, nor even the activists who were one day to establish a network of conservationist pressure groups.

There was little enough interest in preserving individual buildings, still less in maintaining the character of whole areas. When Inigo Jones's once fashionable Covent Garden piazza was overwhelmed by the building of a vegetable market in the nineteenth century, it was seen as a purely private affair, just as it was when the University of London began to spread across Georgian Bloomsbury. Property rights were sacred, and it was up to the individual owner to decide what to do with the buildings that he owned, as much as it was with his livestock, or his bank balance.

While the retired shopkeepers and well-bred ladies who now make up an important faction on the City of London's planning committee can spend hours arguing about their sacred duty to maintain the pattern of the streets that Shakespeare and Bacon once knew in the midst of a firestorm of new development, the New Yorkers of the eighteenth century saw no point in preserving the palisade which gave its name to Wall Street.

Just a handful of structures were charged with enough symbolic significance to make them seem worth keeping, and it was only when a threat came from the outside world that public opinion was mobilised in favour of their preservation. When a German incendiary bomb hit the Palace of Westminster in 1941, for example, there was never any question but that the building should be restored exactly as it had been. Yet in 1912, Aston Webb had been able to demolish the east facade of Buckingham Palace without any questions being asked. And Sir Herbert Baker destroyed the purity of Sir John Soane's Bank of England in a way that would be impossible even to contemplate doing today.

The belief in the idea of progress, with its equation of prosperity and prestige with change, was a powerful one. But when the outlook darkens, physical change starts to seem more threatening, and buildings identified

Trapped in the steel girders of its life support system, a fragment of the eighteenth century awaits its fate in the twentieth, a testimony to our inability to accept the logic of change. Over the course of thirty years, objects thought worthy of conservation have extended from isolated landmarks to banal industrial left-overs with the past, whatever their intrinsic quality, are seen to offer a sense of continuity and stability.

There is more than emotional reassurance at stake. When there is nothing else left to sustain their economies, cities start to rediscover their own history, or at least the history that they would like to have had. They use it as a catalyst for their attempts at regeneration. Careless disregard can give way to painstaking solicitude with the alacrity of a venal nephew discovering a long-forgotten elderly aunt with a legacy to dispose of. It's a pattern that you can see on the largest scale with the increasing reliance of London on tourism, or the smallest in the old mill town of Lowell in Massachusetts, which managed to put itself on the subsidy map by capitalising on its industrial architecture.

Lowell, just twenty-five miles from Boston, was established as a planned industrial city in 1826, but went into steep decline from the 1920s to the 1960s. Senator Tsongas, Lowell's favourite son, set up the Lowell Development and Financial Corporation in 1975. He dropped heavy hints to those local bankers who baulked at contributing to the corporation's $350 000 seed money about the use to which he would put his membership of the House Banking Committee. Downtown was designated a historic district in 1978, part of the National Parks system, and 300 000 tourists a year were drawn to its restored factory buildings scattered between parks and museums. In 1975, the Massachusetts legislature set up the University of Lowell, and in 1978 the city won a $5 million federal grant to encourage the computer company Wang to set up its HQ within its boundaries.

According to Tsongas, Lowell's paralysis in the 1950s and 1960s, which left its original buildings untouched by urban renewal, gave it a better chance to emerge from decay in the 1970s than any amount of new roads or shopping centres would have done. It has attracted $1 billion of outside investment since 1975 – a sum that includes $170 million of federal and state aid – through a combination of American pork barrel politics, which traditionally encourages national politicians to use their position in Washington to boost their home towns, and Lowell's intrinsic qualities.

A disregard for the charms of ancient bricks and mortar is not always what it seems. Tokyo has been devastated twice this century, the first time by the earthquake of 1923, the second by the allied bombing raids that destroyed 700 000 buildings in the firestorms of 1945 and left more than half the city's population homeless. But there was no rush to rebuild the city exactly as it had been, as the Poles did with Warsaw. Not because the Japanese had any less of a sense of their own identity and traditions. Nor because Japan lacked an architectural heritage worth saving. Quite the

Living in the past

contrary. As Kyoto's rich collection of sixteenth-century buildings still shows, Japan's cities had buildings of the highest quality.

But these outward signs did not constitute the essence of the Japanese identity. Japan in the 1850s saw the fate that had befallen China at the hands of the Europeans, in particular in the Opium Wars fought by the British to safeguard their destructive, but lucrative trade. To remain truly Japanese, the country's élite saw its only option was to acquire the steamships, railways and industries of the West, in the process changing on the outside but staying the same inside. Thus, with the exception of a few rebuilding projects, such as the restoration of the Imperial Palace, there was no move to recreate Tokyo as it had been before the wartime bombing.

The form of the city, however, retains its original feudal character even now. The palace, with its vast gardens, its moats, gates and walls, is the void at the heart of one of the most densely built-up cities in the world. Twisting lanes and chaotic tangles of buildings large and small press up to the very edge of the moat.

Arata Isozaki, the best-known Japanese architect in the West, calls Tokyo an overgrown village, and maintains that while the Japanese sense of interior space is well developed, the country has no real tradition of city planning.

With the increasing export of capital from Japan to finance the redevelopment of Western cities, two very different views of the past have come into collision. In London, the Japanese investors who paid an unprecedentedly high price for the old *Financial Times* building in 1987, attracted no doubt by its location next to St Paul's, were mystified to find that a building constructed as recently as 1958 was considered worthy of official protection by being listed as of historic and architectural interest. In the interests of smooth international relations, the Japanese smiled politely and set about complying with the baffling requirements of their hosts.

This is not to say that Tokyo has no interest in preservation. But it is of a very different order from that of London, where there is now an almost general presumption that all new buildings are inferior to all old ones.

Within Tokyo there are indeed a number of surviving landmarks from the past. Tokyo's Central Station, its brick gables modelled on a nineteenth-century original in Amsterdam, inspired enough affection to trigger a campaign to save its familiar outline when Kenzo Tange drew up plans to demolish it. And there are other isolated landmarks of the past in Tokyo that have been retained – the Diet building, the precincts of Keio University and the National Museum of Modern Art among others. When Frank Lloyd Wright's Imperial Hotel outlived its usefulness, the wave of international protest was hardly sufficient to stand in the way of the bulldozers, but a substantial part of the structure was re-erected outside Tokyo as part of a building museum. But these are isolated rarities, a tiny number of exotic specimens maintained as the recreational pursuits of a very wealthy society able to indulge its taste for collecting, whether it is Van Gogh paintings, antique motor cars or Victorian architecture. Still less than they believe in conservation do the Japanese see the issues of context and urban fabric as having any relevance to the contemporary practice of development. The Marunouchi business district at the palace gates, acquired by the Mitsubishi conglomerate in the early years of the century, for example, is quite unlike anywhere else in the city. It has a grid plan and several blocks of classical building modelled on Lombard Street in London as the most appropriate form for a would-be international banking centre. But the whole area has now been zoned to a much higher density, and will quickly see its eight- and ten-storey buildings replaced by clusters of high rises.

These attitudes clearly have much to do with the confidence with which Japan views its future. A wealthy country, which has finally emerged from the insecurity about its place in the world that has dogged it over the last century, it has no need of being reminded of its past glories. And its culture does not recognise the possibility of the anxieties that the West feels about change. The Japan of the 1990s sees things much in the same way as Victorian Britons in the 1890s, Los Angelenos in the 1950s and Houstonians in the 1960s. Life for the privileged can only get better.

The opposing view, put into words by the American critic Vincent Scully, is that whenever we see a building being demolished, we automatically expect that it will be replaced by something worse. It's an attitude born of an age in which an enthusiasm for geriatric architecture moved from the preserve of the art historian to become a much wider concern. A large and well-organised claque campaigns to save elderly buildings from destruction, often not because of their architectural quality, but as a tactic in their campaign to resist change itself.

The crucial transition in the way that old buildings were seen took place at much the same time in both Britain and the United States, at the end of the 1950s. The fate of two buildings in particular, one in New York, the other in London, marked the shift from architectural conservation as a hermetic art, a historical pursuit, to a much wider issue. Both were railway buildings, whose destruction was an indication of the lowering prestige of trains in an era of air travel. McKim, Mead and White's magnificent Pennsylvania Station, completed in 1900, a triumphant reworking of the baths of Caracalla to rival the splendour of Grand Central, and Philip

Living in the past

Hardwick's 1837 design for Euston, the first, and perhaps the handsomest of London's palatial railway termini, were both demolished, despite vigorous campaigns for their preservation which saw the rich and famous taking to the streets waving placards protesting against their destruction. For the first time, nineteenth-century architecture – previously seen as no more than frivolous eclecticism – was treated as an artistic achievement of the first rank, as worthy of preservation as any other important work of art.

As conservationist movements grew in strength, so the motivation for the stage army of pressure groups that sprung up to protect all these buildings was less their individual quality but their very familiarity. The elaboration and quality of their materials, and the role they had to play in providing a sense of continuity in the city were regarded as their greatest virtues. The laws protecting such buildings proliferated. Not just exteriors, but interiors as well were to be preserved, and eventually not just individual buildings but groups of buildings and their settings too. In so doing, it opened the door to a much wider extension of the protection afforded to ancient buildings in both countries, and also the possibility of safeguarding very recent buildings.

With the enactment of federal conservation legislation in 1965, New York City created a Landmark Preservation Commission which had the power to stop external alterations to buildings in districts designated as having special character, historic or aesthetic interest. One of its first acts was to declare SoHo a historic landmark district, and by 1986 the commission had designated 730 individual landmarks and forty-eight historic districts.

In England and Wales, there are now more than half a million entries in the official list of buildings of historic or architectural interest that qualify for statutory protection – that is to say there are penalties for unauthorised destruction or alterations. Permission for demolition is given only extremely rarely, and there is a well-staffed inspectorate continually updating the lists of protected buildings. In the twenty years following the inception of the scheme in 1966, the number increased by a factor of five. A total of 21 460 entries were added to the list for England and Wales in 1986, which by then had reached a grand total of 426 846. Permission was granted for the demolition of just 185 of them.

The listing figures probably substantially underestimate the number of individual buildings concerned, because they refer to entries on the list, rather than buildings. Thus Bedford Square in London, with its fifty-two individual grade one listed houses appears as just one entry. The best guess is that there are already one million listed buildings (Richard Griffith, *The Planner*, vol. 75, no. 19, p. 16).

It is a mistake to see contempt for the architecture of the recent past as a specifically modernist tendency. In fact, disdain for the tastes of their immediate predecessors was part and parcel of the conventional attitudes of the early twentieth century. Sir Harold Nicolson, in his book on Lord Curzon, describes the day that his subject took office as Secretary of State in 1919, paused at the doorway of his office in the Foreign Office, and looked up at the cast-iron beams of its ceiling, camouflaged by Egypto-Byzantine stencilling, and exclaimed, 'How ghastly – how positively ghastly'.

It was an attitude without which Sir Leslie Martin's 1965 scheme to demolish the whole of the Foreign Office and banish traffic from Parliament Square would have been inconceivable.

Each generation, it seems, has to learn to despise its predecessors as an inescapable part of its adolescence, and it is only with maturity that it becomes capable of seeing beyond its prejudices to perceive the real merits of the recent past. The contempt with which the 1990s regard almost all the works of the 1960s, for example, is a precise echo of the view that the Edwardians had of the Victorians, and for that matter that the Victorians had of the Georgians. So it was that the demolition of Regent Street, the heart of John Nash's great scheme for London, was seen as no greater a loss than the demolition of the glass slabs of London Wall. Nash's reputation by the time Regent Street came down in the 1900s was at a particularly low ebb – the subject of amused scorn more than admiration. As late as 1896, H.H. Statham, editor of *The Builder*, found his work laughable. Yet just a generation later the proposed rebuilding of Nash's Carlton House Terrace in 1934 sparked enough of an outcry to lead to the establishment of the Royal Fine Art Commission as an official arbiter of public taste. From that period, the legal mechanisms protecting ancient monuments have expanded vastly. The industrial landmarks of the nineteenth century – docks, bridges and stations by Telford and Brunel and Hardwick – were placed on the register of protected landmarks, just ahead of Sir Giles Gilbert Scott's cast-iron telephone boxes from the 1940s. Eventually even the landmarks of the 1950s, such as London's Festival Hall, were accorded official protection. Now Norman Foster's 1974 Willis Faber building in Ipswich is listed. In New York, both the Seagram and Lever towers were nominated for landmark status in the late 1980s. All that it takes for an eyesore to become a piece of priceless heritage, it seems, is the elapsing of sufficient time.

What nobody could have foreseen was the enormous explosion of popular concern for the buildings of the past, which in Britain at least became a national obsession. By the 1980s, the pace of change had left a legacy not just of empty churches and palaces, but also of power stations, mills, warehouses and even car factories, marooned by the retreating tide of technological history. If the work of leading architects had been considered unworthy of conservation just a generation earlier, even anonymous tram depots and pithead baths now attracted their own dedicated bands of supporters lobbying for their retention.

It is too heavy-handed to call what has happened in Britain a collective failure of nerve, brought on by the realisation that the imperial past offered greater glories than the future. But even an increasingly threadbare past seems like a more attractive option than the realities of the present. Britain is a confused society trapped between its traditional self-confidence and unmistakable signs of economic and political decline. As it slips into the gap between mainland Europe and North America, its influence is waning and its wealth ebbing away.

It is too obvious and too simplified an explanation for the wave of nostalgia of the 1970s and 1980s, which was preceded by a bout of neophiliac enthusiasm for technology and change, but once the 1960s had burnt themselves out, the past seemed like an increasingly comfortable place. Nostalgia, combined with the new interest of ecologists in recycling precious resources, provided a ready-made strategy for the city. Rather than demolishing the redundant traces of the past, Britain set an example for their adaptive reuse. It was a strategy that was seen as providing the emotional continuity that the modern city was held to lack, as well as offering the potential for a richness and complexity that had been expunged from the city by the mechanistic calculation of the functionalists.

Preservation is open to very different interpretations. In the nineteenth century, as academic interest in the architecture of the past matured, so the idea of attempting to return buildings to their original state, by sweeping aside later additions and removing the traces of the passing of time, grew more popular. In sharp contrast to this view of conservation, William Morris was moved to establish the Society for the Protection of Ancient Buildings in 1877. Morris was provoked by the increasingly ruthless restoration of the English cathedrals. In the pursuit of so-called authenticity, fine Perpendicular work was destroyed to be replaced by Victorian interpretations of the original early Gothic. In the process, great works of architecture were irretrievably damaged in the same way that an over-restored oil painting loses all sense of the original. Inspired by Ruskin's romantic attachment to the charm of the patina of age, the society drew up its own set of principles for the care of old buildings with the minimum of violence. When alterations had to be made for the purposes of maintaining structural integrity, Morris believed they should clearly be seen as new, otherwise the original was diminished. If that meant that the results looked like a patchwork quilt, then so be it. It was an argument that has had considerable force in Britain.

No matter how skilful the work of the twentieth-century craftsmen who seek to restore buildings to their original condition, the result can never be other than a replica. Like a Greek temple, rebuilt to give tourists something more obvious to marvel at than piles of mossy stones, restoration of this kind ensures that the old has irrevocably gone. The new may be beautiful, but, like Williamsburg – the Virginia township that the Rockefellers demolished so that they could rebuild it exactly as they thought it ought to have been – or the English Gothic of York Cathedral rebuilt after a fire, it will have taken on a new meaning, a monument to the twentieth century's inability to accept the consequences of catastrophe. We childishly believe that no setback is so serious that we cannot wipe out its effects with a bit of fund raising and volunteer work.

When a society does opt for building a complete replica of what has gone – as the Poles who worked from old photographs to rebuild the centre of Warsaw did after the war – there are difficult questions to be answered. Should it decide to leave new plasterwork carefully cast from surviving fragments of the old, looking sharp, clean and new? Or will it be faked to look indistinguishable from the real thing? Should buildings be frozen exactly as they were at the point immediately before they passed into the hands of the conservers? Or, where details of a building have been destroyed, should the surviving authentic sections be placed in their original position in a neutral background, like mosaic fragments?

Buildings lose their spirit when they are turned into museums. That fragile quality that reflects their life is easily extinguished through much less dramatic means than physical destruction. There are few sadder sights, for example, than the Rietveld House in Utrecht, scrubbed clean of every trace of life and the people who lived in it in the name of restoration. Pilgrims are allowed to pad through the place in tightly controlled groups, treading gingerly through the kitchen in special felt overshoes, as if they were lunar explorers.

In the climate of the energy crisis of the 1970s, the sheer effort and resources that had gone into constructing buildings seemed too precious to discard, whatever their intrinsic aesthetic merits. A great deal of effort was expended on propaganda which set out to prove, not always very convincingly, that recycling old buildings was more economical than constructing new ones. Certainly it was true that retaining elderly buildings could offer the chance of providing qualities that new buildings would find hard to equal. Skills had disappeared, materials had become hard to come by, and

Living in the past

our anaemic society finds it impossible to justify the sheer abundance of space that the Victorians could.

From an architectural point of view, this produced a divide between those buildings restored by purists, where the whole point was to maintain as far as possible the character of the building as it had been at the time it was built, and at the other extreme those who take existing buildings as the starting point for more drastic surgery, making it entirely clear that these are not ancient survivals, but hybrids.

The restoration of Boston's Quincy Market typifies the most cavalier approach to the past. Peter Faneuil built the original market hall in 1742, but its present form reflects Charles Bulfinch's enlargements of 1805, while the lower buildings were designed in Greek Revival style by Alexander Parris in 1826.

Benjamin Thompson, the architect who converted the market into a modern shopping mall, claimed that 'Our goal is genuineness. It is solid wood not plastic veneer, it is the real cobblestone street on which earlier generations walked. It shows the marks of time, treads worn by generations of feet. Do not improve on history, do not restore back to a fixed cutoff point, history is richer than any one period or style. When repair or replacement of building elements is required, new materials should be subtly distinguished from the original'. All of which sounds as if it was precisely what Morris had in mind.

But despite these words, Quincy Market has actually been the subject of the most ruthless rebuilding imaginable, in which very little is left of the original structures. Purists see the cavalier treatment that the market suffered at the hands of Thompson in the name of restoration as almost as bad as total destruction. Yet the huge popular success of the project helped make conservation of a sort respectable in America.

As well as setting up legal protection for buildings, governments have poured substantial resources into maintaining them. In 1981 the United States began to offer three different types of tax credit, twenty-five per cent for work to restore designated historic landmarks, twenty per cent for buildings of any kind that were forty years and older, and fifteen per cent for thirty-year-old buildings. Work carried out to earn the twenty-five per cent credits had to be to the standards set by the Advisory Council on Historic Preservation, administered by the National Park Service. Conservationists pointed out that developers worried about delays of going through the designation process necessary to earn National Register status, settled for twenty per cent, not twenty-five per cent, and carried out the work with no controls. The Secretary of the Interior drew up a ten-point standard. To qualify for the tax credits, projects must pass on all ten points. Standard three required that 'All building structures and sites shall be recognised as products of their own time. Alterations that have no historical basis and which seek to create an earlier appearance shall be discouraged', clearly an idea inherited from Morris's SPAB. Standard nine states 'Contemporary design for alteration or additions to existing properties shall not be discouraged when such alterations or additions do not destroy significant, historical, architectural or cultural material, and when such design is compatible with the size, scale, color, material and character of the property, neighborhood, or environment'.

In the United States, the status of historic buildings is far more fragile than it is in Britain, mainly because of the conflict between landmark protection and zoning statutes. It took a Supreme Court case in New York to rule that the bankrupt New York Central Railway Corporation had not been deprived of its constitutional rights when the city's Landmark Commission stopped it from demolishing Grand Central Station to sell the site for an office development. And the court only backed the conservationists on the understanding that the company was allowed to put its development rights up for sale for transfer to other development sites. The effect of this was if anything to increase the congestion on key sites, to make Manhattan still more of a sunless maze than ever, and to reduce the remaining landmarks to pointless survivors lost in a bleak forest of office towers.

Grand Central, so far still intact, has some visual power left, even if it is densely ringed by high rises now. But the battle on Park Avenue over the future of St Bartholomew's Church highlights the difficulty of legislating to protect the character of ancient buildings in a highly charged property market, where air rights change hands for up to a hundred dollars per square foot. St Bartholomew's, an Italian Romanesque church, is protected by landmarking; but, undaunted, it planned to build an office tower on top of the chapter house next door. Just as the Vuillard Houses, two surviving nineteenth-century houses of exceptional charm, are dwarfed by the sullen Helmsley Palace Hotel immediately behind, so a tower on top of the church's chapter house would have been a grotesque device rendering the original building meaningless.

Other American cities have tried to evolve more sensitive zoning systems to protect their historic buildings. In San Francisco, regulations were carefully drafted to encourage developers to leave landmarks alone. They allow for the transfer of development rights above listed buildings to a zone well away from the historic core of the city. San Francisco also allows for non-contiguous floor area ratios, which means that development plots can be assembled in such a way as to leave historic buildings intact, and in a sensible context.

Even Los Angeles, a city in which councilmen have been known to suggest that those who want to see old buildings should go to Europe, began to worry about architectural conservation in the 1980s. Bertram Goodhue's 1926 Public Library in downtown, almost as much of a landmark as City Hall and the Union Station, was badly damaged by arson. Its restoration was only achieved by the extension of hefty zoning concessions to Robert Maguire of Maguire Thomas, developers of I.M. Pei's so-called Library Tower, the tallest building in the city. Maguire was allowed 2.5 million square feet of office space over seventy floors in exchange for a $20 million contribution to rebuilding the library. The Roosevelt Hotel in Hollywood with its Hockney-decorated swimming pool, the first home of the Academy Awards, and the Beverly Hills City Hall were both the subject of careful conservation programmes. Spring, Broadway and Seventh Street are designated historic districts now.

In France, with a tradition of clean-sweep redevelopment that goes back to Louis XIV and Haussmann, a concern for old buildings took off rather later than in Britain and the USA. It was only after the demolition of Les Halles in the early 1970s that conservation began to be seen as an important issue, though there had been earlier rehabilitation of run-down seventeenth-century tenement buildings around the Marais. The destruction of Les Halles – seen in retrospect as the tragic loss of one of the city's finest nineteenth-century landmarks – led directly to the curious idea of turning the Gare d'Orsay into a museum in which to hang not just large chunks of Victoriana but the delicate impressionist paintings from the Jeu de Paume collection.

The Orsay station and hotel buildings, built for the 1900 International Exposition, designed by Victor Laloux in the most florid Beaux Arts manner, was placed on the French historic buildings inventory in 1973, immediately after the demolition of Les Halles, and classified as a national monument in 1978. Set against Baltard's iron and glass pavilions at Les Halles, the Gare d'Orsay looks absurdly frivolous, but rather than risk losing any more monumental nineteenth-century buildings, it was brought under the conservationist umbrella without delay. Preliminary planning permission already granted for a hotel and conference centre tower designed by Le Corbusier was revoked, and a 500 000 square foot museum within the existing building was proposed instead.

The question of what to do with the landmarks of the past became more and more acute as the 1980s came to an end, as ever younger, larger and sturdier buildings became redundant. What had once been icons of the modern world turned into derelict ruins when they had outlived their usefulness.

Fiat's Lingotto car factory in Turin, where modern mass production of cars first came to Europe, was the most conspicuous example. The entire plant was empty by the middle of the 1980s, just sixty years after it was built, and Fiat was forced to consider what to do about Matté Trucco's vast structure, more than one third of a mile long. Roland Barthes, author of the questionable proposition that you can class the production of a motor-car in the same league of creative endeavour as the building of a medieval cathedral, would certainly have recognised the Lingotto factory as possessing the authentic cathedral-building spirit. If it had closed ten years earlier, the structure would undoubtedly have been demolished. But by the 1980s, the climate was right for such a building to be seen as a potential resource rather than a hindrance. It had been largely responsible for Turin's prosperity as an industrial centre in modern Italy, and simply to dispose of it was inconceivable. The company set its heart against demolition, and began thinking what to do about the vast tracts of land and buildings that make up the Lingotto. It is not simply a question of preservation, even preservation on the biggest scale imaginable. The factory, with its endless grid of columns, is of such a size that it could not possibly be put to one single new use. It is big enough to house a small town with ease. And just as important as the historic structure itself is its impact on Turin's fabric. The factory is part of a thick swathe of industrial buildings and railway lines that cuts Turin in half, making it impossible to get from one side of the city to the other without long detours. Lingotto's closure is, or so Fiat believes, a chance to get to grips with a wholesale reordering of Turin. Renzo Piano's solution involved a huge mixture of uses – ranging from galleries to playgrounds, and universities – and it was enough to persuade Fiat to attempt its gradual implementation.

The same kind of problems were being faced from Sydney's Circular Quay to Battersea Power Station in London, from Union Station in St Louis to the Manchester Royal Exchange. It is the landmarks of the industrial revolution which are now occupying most of the attention of the conservationist movement. In Manchester, the old commodity exchange is now a theatre with a steel stage and auditorium that looks like a space ship sitting inside the nineteenth-century trading room, its clock and dealing boards still intact exactly as they were on the day that the market closed for good. In St Louis, what was once the busiest station in the United States has been turned into a sprawling hotel.

These large-scale recycling projects have turned into spectacular pieces of urbanism, more Cecil B. de Mille than town planning, and are perhaps the high-water mark of conservation.

Conservation at its height was seen as an uncomplicatedly good thing, a nebulous enough concept to appeal to both the traditionalist conservatives with their dislike of new buildings and the anti-development radicals on the left who saw the issue of historic buildings as another weapon in their campaigns.

In London, the group which sought to stop the building of offices on Coin Street focused on the preservation of the clumsy OXO tower simply as the means to prevent this new development. At the Covent Garden Opera House, the preservation of a terrace of not very distinguished nineteenth-century houses became a weapon used by the Covent Garden Association in their battle to stop the redevelopment of the area. Even more poignantly, Peter Palumbo's attempts to build Mies van der Rohe's only design for the United Kingdom on the Mansion House Square site, became the focus of a 25-year-long struggle over the shape of the City. In the early 1960s, Palumbo was actually commended by the City Corporation for his public spirit in bringing such a distinguished piece of architecture to London. But he was told that he could not start demolition until he had secured control of all the properties. Twenty years later, when Palumbo had finally completed the painstaking task of acquiring all the leases, these humdrum Victorian buildings were propelled centre stage as part of London's priceless heritage, part of the pattern of twisting lanes and ale houses that Milton and Shakespeare had frequented, it was claimed.

How should one interpret this violent turnaround? Was it a loss of nerve? Those who see Mies van der Rohe's chaste elegance as superior to the pattern book Gothic of Belcher would certainly present it as such. On the other hand, the suggestion that sentimental views of the past should not be allowed to stand in the way of progress underwrote the ruthless commercial attitudes of the hit-and-run developers of the 1960s. And indeed this latter view is precisely how a strain of populists did seek to present it.

But if both left and right were able to present the Mansion House saga as a simple case of history versus insensitive development, the arguments became even more complex when the impact of gentrification began to make itself felt in London and New York. Gentrification leads to lower population densities than those which existed before – gentrifiers like to have a couple of bathrooms and larger living rooms than their predecessors. The endlessly retold story of the lofts of Lower Manhattan, once presented as a simple tale of saving old buildings and bringing life back into the neighbourhood, then a more complex battle between newcomers whose ability to pay higher rents actually contributed to the process of the decline of manufacturing industry, was echoed all over London, and nowhere more so than in Spitalfields.

'Doomed and grimly magnificent,' wrote Ian Nairn of the area in 1970, when London's early eighteenth-century new town, hardly touched since 1750, looked to be on its last legs. Christ Church, Hawksmoor's master-piece of the English Baroque, shuttered and barred for want of money to restore it, loomed over the tiled roofs of the Huguenot weavers' houses of Fournier Street. It was a sight as full of pathos as an engraving by Piranesi. Meths drinkers sprawled in ornately carved classical doorways. Rubbish from the fruit market spilled over the cobbles, and piled up outside the once splendid merchants' houses of Spital Square.

Two centuries of neglect since the prosperous had fled from London's East End ensured the survival of every detail – from Georgian shop fronts to eighteenth-century paintwork. But it had also left the red-brick streets of Spitalfields like rotten fruit, ready to fall at the first disturbance.

It was the largest surviving area of its date in London, but Nairn assumed, perfectly reasonably, that it was all bound to go – 'not only because rehabilitation would be difficult, but because nobody loves it'. Now that conservation is taken for granted, and so many of the houses of Spitalfields have been restored to single-family splendour, it is worth remembering Nairn's words as a measure of how much has been achieved, most of it by the Spitalfields Trust – a group started by the architectural historians Dan Cruikshank and Mark Girouard, by squatting in two early eighteenth-century houses in Elder Street in 1977 to rescue them from demolition.

As the trust saw it, the remains of Spitalfields were too fragile to leave to the bureaucracy of the state. Sub-dividing these houses for municipal flats might save the exteriors, but the precious panelling, staircases and flagstones inside, which in many cases had survived intact, would have to be sacrificed. Their essential qualities could only be preserved in the hands of enthusiasts who would live in them in the way that they were originally built. Central heating, fitted kitchens and internal partitions were all out. Even electricity caused the most extreme purists a certain amount of heart-searching.

The trust started buying properties and selling them to approved pur-chasers, who covenanted to restore them faithfully. To ensure that the dis-placed sweatshops were not driven out of business, it also built low-rent workshops nearby.

But the picture is by no means one of the simple triumph of the forces of sweetness and light over philistine developers. The trust's playground, in which its members dedicated years of backbreaking toil to the restoration

Living in the past

of their homes, with very much the same eccentric enthusiasm that a train spotter would lavish on a steam engine, runs along one of the most unstable urban fault lines in Britain.

Two utterly different worlds which live in the closest proximity entirely fail to meet here. To the west is the City, with some of the highest land values in the world, bursting out of its straitjacket. A few yards further east is Spitalfields, where 24 000 Bengalis have made their homes, successors to two earlier waves of immigration, the Huguenots and the Jews. The conditions in which some of them live, subject to brutal racist attacks, and in the most overcrowded streets in London, suggest Dickensian squalor. But Brick Lane, the area's main artery, has nonetheless become one of the most vital streets in the capital, a memory of an older kind of urbanism, before high streets were crushed into chain store uniformity, where people lived above the shop, and restaurants and cafés were open into the small hours.

The story of what happened here over the last decade is of far more than local interest. It has a message for all attempts at urban renewal through architectural conservation.

The local social worker Charlie Forman, a strong critic of the trust, maintains that the saving of Spitalfields had nothing to do with what he calls the middle-class aesthetes of the trust. To Forman, the saving of Spitalfields has been the construction of a thousand social houses for rent in the area in the teeth of determined efforts to displace the Bengalis to make way for offices, the halting of the sell-off of municipal housing, and the overturning of a racist housing allocation policy by Tower Hamlets Borough Council.

'The reality of restoring the houses had a human cost. The trust's vision was incompatible with public housing, and the inevitable result was that Bengalis would not be living or working there. They would be replaced by owner-occupiers rich enough to afford the fine detailing of replacing Georgian internal features.'

As Forman sees it, the trust has gone further than simply excluding tenants from the houses its members have acquired. 'The trust has created a market, and prices for land are rocketing, and that makes other public housing impossible. If the trust really wants to save the architecture, it should have sold the houses on to the associations.'

There have been some signs of a withdrawal of official tolerance towards the preservationists. The shift in Britain may have come with the hostile reception to the City of London Development Plan of 1985. The plan called for strict controls to preserve the city as it was, with a ban on large-scale developments, changes of use, and alterations to the existing street pattern. It misjudged its timing badly. After a decade in which there was automatic presumption that conservation was in the best interests of the community at large, this kneejerk reaction was questioned for the first time in a serious way.

The reaction to the City's planning draft from many of the developers was hostile in the extreme, and the Centre for Policy Studies commissioned a report from six experts which came out violently against both the plan and the attitudes behind it. They saw it as a straitjacket, threatening the very survival of the City as Britain's most precious financial asset: 'New organisations are not going to put up with refurbished buildings lurking behind Victorian facades. The philosophy behind the plan unfortunately illustrates the national malaise of looking at the past, and not the future, which is the root of Britain's economic decline. The plan is based on superficial analysis and outdated ideas.' And indeed, the plan was withdrawn and substantially revised. It was perhaps in part a reflection of the boom that London was going through in the 1980s, and the shortlived rush of optimism about the future. Clearly the past is going to go on having an important part to play in the shaping of the city. But our views of the past, and our judgements of the quality of its remains, are permanently provisional.

A roof over their heads

9

The 1980s was the decade in which the retreat from public housing turned into a rout. With a remarkable degree of unanimity, governments in America, Britain and France decided that the policies of the post-war consensus on housing had been disastrously misguided.

Ronald Reagan cut the Department of Housing and Urban Development's budget from $35 billion in 1981 down by eighty per cent to $7 billion in 1988. The number of homes built with federal assistance in America dropped from 550 000 in 1976, to 225 000 in 1981, and to little more than 100 000 in 1985. In Britain, local authority house building came to a virtual standstill. From a peak of 300 000 homes a year, the programme declined to 100 000 units in 1977, and was down to a mere 15 000 by 1989.

What made the shift against the public provision of housing politically possible in Britain was the widely accepted belief that it had been an ignominious failure. The National Health Service, once a twin pillar of the welfare state alongside the public housing system, was spared from the sharpest attentions of Mrs Thatcher's radical Conservatism thanks to the wide measure of popular support it still enjoyed. Council housing no longer had such support. The perception of public housing in Britain had declined rapidly from its heroic period in the post-war years, when it was regarded as a crusade to give the bombed out victims of the Blitz a better future, to share the catastrophically low esteem with which the housing projects are held in America.

A masochistic outburst of architectural myth-making in both America and Britain conspired to help the process along. The ultimately self-regarding determination of architectural theorists to show that form was more important to a building's performance than budget or management policy allowed even the dynamiting of the Pruitt Igoe flats in St Louis to be seized on as evidence that the ills of post-war development were fundamentally architectural. And in the process it was assumed that public housing was in itself a fundamentally flawed building type. Actually, the fact that Pruitt Igoe turned out to be a disaster had nothing to do with the modern movement. As the *St Louis Post Dispatch* pointed out at the time, its destruction in 1974, fifteen years after it was completed, can be explained because 'there was no maintenance fund, and the broken windows let in wintry air freezing water and bursting the pipes'. The development was the victim of brutal budget cuts while it was still under construction, suffered appallingly bad management, and was occupied almost entirely by poor blacks without the resources to make life in Pruitt Igoe tolerable.

This did not stop Charles Jencks from claiming to see the dynamiting of the development as representing the death of modern architecture. Too many people who should have known better believed him, and too many local authorities were seduced into assuming that dynamite could provide a quick and painless solution to their housing management problems too.

The shift against public housing took place despite, or perhaps because of, glaring evidence from all sides showing that the difficulties which millions of ordinary people faced in finding somewhere to live were as intractable as ever. The precise number of people who literally have no roof at all is the subject of endless and largely inconclusive argument between governments who profess to see the homeless as a minor, if annoyingly conspicuous problem, and housing activists, to whom the phenomenon is the denial of a basic human right. The 1990 US census went to extraordinary lengths to come up with a definitive answer. It equipped its enumerators with torches to search back alleys and behind the air conditioning extracts of downtown stores to track down the ragged army of street people. Until their findings are published it's impossible to be certain, but the best guess for the country as a whole is that two million people have no permanent home The British census authorities trained their staff to carry out an equally thorough search in 1991. In 1986 the UK was conservatively estimated to have 120 000 homeless people. Apart from the highly visible escalation in the number of people living in cardboard boxes at London's mainline stations, in the undercroft of the South Bank arts centre, and in West End shop doorways, – the 1991 census found 2500 of them – 9000 households in the capital were lodged in squalid but costly private bed and breakfast hotels, and 13 000 more were in hostels. In 1981, 18 000 households were accepted as homeless by London local authorities, who spent £5 million putting them up in cheap hotels. Their numbers have certainly not decreased since then.

So firmly established has the encampment of street people living in cardboard shelters underneath Waterloo Bridge become, that the flames from their camp fires night after night have charred the bridge arching gracefully up over their heads, threatening seriously to weaken its structure. The authorities were alarmed enough at the end of 1990 to carry out emergency checks.

Despite the conspicuous lack of success of the giant shelters that Mayor

A roof over their heads

Koch opened for New York's homeless, and the outrage against raids by the Los Angeles Police Department on the makeshift bivouacs that give the eastern edges of downtown the look – and the stench – of a Californian Bombay, the British government attempted precisely the same strategies. But even as it found the £15 million needed to open enough hostels and night shelters to let the Metropolitan Police sweep the derelicts and beggars out of sight of appalled tourists with a clear conscience, it admitted that it was trying to deal with a worldwide phenomenon, which nobody fully understood.

The street people are only the most obvious casualties of the wider housing crisis. Equally dismaying is the dawning realisation, in both America and Britain, that the private sector cannot supply large numbers of people in ordinary jobs with decent, affordable housing.

The housing market is back where it was one hundred years ago, when, following in the footsteps of the London County Council which, inspired by the charitable trusts like the Peabody and Octavia Hill, pioneered municipal housing in the 1890s, Britain began the first national housing programme in the world. It was based on the conviction that since private enterprise had shown itself incapable of providing decent homes for large numbers of the British people, there was nothing for it but a massive intervention by the state to do the job instead. As Britain's housing policies matured with the building of the new towns, they became increasingly egalitarian. Unlike the American system of federally funded housing which was never meant to be more than a last resort, designed for the vigorous but temporarily poor who would be moving on as soon as their circumstances improved, British council housing was conceived in terms of social engineering, a means of building a broadly balanced community. Just as Britain socialised medicine and education, so it socialised housing, in the belief that unless the whole community used these facilities, they could not work. The local authority expected to house doctors and teachers, bus drivers and waiters, as well as the unemployed, the old, and the single-parent families.

Despite the hostility of the Thatcher government to social housing, it was the Conservative administration of 1951 which pushed the annual house building programme through the 300 000 barrier. And it was another Conservative government, with Sir Keith Joseph, Margaret Thatcher's John the Baptist, as its housing minister, that found the money for the huge subsidies needed to embark on a high rise housing programme in the 1960s.

In the inter-war period, Britain demolished 250 000 slums and built 300 000 council homes; public housing rose from zero to ten per cent of the total. By the time the clearances finally ground to a halt at the start of the 1980s, nearly two million substandard houses, the homes of around five million people, had been demolished and three million more improved with government grants. Yet in 1979, the Greater London house condition survey showed that 640 000 dwellings, twenty-five per cent of the total, were in some way unsatisfactory. And 250 000 of them were actually unfit for human habitation.

The same pattern of slum clearance followed by subsequent decline was repeated up and down the country. Glasgow's East End was typical. In 1900 the area consisted of stone tenements, four storeys high, with eight or twelve small flats on each close. These buildings were put up by private landlords, close to the workplaces, or along the transport routes to get to them. Glasgow's tenements were particularly small. Ground floors often had commercial and workshop space, and the small back courts were colonised by the workshops. Rent controls, tax and subsidy policies, in force since 1915, left owners unable to carry out repairs or improvements. With whole families living in two-room apartments and sharing lavatories, homes that had always been substandard grew steadily more ramshackle.

Such was the resentment of residents and their political representatives against the conditions in which they were obliged to live, that any policy but clearance and total rebuilding would have been impossible. Slum clearance began in the 1930s, restarted after the war in the 1950s, and was complete in the 1970s by which time 100 000 people, some seventy per cent of the East End's residents, had been rehoused. After Tower Hamlets in London, Glasgow's East End now has the highest percentage of public housing in Britain. Yet the post-war estates in both areas have become as synonymous with poverty and deprivation as the slums they replaced.

Glasgow District Council doesn't have the money to maintain its housing. All it can manage is repairs. It responds when called out by the tenants to deal with damp or broken windows, but it can't stop its buildings from deteriorating. And it faces a slide back into the same decay that overwhelmed the private landlords of the 1920s.

In the post-war years, Labour and Conservative governments fought election campaigns on their readiness to out-build each other's council housing programmes. To reach their 300 000-a-year target, the Conservatives had to cut the standards to which they built houses, a decision that was to store up problems for the not very distant future. In an attempt to undo the damage, the 1961 Parker Morris Committee looked closely at what council housing should offer in terms of floor area, the relationship of one room to another, and even the amount of storage space in the kitchen, and the extent of tiling on the bathroom walls. Previous

A roof over their heads

attempts to regulate house design stuck to simple tables of minimum areas for each room. Parker Morris spelt out in lucid and humane terms that the quality of life possible in those rooms was just as important as their size. Its advice became mandatory in 1967, but by 1981, Conservative philosophy had already undergone a sea change, and the environment minister at the time, Michael Heseltine, abolished centralised standards, describing the move as 'a quantum leap' that would give the local authorities discretion to build what they wanted.

The assurance sounded hollow to local authorities who believed that their new-found freedom would force them to reduce standards that were already at a minimum. Too many council estates were perceived as grim and unattractive, if not actually falling to bits. They were criticised as socially damaging, with families forced to live high off the ground. In fact, flats of all types account for only one third of the entire council stock – or at least the stock before the sell-off programme of the 1980s started – the other two thirds being two- and three-storey houses. And of those flats, blocks of five storeys and higher accounted for less than ten per cent of all council housing. That is to say, no more than 500 000 British households live in blocks five or more storeys high. It's a substantial number, but one which certainly presents a very different picture from the hysterical branding of public housing as made up entirely of high rise slums that marked the formulation of public policy in the 1980s.

While there are many conspicuous examples of unsightly and unloved blocks from the 1960s, this is not the whole picture. Very often, local authority housing was designed with more care, skill and imagination than its private equivalent. In the pursuit of building a socially mixed community, local authority architects tried to create it in a physical sense, grouping houses into forms that seemed, to them at least, to express the possibility of sociability. The new and expanded towns, and the larger estates, are full of terraces and squares, planned around local schools and shops. The most sophisticated local authority architects employed urban designers and landscape architects, offering an attention to detail that no private house builder could match.

The reaction against what were seen as the drab and depressing streets of the big cities led the local authorities to try to soften this image of the town by building traffic-segregated projects, with large areas of green.

These brave visions foundered in neglect, vandalism, damp and rotting concrete. It's worth asking whether these failings would have been any less pronounced in the kind of housing that was demolished to make way for the redevelopments of the 1960s. The answer is probably no. But the difference between a street of houses and a block of flats is that the block

forces its inhabitants to rely on each other. Without a strong sense of social cohesion, there is no pressure for all the residents of a stair, or a lift lobby to clean it. In the Scottish tenements, a system enforced with local bye-laws demands the occupant of every flat to take a turn to sweep the common parts clean. A cardboard notice pointing out your obligations circumnavigates the whole tenement every month, before returning to hang on your door handle to remind you it's your turn again. But in England there is no such discipline.

Some researchers, notably Oscar Newman in America and the British geographer Alice Coleman, have attempted to trace a direct link between the form of a house and the behaviour of the inhabitants. Newman's *Defensible Space* uses the highly detailed records of the New York Housing Authority's own police force to justify the application of the concept of territoriality to housing design. His findings, followed a decade later by Coleman's, have broadly been that the regimentation of the traditional nineteenth-century street provides a much more appropriate context for high-density living, with its clearly defined hierarchy of public and private space, and that efforts to replace that sense of continuity of fabric with object buildings, free floating in landscaping, ideas ultimately derived from Le Corbusier, have been disastrous.

But it is equally plausible to argue that the stress experienced by those who live in social housing has more to do with their poverty than it does with the physical or architectural quality of their surroundings. The mundane issue of having enough money to keep the heating on matters more than whether the exterior is made of concrete or brick, or whether they are arranged in terraces or dotted over parks.

There are more logical grounds to attack the way that the housing programme was carried out. In the London Borough of Camden, for example, the end result of its slum clearances in the 1970s was a net gain of 478 homes, achieved by high densities. But that gain was more than cancelled out by the loss of accommodation suffered during construction. Even more worrying were the problems caused by the poor standards of supervision during construction, using complex and often untested building technologies. Because of the massive scale of schemes in the sixties, minor problems, multiplied through thousands of units, were to prove enormously costly to resolve.

By the time that the system-built Ronan Point block in East London collapsed, like Pruitt Igoe seemingly symbolising all that was wrong with the public sector, there were plenty of other troublesome teenaged local authority housing schemes. Despite continuing overall shortages, caused mainly by the ever diminishing size of the average household rather than

A roof over their heads

absolute population growth, the less popular blocks became harder and harder to persuade people to move into. Poor management started a vicious spiral of decline. Otherwise tolerable estates with a large number of boarded-up flats made all those with sufficient self-confidence and bargaining power refuse to move in. Whether sanctioned by official management policies or not, these quickly became ghettos.

Despite the growing number of those prepared to sleep rough, something like 100 000 council houses were standing empty in Britain in 1990. To tackle this problem, the government's first response was to switch its efforts into the rehabilitation programme, both for owner-occupiers and for local authority projects. Grants for basic amenities had been available since 1959. The 1974 Housing Act took a different tack, its aim being to reduce social stress by putting money into improving the quality of housing in designated areas, which could be spent in a number of different ways, some of it on rehabilitation, some of it on new building. Much effort and enormous amounts of money have gone into reshaping the legacy of the 1960s and 1970s, remedying technical faults and mitigating the effects of poor social policies.

Large swathes of housing, much of it less than a decade old, were comprehensively remodelled to overcome damp or deteriorating cladding. Even the most architecturally celebrated projects have not escaped. In Milton Keynes, Norman Foster's Bean Hill housing scheme had its corrugated metal facades reclad, and pitched roofs built on top of its original flat roofs. In Warrington, James Stirling's large scheme was demolished altogether. It was a victim of the shifting policies of the new town's administration which allowed what had been a showpiece to deteriorate into a frightened, lowering enclave marked by the ubiquitous presence of large dogs chained to the balconies in an attempt to provide some protection from neighbours and marauding outsiders.

The danger inherent in the rush to demolish the municipal blocks of the 1960s is that it provides a convenient scapegoat for some of the not very attractive realities of daily life. Compare, for example, Warrington Crescent, the London street in which I used to live, a white, stucco-faced, neo-classical street, built originally as vast houses that rambled over six floors from basement to attic. Long since turned into flats, the street has been through some difficult periods. For years the freeholders, the Church Commissioners, spent so little on maintenance that rot and damp ran riot.

Now, two-bedroom flats change hands for £250 000 and the street is, so we are expected to believe, the very model of what urbane, decent housing should be. Yet, in its scale and density, it is very similar to Stirling's Warrington blocks which are being demolished less than twenty years after they were built. My old street is a mix of relatively affluent owner-occupiers, elderly tenants, and a few squatters. Like Warrington New Town, Warrington Crescent is still full of litter. The so-called traditional building materials that the Victorian jerry-builders used to throw up the street are so ramshackle that it costs between five and ten thousand pounds per flat each year to maintain the fabric of the building. Yet nobody is suggesting that these should be demolished; they are listed buildings and part, so it seems, of our irreplaceable architectural heritage.

Meanwhile in Warrington, a repairs programme which involves spending rather less money per unit is seen as an intolerable financial burden, and as sufficient justification to demolish all one thousand homes. Perhaps the real reason that the Warrington estate is being demolished is because the people who live in it lead lives that are bleak, and will be bleak whatever they live in. But by demolishing their present homes, there is at least the illusion of the possibility of change.

The provision of social housing in France closely mirrors the British experience. France has a much larger private rental sector which accounts for twenty-five per cent of the total housing stock, compared with ten per cent in Britain. The French system for building social housing, the *Habitation à loyer modéré*, was set up in 1953 and has built three million homes, compared with six million put up in the UK. They are administered not by political authorities but by housing associations, of which there are 678 (as opposed to the 458 local housing authorities in Britain), which tends to reduce the remoteness and bureaucracy with which they are administered.

As in Britain, it is the big schemes that have caused difficulties. There were riots involving tear gas and looting in 1981 at Les Minguettes in the suburbs of Lyons, one of the largest French housing projects. Built between 1960 and 1976, it had 2200 dwellings vacant out of a total of 7500 in 1982. And that unrest continued sporadically into the 1990s.

The big schemes account for one third of the French projects, and the government is spending £50 million a year to improve their physical condition, with another £20 million on social development in 150 of them. The strategy is to abandon the most uneconomic properties. Some have been demolished, and a block designed by Le Corbusier at Briey la Forêt in Lorraine was closed in 1985, with just nine of its 339 flats still occupied..

Federally funded public housing began in the USA in 1937, conceived as a means of providing the deserving poor with temporary homes while they set about getting something better. It has burgeoned into 1.3 million units, home to perhaps four million people.

A roof over their heads

In fact the public housing projects have become overwhelmingly occupied by poor blacks with minimal social mobility. The Chicago Housing Authority, for example, accommodates 37 000 families, seventy per cent of them headed by women and ninety-five per cent black. The dismal condition which a more than usually incompetent administration has let them reach can be gauged from the fact that in 1990, 6000 of its apartments were empty despite a 40 000 strong waiting list.

In Washington, the US Department of Housing and Urban Development (HUD) estimates that 70 000 public housing units all over America are currently boarded up and that a thousand of them are demolished every year. The large public housing authorities claimed that $20 billion was needed for urgent repairs to the public housing stock. But it wasn't simply that the government was trying to make do with less money, it wanted to spend its reduced budget to do different things.

What had really changed was the official view of the nature of the housing problem, and how best to go about solving it. From the perspective of the conservative governments of Britain and America, the state had no business getting involved in the provision of a subsidised rental housing for the broad mass of people at all.

This was a huge reversal, one which ran directly counter to more than fifty years of public policy towards housing supported by both main political parties. The Conservative government in Britain was now actively trying to stop local authorities building houses themselves, and to play what was officially described as 'a strategic role' instead. The Conservative view was that the state provision of housing had created a culture of welfare dependency.

The 1981 UK census showed that one third of the British people lived in social housing, twice as many as the French. To the Conservatives, who were by now presenting themselves as the party of home ownership, this was anathema, and they committed themselves to a vast sell-off of council housing. Every tenant was given the right to buy their council home, and offered substantial discounts as an incentive to do so. Labour objections were briskly dismissed, not least by the more prosperous Labour-voting council tenants who saw the scheme as a chance to enjoy some of the same capital gains that had buoyed the middle classes through the inflationary 1970s.

During the Thatcher years, more than one million local authority homes, most of them houses rather than flats, were sold to their tenants. It was a change almost on the scale of the eclipse of private rented housing, which saw 2.5 million homes move from renting to owner-occupation in the twenty years from 1960. The second Conservative initiative was to increase the number of homes available for rent. Controls have been lifted for new lettings, and council tenants now have the right to insist on transfer of their properties to housing associations, cooperatives or private landlords – a right that is likely to be more rhetorical than real.

The Conservatives switched responsibility for the provision of social housing away from the local authorities to the housing associations. In ten years the housing associations doubled their stock of houses. By 1981, they were doing ten per cent of all rehabilitation and twenty per cent of public sector rehabilitation. By 1991, the housing associations had overtaken the local authorities in building new homes. At the same time, the government has reduced its grants to housing associations, to make them rely more on private capital, and in the process to submit to the discipline of the marketplace.

The effect of the Conservative changes was to reduce council housing in Britain to a rump, occupied by the poorest, those least able to find an alternative. It's a change which may be attractive for those who bought their homes – provided they are in a position to go on meeting their mortgage repayments – but leaves a substantial sink of substandard public housing, on the American model, while maybe the very poorest, as in France, can't afford to stay in social housing at all.

With the emphasis on the private sector, it is worth looking hard at what it has to offer. The perceived benefits of owning your own home which the Thatcher government had as its ideal is based on the experience of the constant, and often spectacular growth of property values in the 1960s and 1970s, which gave a whole class the impression, illusory or not, that they were acquiring substantial personal wealth. The impact of a few years of very high interest rates, accompanied by falling property values and soaring mortgage foreclosures in the early 1990s, will create a very different attitude to home ownership.

Home ownership costs society a great deal. Between 1978 and 1986, the price of mortgage relief in the UK more than doubled in real terms to about £4.5 billion. Taking into account the extra costs to the exchequer of capital gains tax exemption and discounts on council house sales, it was over £9 billion, which compares with the £4 billion annual subsidy to council tenants.

Quite apart from the question of the form of tenure for housing is the equally sensitive issue of where new housing is going to be built. The pressure on land in Britain from private house builders looking for sites in the ever widening ring around London that has absorbed most of the nation's population growth has been intense. This is precisely the area that is

A roof over their heads

protected by the great sacred cow of the British planning system – the green belt, which has placed strict restrictions on new development since 1945. A propaganda campaign mounted by one developer to press for more sites to be released for development claimed that the green belt has put up the price of an average house in Southeast England by nearly £4000. But neither the Conservatives nor the Labour Party have dared to loosen the grip of the belt, which prosperous suburban home-owners already in the area see as the best defence against an influx of newcomers spoiling their leafy villages.

The response, by a consortium of volume house builders in the mid 1980s, was to identify a series of sites for private new towns on land in or beyond the green belt, usually scarred by old gravel pits, which they worked hard to present to the government as the best way to reduce the pressure for land. Building on a few concentrated sites would be less damaging to the environment as a whole than gradually nibbling away all over the green belt, they argued. The consortium drew up plans for towns that would be built over ten years on sites of around 700 acres, with 4800 houses for sale that could house a population of 12 500. There would be primary and secondary schools, a health centre, a modest shopping centre, some offices, a village hall, pub, library, leisure centre, and a couple of industrial estates – very much a privatised and scaled-down version of the public new towns, and recognisably descended from Ebenezer Howard's ideas.

But comfortably suburbanised country-dwellers reacted with horror, panicking the local authorities of Berkshire, Hampshire and Essex, into unrelenting opposition to development in any form.

The difficulty that the private housing market has in meeting the aspirations of people is not confined to Britain. According to the Joint Center for Housing Studies at Harvard and MIT, the average American thirty-year-old spent fourteen per cent of his income on a mortgage in 1955. But in 1987, the equivalent thirty-year-old was spending forty-four per cent of that income. For a substantial number of Americans, that is not enough to buy a house. As a result, police and firemen cannot afford to live in the small towns they serve when they have been commuterised and, just as in London, the service economy is threatened when restaurants have to close early so that staff can get home to far distant suburbs.

American cities don't have green belts, but they do have zoning restrictions which have been used very much in the same way, to keep all but the most affluent newcomers out. By specifying minimum lot sizes, and even the costs of the houses on them, American communities have kept themselves racially homogeneous – and made the provision of economical housing very difficult. The constitutional legality of using zoning in this way has been attacked in a series of challenges, and one judgement in particular, the Mount Laurel case in New Jersey, seemed to outlaw the practice, and insisted instead on the provision of inclusionary zoning, that is to say, imposing a duty on municipalities to write zoning codes in such a way as to mandate the inclusion of a certain proportion of low cost homes.

Another approach has been to change the zoning rules controlling the way a house is positioned on its lot. Rather than insisting on minimum clearances between the house and the lot boundaries, what is called zero lot line legislation has allowed the standard small lot size to drop from 7500 to 4000 square feet by positioning houses on the lot edge itself.

Yet to a large number of Americans, families earning less than $30 000 in 1990, this is of little comfort. There remains a substantial gap between what their income can buy and the cost of the average American dream house. It can only be bridged if the state increases people's incomes or reduces the costs of their homes.

Finding ways of doing that in a way that Americans find acceptable has been a recurring preoccupation of the architectural profession in the US. The president's commission on housing in 1982 attributed twenty-five per cent of sales price of new housing to unnecessary regulatory burdens, and there is heavy pressure from the builders to relax building codes to allow for cheaper construction techniques. Very much the same development took place in Britain in the 1980s, with the disastrous starter homes – blocks of studio bedsits, aimed at first-time buyers, with furniture and fittings included in the cost of a prearranged mortgage. The resulting units turned out to be very hard for their first purchasers to resell.

In the bleak New Jersey town of Ashbury Park, Steven Winter tried to build a high-quality $50 000 house, all that the majority of people who live in the area can afford. He found, however, that it couldn't be done without a subsidy. The Rouse Enterprise Foundation, set up in 1982 by the much publicised shopping centre developer James Rouse, concerned itself with the rehabilitation of run-down housing for families with an income of $10 000 or less. Implicit in the foundation's work was the relaxation of building regulations, self-help, salvaged materials and the building of houses to standards that did not reflect the generous incomes of middle-class lifestyle.

Other ways of approaching the same problem are demonstrated by William Rawn – the architect hero of Tracy Kidder's book *House* – who has worked in South Boston for the Bricklayers and Laborers Non Profit Housing Company. The city supplied land for just $1, and eighteen first-time owners won through a lottery the right to buy the houses at $69 000, fifty per cent below market cost, with safeguards to ensure that they are not

A roof over their heads

resold at the market value. Similar complex arrangements to produce low-cost houses for sale have been drawn up in many American cities.

In the absence of federal subsidies, and with the reluctance of voters to pay higher taxes, American cities have haggled endlessly with developers in the hope of persuading them to accept the burden of financing affordable housing. San Francisco insists on one subsidised house as the price of permitting every 1125 square feet of downtown office space. In New York, $400 million of the revenue the city earned from the World Financial Center development and from the neighbouring Battery Park apartments will go towards subsidising low-income housing elsewhere in the city. The idea that the rich and the poor should live side by side – an issue that in America is complicated by the question of race – is clearly not part of the agenda. Indeed, exactly the opposite is taking place.

Gentrification is not simply a matter of restoring lofts and doing up old brownstones. The process dates back at least to the attempt to resurrect Philadelphia from 1963 onwards, in the city's Society Hill area. The wealthy moved into the area, buying early eighteenth-century houses and restoring them, some encouraged by a sense that this was the cradle of America which had been allowed to slide into decay.

The takeover of rotting neighbourhoods by an influx of more affluent newcomers is inevitably presented by developers and conservative politicians as a sign of inner-city revival, evidence that the young and active are once more living in the city centre. But the real meaning of gentrification is very different. Peter Marcuse, a planner at Columbia and a former chairman of the Los Angeles city planning committee, found chilling evidence that gentrification in New York City at least is just another version of white flight. But instead of moving out to the suburbs, here the flight is from the Bronx, Brooklyn and Queens into the gilded stockade of Manhattan.

The condominium apartment towers, Trump, Metropolitan and Museum, were as much the landmarks of the changing social territory of the 1980s as the sandblasted loft walls had been in the 1970s. They were based on a mixture of Hollywood glamour and Le Corbusian fantasies of metropolitan life: restaurants, health clubs, chauffeurs' waiting rooms and wine cellars all formed part of the appointments of the New York condominium towers. They were built by tycoons shot through with egotism. Harry Macklowe, developer of the Metropolitan Tower, kept a chart of all the condominium towers in the city, and was quick to buttonhole visitors with claims that his sixty-five-floor tower was actually seventy-eight floors high, and so taller than the Trump Tower. Macklowe worked this conjuring trick by the simple expedient of skipping floors 17 to 29 on the lift button. Meanwhile, Trump dressed his doormen up in Cossack outfits, bearskins, and in approximations of the tail-coated waiters at the Connaught. These apartments are places dedicated to consumption, in which the giant kitchen with its glittering array of high-tech equipment is never used because breakfasts are catered and lunch and dinner are taken in restaurants.

Gentrification is not the product of an influx of additional well-to-do residents. In fact New York has fewer of them now than it did when the gentrification process started. Between 1970 and 1980, the number of people with a college degree living in New York City declined in absolute numbers from 813 563 to 776 557. But their spread across the five boroughs was very uneven, so that while Manhattan increased its number of college-educated residents by 22.9 per cent, in the Bronx it went down by 36.1 per cent. Gentrification has less to do with people deciding to come back from suburbia than with the reshuffling of people who already live in the city. It's the children of blue-collar workers in the Bronx who go to college and graduate to a loft in Manhattan, or more likely a formerly rent-stabilised apartment gone co-op on the Upper West Side, who are displacing people very much like their own parents.

The New York City triennial Housing and Vacancy Survey, conducted for the city by the US Bureau of the Census, found that the city had demolished 154 722 homes between 1970 and 1981, that in the same period 21 186 were condemned, and that 99 189 were burned out, boarded up, or exposed to the elements (a total of 275 097), while 22 149 were converted to non-residential use, and another 23 754 were merged with another residential unit. In all a loss of 321 000 units, that is 31 000 units abandoned every year for eleven years.

The Bronx in 1970 had 17.5 per cent of the city's households and Queens had 24 per cent, yet Bronx had 44 per cent of the city's demolished buildings in the next eleven years, and Queens only 3.6 per cent. The effect of abandonment is to make it more and more difficult for people living in the boroughs affected to stay on.

Whole areas of the city are notorious for their resemblance to the blitzed areas of post-war Berlin, and the rot spreads quickly. Those who can move do so, either to gentrifying enclaves in their own boroughs or, if they can afford it, into Manhattan, where they compete with the people who are drawn into the city to find work or to study.

If you put the two together – abandonment and gentrification – between 41 000 and 100 000 households are displaced every year in New York. In 1981, Le Gates and Hartman put the figure at 2.5 million per annum in the US as a whole, working with local figures from Denver, New Orleans,

A roof over their heads

Portland and Seattle. Research in the US suggests that gentrification affects the white, lower middle class in socially heterogeneous neighbourhoods, not low- or very low-income areas. It is not, broadly speaking, a product of large-scale movement between cities. The overwhelming majority of people who move out of gentrifying areas, and who do not stay in or near the same neighbourhood, stay in the same city.

The mirror image of gentrification is the tendency for those Americans who can afford it to live in surroundings further and further removed from the traditional idea of the city, or even the traditional idea of the suburb. According to John Herbers in *The New Heartland*, one of those alarmist books of pop sociology that America throws up every so often, the country is in the midst of a bout of change as great as the migrations first from farms to the cities, and second from cities to suburbs. The new non-metropolitan metropolis, exurbia, is a settlement with a population of 150 000 people spread out over 250 square miles, where downtown is a strip ten miles long, and the residents think nothing of an eighty-mile commute to work. In New York, Los Angeles, London and Paris – and, in a different way, in Tokyo – the 'city' in which the majority of people live is neither the old centre, the preserve for the most part of the wealthy, nor the ghettos and poorer inner suburbs; it's the new suburbs.

Suburbs have never had much appeal for architects. In the early years of the twentieth century they were horrified by the monotony of the mean streets of suburban London and New York, a little later they were equally appalled by the apparently endless sprawl of Los Angeles. Yet they have learned to love both of them, now that they are both in different ways threatened, and they have found a new kind of suburbia to worry about, even more amorphous, even more shapeless than all its predecessors.

Le Corbusier claimed that in reality the garden city leads to an enslaved individualism, a sterile isolation of the individual. 'It brings in its wake the destruction of social spirit, the downfall of collective forces, the annihilation of the collective will,' he wrote in *La Ville Radieuse*.

Lewis Mumford attacked post-World War Two suburbia because, 'it caricatured both the historic city, and the archetypal suburban refuge, a multitude of uniform, unidentifiable houses, lined up inflexibly at uniform distances on uniform roads in a treeless communal waste' – a picture of a wasteland that is close to the descriptions of the nineteenth-century suburb which in its day was just as unpopular.

The same condescension still comes from the American Institute of Architects, which claims that 'These new areas are populated by transient, career-minded families who have not developed allegiances to these areas beyond a concern for property values. There is also little interest in

The 1980s saw America, Britain and France all abandoning their earlier commitment to social housing. Nowhere was the shift in policy more violent than in Britain, where local authority house-building came to a virtual halt, and more than one million council homes were sold to their occupants. Those state funds that continued to go into house-building were channelled to housing associations, while attempts were made to resuscitate the long moribund private rental market. In London's docks, just as in mid-town Manhattan, high-rise housing came to mean expensive private housing, not municipal rented flats

supporting nearby cities that at one point would have been the center of employment for outlying areas.'

What they describe is a variation on the phenomenon that has overtaken the more accessible of Britain's small towns and villages, where the cottages of the poor farmworkers and artisans have been taken over by affluent urbanites who work elsewhere, whose children do not attend the local school, and whose very presence is displacing those of the older community who have not already moved on. The result is that the local school suffers a catastrophic drop in its rolls, the village pub closes and is turned into a weekend house, the shop probably disappears too, and nobody protests more forcefully than the newcomers whose presence has made these developments inevitable. In America, exactly the same kind of people lament the erosion of the city core, even as they move out.

The architectural messiahs of housing are still with us. Christopher Alexander is the latest in this recurring species. 'There is no doubt that the alienation and despair which many people feel is created at least in part by the depressing burden of this mass housing in which people are forced to spend their lives,' he claims. With the stark and often tragic evidence of the failures of Britain's post-war housing experiments all around us, who can say that Alexander is entirely wrong on this count. But it is not only the excesses of welfare state paternalism and the attempts of middle-class architects to carry out social engineering on a grand scale to a helpless working class that Alexander is talking about. He is equally critical of the free enterprise approach to housing. This is the custom of mass-market builders in America, and for that matter in Milton Keynes, of laying waste to acre after acre of agricultural land with deserts of neatly ordered suburban homes.

'Such houses', he claims, 'are identical, machine-like stamped out of a mould and almost entirely unable to express the individuality of different families. They suppress individuality, they suppress whatever is wonderful and special about any one family. Placed and built anonymously, such houses express isolation, lack of relationship, and fail to create human bonds in which people feel themselves part of the fabric which connects them to their fellow men.'

To put his ideas into practice, Alexander gets to play with the hapless Mexicans. Under the impression that he was bringing them western expertise, Alexander was allowed into a village in northern Mexico where, in a process that he bathetically describes in his book *Production of Houses*, he tried – and singularly failed – to build just five houses. In fact Alexander is producing just another variety of the professional arrogance which he claims to be against.

A roof over their heads

The truth is that the market does provide an infinite variety of aesthetic expression for homes. The messages that people use their homes to express may not be very comforting for the metropolitans – Milton Keynes has a weakness for thatched roofs, the suburbs of Houston betray every kind of fantastic dream from Scots baronial to New England fisherman's cottage – but the choice of a house is a chance to reflect these fantasies about life, dreams which are ignored by those who shape the high culture of a society at their peril.

Walt Disney as a city planner

10

The expo is to the city what fast food is to the restaurant. It is an instant rush of sugar that delivers a massive dose of the culture of congestion and spectacle, but leaves you hungry for more. The expo is Disneyland's alter ego, an insight into the gaudy mixture of the mundane and the fantastical that still lies close to the surface under the banality of the modern city.

Architecturally, expo sites are dominated by tortured pieces of structural gymnastics and giant mechanical toys. They are criss-crossed by monorails and robots, dotted with lakes and fountains, and adorned with bad art and worse sculpture. There are places to sit and places to drink, cinemas, theatres, fireworks and lasers, giant domes and inflatable tents. There is entertainment, and work, spectacle and sociability. In fact, in vulgarised, hysterical microcosm, the expo *is* the city.

For what are inevitably presented as eminently sensible reasons, enormous sums of money are poured into expos. Mayors underwrite them because they fill the hotels and bring free-spending visitors. Developers hope that they will boost the value of their land. Planners see them as catalysts for long-term urban development.

Yet none of this will happen unless the expo has the kind of elusive and entirely unsensible qualities that attract visitors in their millions. The expo is a licensed carnival for which the usual tidy financial criteria that business and government use to filter their attitudes to the city do not apply.

Their organisers know that they are looking for magic and, not being magicians, they are in no position to turn down any idea, no matter how outlandish, just in case it's the one out of a hundred which finally does deliver the goods.

The expo functions as if all the public life of a city were concentrated into one hysterical compound like so much cake icing, beyond which is the private world of suburbia. Outside the gate, expediency squeezes out all considerations but utility and economy. Inside, as if to compensate, there is nothing but spectacle. Monumental architecture which has been abolished on the outside is permissible here only on licence.

Siegfried Giedion claimed that the first modern fair, the forerunner of the expo, was Paris's *première exposition des produits de l'industrie française*, held in 1798 on the Champs de Mars, the site on which the Eiffel Tower was to rise ninety years later. There were just 110 exhibitors, and apart from a tethered hot-air balloon hovering overhead, most of their wares would seem mundane enough today. The displays of cotton yarn, watches, paper and cloth were worthy, if hardly spectacular evidence of the accelerating pace of the industrial revolution, and the destruction of the craft guilds. But half a century later the exoticism of London's Great Exhibition of 1851, the first genuinely international exposition, was another matter. Alongside the steam engines and weaving machines, the wax flowers and musical instruments, were archaeological plunder from ancient Egypt, stained glass, furniture, fountains, indoor trees, and prodigious creations in bentwood, tin plate and cast iron. Despite the strictures of those critics who saw the exhibition as stark evidence of the rape of craftsmanship by the machine age, six million paying customers came to see the Venus de Milo carved in butter.

But it was Joseph Paxton's prefabricated structure, built in just six months and covering an awesome 800 000 square feet, rather than its contents, that was to haunt the imagination of the nineteenth and twentieth centuries. More than a building, it inspired a completely new architectural type with its promise of all that the industrial world could achieve – the great iron and glass exhibition hall.

It was a condensation of many different kinds of urban space – promenade, piazza and forum – into a single gigantic object. As developed by the French, the exhibition hall quickly became an essential part of the modern city, put to work in a range of different contexts from the convention centre to the department store, two building types which both have their architectural and commercial roots in the world's fairs. But this was only one aspect of the legacy of the expo. Even more intriguing was the scope it gave for exploring various definitions of the city. It was the arena in which Robert Moses met Walt Disney, and where high art collided head-on with popular culture. From the first Paris exposition to the Brussels Expo of 1959, from the City Beautiful of Chicago to the starry-eyed futurism of New York in 1939, from the welfare-state optimism of the Festival of Britain in 1951 to the grim corporate vision of New York in 1964, each of the fairs sloganised a particular view of urbanism.

The Paris *Exposition Universelle* of 1889 was an even larger and more flamboyant event than London's Great Exhibition. Attracting all of 28 million visitors, its swaggeringly ostentatious national pavilions set the precedent for future fairs, culminating in the glum confrontations between German and Soviet exhibition architects in the 1930s, and their Cold War reprises in the 1960s. Alongside the engineering *tour de force* of Eiffel's famously controversial tower – the 'useless monstrosity' so angrily denounced by its contemporaries – and the vast clear spans of the Halle des Machines, a crop of bizarre new structures made their startling, if temporary presence felt on the Parisian skyline. Ignored as kitsch by the more squeamish of architectural historians, it is the fantastical aspects of the exposition, the replicas of the pagodas of Angkor Wat, Senegalese villages and Indochinese palaces, which could be seen incongruously silhouetted against the dome of Les Invalides, that were to have as much of an impact as Eiffel's engineering brilliance.

Once inside the turnstiles, paying customers could wander along a replica of a twisting street in old Cairo, past a reasonably faithful reconstruction of the Bastille and the Faubourg Saint Antoine, in which they could pause for refreshment in an open-air café. Elsewhere, Charles Garnier, architectural consultant to the exposition, had the chance to pursue a curious obsession building his personal Ideal Home Exhibition in the shape of a series of highly detailed archaeological reconstructions of Houses Through The Ages, from Etruscan villas to specimens of Gallo-Roman, Moorish and Red Indian homes. In the age of the grand tour it was the nearest that the masses could get to foreign travel: Disneyland before even the animated cartoon, let alone Mickey Mouse, had been thought of. Indeed, a century later a troupe of international celebrity architects were still pursuing the same sort of fantasies, drawing up plans to build hotels for Euro Disney at Marne-la-Vallée on the edge of Paris in the form of Wild West villages, Santa Fe-style lodges, and ski resorts from the Rockies.

But the exposition was more than uncomplicated escapism and had a didactic side too. There was a full-size replica of a slum tenement, set up inside the City of Paris's pavilion, through which the curious could wander on specially constructed walkways and bridges, before viewing the municipal solution to the problem, *La Maison Salubre*, with its water closets and main drainage.

Above all, the early European fairs were a chance for the engineers to let rip with technological invention of a quite remarkable order, outdoing each other with spectacular but outlandish structures. Paris's Halle des Machines in particular, with its self-propelled overhead viewing platform, was in itself as much of a mechanism as it was a piece of architecture.

The early expositions were quite outside the normal experience of city life and were never intended to be more than temporary diversions from it. But the idea that a fair could be planned in such a way as to have a permanent impact on the shape of a city wasn't long in coming. It was Barcelona's World Exposition of 1888, sited in the Ciutadella Park, which finally pushed the Catalan capital out of its medieval walls. The preparations for the fair included laying out a grid of boulevards and streets for Barcelona itself that the Catalan engineer Ildefons Cerdà had proposed thirty years earlier. Influenced by Haussmann's Paris, but adding significant inventions of his own, Cerdà's plan was to build square city blocks with champfered corners that had the effect of creating a network of streets interspersed with squares. And with the boost of the fair, Barcelona was able to transform the overcrowding of its ramshackle, multilayered, medieval core into a modern city in a single generation.

The entrepreneurs behind the Chicago World's Fair of 1893 were interested in its impact on the long-term future of the city as much as in the event itself, not least because of its effect on the value of their own property. The fair was intended to be more than a temporary architectural freak show, it was meant to point the way towards a reshaping of the whole city. Daniel Burnham drew up the masterplan for building the fair on Jackson Park, an undeveloped site on Lake Michigan, around an artificial lagoon. He believed that what was needed in Chicago, a city which already had a dozen skyscrapers and more than its share of engineering triumphs, was a centre with the architectural dignity that American cities acutely missed. Burnham saw the Columbian Exposition as a model for rebuilding Chicago itself. With Frederick Olmsted directing the landscaping, he prepared a formal, beaux-arts layout which placed two stipulations on the collection of mainly East Coast architects who designed the individual buildings. Everything had to be white, and classicism – albeit of the most over-ripe, feverish variety – was the architectural style of choice.

The whole complex was planned on a gigantic scale. The dome of the administration building, for example, was more than a match for St Paul's – in size and self-confidence if not in skill. But despite the monumentalism of the fair, its flimsy plaster and lathe buildings were never meant to last. Only Charles Atwood's Fine Arts Building outlived the fair. But the ponderous grandeur of the architecture – with its axes and esplanades, and the deference that individual architects paid to overall effect above individual impact – provided a model for American planning until World War Two.

The fair marked America's coming of age as an industrial power. But if the organisers took a high cultural tone, it was the gum and popcorn vendors who made fortunes. Venetian gondolas were imported to ply the artificial lakes, while rickshaws carried well-to-do visitors around the fair in comfort. Washington Gales Ferris devised the first ferris wheel especially for the fair. With its 250-foot diameter, and thirty-six cabins, each holding forty people, visitors were offered the same kind of perspective of the fairgrounds and the skyscrapers of Chicago's loop that Eiffel's tower gave visitors to the Paris exposition. From vertiginous cabins, they could gaze out across a dizzying landscape that certainly looked much more like the city that Burnham was after than the attraction parks studded with isolated buildings that formed the pattern for later fairs. That is not to say that there weren't plenty of bizarre pieces of architectural showmanship on the site. The Naval Exhibition, for example, was housed in a building shaped like a battleship. There was a minaret complete with muezzin calling the fair to prayer, and belly dancers, scorpion eaters and snake charmers wandered amongst the crowds. And the British pavilion was patterned after an English country house – a tradition that was still alive a century later when Mrs Thatcher's government organised its own exhibition in Kiev in 1990, drawing enormous Soviet crowds to a replica of a British shopping street, and an archetypal British home.

Chicago, however, had rather more progressive tendencies. There was a women's building, designed after a national competition limited to women architects, which had a kindergarten, and was ornamented from top to bottom by female sculptors.

New York has staged two world's fairs this century. Wallace Harrison's Trilon and Perisphere provided a soaring landmark for the first in 1939, reflecting a world still lost in adolescent wonder at Nylon, chrome, motorcars and air conditioning. The live TV broadcast was introduced to America here. Norman Bel Geddes designed Futurama, the enormous General Motors display, that proudly claimed to be the city of tomorrow – its 500 000-scale model buildings, its one million trees, and 50 000 cars – 10 000 of which actually worked – defining the idea of the modern world in the popular imagination. The models were magnificent, but they reduced the individual to the scale of an ant, paving the way for Robert Moses to start driving expressways through the Bronx, and demolishing swathes of Manhattan for the building of the Lincoln Center during the 1940s and 1950s.

By the time of the 1964 New York fair, once more dominated by Robert Moses, the dark genius of urban renewal, the city of tomorrow had gone senile. Moses distrusted modern art, and his one attempt at involving the younger generation of artists ended in embarrassment. Andy Warhol painted '13 most wanted men', a mural that caused a brief scandal before being obliterated on orders from Moses and with the acquiescence of Philip Johnson who had organised the commission. Moses was much more comfortable recruiting the old men who had worked with him on the 1939 expo, and the public was predictably underwhelmed by the results. The crowds still went to Flushing Meadow, but came away a little blasé, not to say bored with what it saw of the fair.

Moses liked to strike a high spiritual tone. He offered sites free of charge to the Mormons and Christian Scientists, who in the event found themselves crushingly upstaged by the Catholics. Pope Paul VI loaned the fair Michelangelo's 'Pietà', not moved since it had been installed in the Vatican in 1499. It was shipped across the Atlantic and placed in a theatrically lit, blue velvet-lined enclosure through which sightseers were propelled on a moving walkway. GM, which had produced Futurama with its extraordinary image of the high-rise city for the pre-war fair, revealed the imbecilic nadir of the American dream of order in 1964. It chose to display a model of a self-propelled jungle road builder, a factory on wheels designed to slice through virgin forest leaving an elevated superhighway in its wake, that could have been a metaphor for Vietnam.

But the 1964 fair was very significant in one way at least. It marked the convergence of the expo tradition with that of Disney. Walt Disney had set up his first theme park in California nearly ten years earlier, and in the run up to the fair he offered his services to several of the big commercial exhibitors. He devised a troupe of animated dinosaurs for the Ford pavilion, and a chorus of walking talking dolls for Pepsi who sang the joys of cola in a dozen languages. But Disney wasn't just interested in a role as a technician. There had always been something of an Ebenezer Howard about him, a utopian dream to rebuild the city as it should be, not as it actually was. The traffic wasn't all one-way. Disney was closer to the architectural taste culture than he seemed. He had many architects as friends, and people with architectural qualifications assumed many of the most important roles in the Disney empire.

After the '64 World's Fair, Disney hired William Potter, who had been one of Moses's aides, to help run his Californian empire. Disney, who had moved far beyond animation and film, had an abiding passion for planning the ideal city. He had initially hired William Pereira, architect of Los Angeles's international airport, and the Bank of America pyramid in San Francisco, but the relationship was not a success and Disney took over the job himself, dictating his ideas to a draughtsman. The early drawings make Disneyland look very much part of the beaux arts tradition: a circle, divided radially into segments. Despite the disdain that Disneyland was treated with in its early days, it represents a very considerable planning achievement – one for which the credit must go in large measure to Disney himself.

Disney dismissed his rivals, claiming that other parks had grown by haphazard accretion around a hotdog stand and a merry-go-round. The world's fairs, he said, were poorly planned clusters of individual, highly competitive exhibits, that were guaranteed to produce fatigue. Worst of all, as far as Disney was concerned, were the museums.

Walt Disney as a city planner

Disney's key to planning his park was 'The Wienie', the reward an animal trainer tosses to his dogs to teach them new tricks. In the Disneyland context, the castle is a wienie, there to draw people down Main Street, and the rest of the park is littered with more wienies to keep people moving, from the Rocket to the Moon to the Mark Twain Steamboat.

The greatest ingenuity was lavished on Main Street. Disney wanted it to have a dream-like character, which he acheived by scaling every brick and tile and gas lamp down to five-eighths actual size. But it also had to accommodate functioning shops. So the ground floor is ninety per cent full size, the second is eighty per cent, and the third is sixty per cent. It has the toy-like quality that Disney was after, but it also accommodates the cash-generating shops, and the apartment that Disney had made for himself above the fire house.

Disneyland is almost as much part of the conventional demonology of the metropolitan intellectual as suburbia. It is inevitably presented as the epitome of the lifeless and the slickly commercial. Yet it is by no means clear that the technological spectacle of the world's fairs has anything qualitatively different to offer. And the struggle by cities all over Europe to persuade Disney to choose them as the site of the first Euro Disney, with inducements worth millions of dollars, suggests that Disneyland is not entirely unpopular. The comparison is kitsch, but there are clear parallels between classical shrines, Mayan temple sites and pilgrimage centres tended by a priestly order with Disney. It has become a safari park to preserve the endangered remains of the city.

In Disney's hands, the amusement park has moved on from the unselfconscious level of popular entertainment to what aspires to high culture by employing academically respectable architects. You don't have to swallow Disney's world view to see that what he is doing is astonishing, the urban equivalent of NASA. Most ideal worlds stay on paper, Disney has built his.

The latest developments at Disney World in Florida, giddyingly blend reality with fantasy. The MGM Disney theme park has fully equipped studios, sets and sound stages which make films, side by side with Great Moments at the Movies, presented by Sears. Disney's imagineers have rebuilt the sets from *The Wizard of Oz*, and the claustrophobic labyrinths of the spaceship Nostromo from *Alien*. They form the backdrop for platoons of robots and a sprinkling of live actors who turn *Singing in the Rain* and *Raiders of the Lost Ark* into predigested bite-size chunks for the shortened attention spans of the video era. Gene Kelly, James Cagney and John Wayne feature as all-talking all-singing waxworks, doomed to go on repeating their lines in twenty-minute cycles.

In a theme park that could have been devised by Roland Barthes, visitors who have paid their $115 for a five-day passport to Disney World are admitted through studio gates into a living and breathing mirage, a surrealist reconstruction of the palm-lined Hollywood Boulevard of the 1920s and 1930s, before old age had started to stain its plaster facades, before the Oscar ceremony moved out of the bankrupt Roosevelt Hotel, and before the balance of power shifted from the producers to the agents. The original Hollywood is dead, its agonies marked by a massive redevelopment plan that has turned the few surviving buildings from the 1930s into a backdrop that divides one parking lot from another. In its Disney incarnation, Hollywood Boulevard is lined with squeaky-clean art deco. With the same endless attention to detail that characterises Disney's Main Streets in Tokyo, Los Angeles and Paris, reality has been improved on. A boulevard that in the flesh is a tired, jaded strip, just one building deep, where tourists wander aimlessly looking for some reason to justify the price of their bus ticket, has been turned into a stage set that depicts another stage set. Sears, which sponsored the park, has built what it calls a 1930s vintage store, equipped with period merchandise.

In California, the pedestrians are mad, bad, or from out of town. In Florida, aspiring starlets are paid to walk up and down a facsimile of Hollywood Boulevard, looking like aspiring starlets. Students masquerade as the hawkers selling maps to the stars' homes who in reality are unshaven derelicts. Disney's imagineers have not shrunk from improving Hollywood's physical layout. In California, Grauman's Chinese Theater stands slightly off the boulevard. In Disney's version it has moved onto the axis to serve as the gateway for the Great Moments ride. This is a fantasy wrapped in a fantasy, a painstaking recreation of something that never existed.

Without a trace of irony – how could there be room for yet another layer? – the Star Tours ride proclaims 'The Adventure is Real'. With George Lucas's help, the imagineers have built a forty-seater flight simulator that looks like a battle-scarred star fighter. By the ticket desk, R2-D2 greets the paying customers while attempting running repairs. Those visitors who manage to hold down their breakfast as they lurch around the universe can repair to the Sound Stage Restaurant afterwards to savour the atmosphere of an alcohol-free wrap party. They can stand in line for the Video Theater, which recreates the audience participation TV shows of the 1950s, the sound effect studios, the epic stunt theatre, or risk a trip along Catastrophe Canyon for a hallucinogenic series of simulated flash floods, earthquakes and hurricanes.

Disneyland was born in 1952, when, according to Walt Disney, amusement parks were still 'dirty, phoney places, run by tough-looking people'.

Disney set about building his alternative with all the enthusiasm of a British planner drawing up a master plan for a new town. As a first step, the Stanford Research Institute was commissioned to look at suitable sites within the Los Angeles area, taking into account topography, utilities, zoning, tax rates, smog incidence and the freeways. They selected a 160-acre parcel of orange groves in Anaheim, just twenty-seven minutes' drive from city hall on the new freeway.

The amusement park trade claimed that a park without a ferris wheel, no roller coaster, no beer concession and no hotdog stands was unworkable. The banks wouldn't lend Disney any money – amusement parks were in their senility, they said. But Disney struck a deal with the newly established ABC TV network to promote his new venture, and as a result Disneyland had more than one million visitors in its first six months, grossing $195 million in the first ten years.

The other vital ingredient was Disney's nothing-is-too-good-for-them approach to handling his customers. The targets in the shooting galleries are repainted every night, cleaning teams scrub the gum off the walkways with putty scrapers – a technique that Disney gave the world – and 800 000 plants are replaced each year because the organisation doesn't believe in putting up 'keep off' signs. Even more crucial is the relentless cheerfulness of the employees, and their dress code. Even in the 1950s, 'bright nail polish, bouffants, heavy perfume, jewellery and unshined shoes' were prohibited. The personnel manager called for 'no low spirits, no corny raffishness, and the ability to call the boss by his first name, without flinching. That's a natural look that doesn't grow quite as naturally as everybody thinks'.

Walt Disney was never completely happy with his creation. What particularly irked him was the knowledge that the hotels and concessions that had set up around Disneyland since it opened were making twice as much money out of the visitors as he was inside the turnstiles.

Disney World, launched in 1971, was the result of years of planning and secret land deals to solve that problem. After a great deal of negotiation, and purchases through anonymous nominees, Disney assembled forty-three square miles at Lake Buena Vista, ten minutes drive southwest of Orlando. It was remote enough to keep the outside world far enough from the front door to prevent any unauthorised off-limits spin-offs. It was a chance to do things on Disney's terms, and to realise his extraordinary dreams of building something that was closer to a genuine city than a facsimile of one. With 23 000 permanent jobs and 20 million visitors a year – almost as many as London attracts – Disney World by most definitions *is* a real city.

Epcot, Disney's most extraordinary vision of an urban utopia was originally intended not simply as a place people came to visit, but a settlement which people actually lived in. Disney's dream was of a city with 20 000 residents and a fifty-acre central hub, enclosed in a glass dome that would keep the weather out. Skyscrapers would pierce the dome, along with a monorail, vacuum-tube trash disposal and central computer, all the usual futurist bric-a-brac in fact. This would hardly have been a democratic utopia. Disney was not much concerned with the idea of representative local government. He wanted to ban all pets, and planned to enforce a strict dress code on residents, who would also have faced expulsion for drunkenness or unmarried cohabitation.

Disney told one of his biographers that 'I don't believe in going out to this extreme blue sky stuff that some architects do. I believe that people still want to live like human beings. I'm not against the automobile, but I just feel that the automobile has moved into communities too much. I feel that you can design so that the automobile is there, but still put people back as pedestrians again'. Disney claimed that 'In Epcot there will be no slum areas because we won't let them develop. There will be no landowners, and therefore no voting control. People will rent houses instead of buying them and at modest rentals. There will be no retirees, everyone must be employed'.

The chairman of Walt Disney Productions in the late 1970s was Ray Watson, a man who had trained as an architect, and was a former president of the Irvine Ranch Company, Orange County's vast new town. Watson became an independent developer whose architectural trademark was market research, which he used to determine consumer preferences for facades, lot sizes and floor plans. He first met Disney, who wanted an outsider's opinion of what he had come up with so far for Epcot, in the late 1960s. Watson talked him out of building houses for rent in Epcot, and, on the strength of it, joined the Disney board in 1973. A scaled-down version of Epcot was eventually opened as a theme park in 1982, though at a cost of $1.2 billion it was still an enormous undertaking.

In the 1970s, Disney had drawn a distinction between the theme parks at Disney World and the hotels. Fantasy stayed inside the fence, and once you were outside the gate you were back in the real world, such as it was. Disney leased land to the usual hotel chains, and they built the boxy high rises that line Hotel Plaza Drive. He built the Walt Disney World Village shopping centre with its Los Angeles suburban, cedar-shingled roofs. But the development of Disney World itself was a long-drawn-out process, and as time went on, the emphasis began to change. Disney and his heirs began building more and more attractions on the monorail loop designed to whisk visitors from their A-frame concrete contemporary hotel to Main Street. There are already three theme parks and 14 000 hotel rooms. There will shortly be a fourth, reportedly involving animals, and another 5000 hotel rooms.

Future World followed the Epcot Center in 1989. Alongside is the World Showcase, which offers national tourist offices with deep pockets a chance to sponsor exhibits extolling the charms of their lakes and mountains – to the tune of $25 million for a ten-year licence. Just like everything else at Lake Buena Vista, these are continually being remodelled. There is nobody to designate the attractions as landmarks, nobody to ensure that they remain in their authentic, original condition. In the same way that Disney was able to create his own version of city life without muggers or urban blight, he was able to keep the conservationists out of his world too.

The Disney approach is now beginning to spill into its hotels. The company is attempting to mix high and low culture by building what Peter Rummel of Disney Development calls 'entertainment architecture'. The Grand Floridian, a 900-room hotel built on the monorail system on the shores of the Seven Seas Lagoon, between the Magic Kingdom and the Polynesian Village Resort, was one of the first examples. Disney claims that the Floridian's wide verandahs, intricate latticework and balustrades take guests back to the nineteenth century, when similar such Victorian resorts catered to the northern carriage trade. The Grand Floridian also has the bizarre spectacle of a Victorian railway station to link it to the monorail line that circles Disney World.

Michael Eisner, Disney's successor as chairman of the company, has courted both academically respectable and critically fashionable architects to design hotels for the company. Michael Graves, who completed two hotels for the company at Disney World in 1990 – the twelve-storey, 760-room Swan resort and the adjoining Dolphin – is the most conspicuous beneficiary of the new policy.

Financed by Metropolitan Life Insurance, which has its own health exhibit in the park, Tishman Realty and the Japanese Asoki Corp leased the land from Disney to build the $375 million Dolphin. It has a 200 000 square foot meeting and convention hall, built in a deliberate attempt to pull in yet another audience for Disney World. Clearly the market is a lucrative one. Tishman, which has worked on Disney World since it started, was so concerned by Disney's unexpected decision to allow a competing hotel into the kingdom that it sued Disney for $1 billion in 1986 before coming to terms.

The Dolphin hotel and convention centre (named for reasons that will be only too apparent to anybody who has seen the fifty feet high, steel-reinforced fibreglass marine mammals on the roof) is, at least for the moment, the biggest in the entire state of Florida. Robert Stern has also built two hotels for Disney World, the Yacht Club and Beach Club, next door to the Swan, as well as what they call a Casting Center – though anywhere else it would be described as the personnel department. Stern is also building one of the six hotels that will open at Euro Disney at Marne-la-Vallée outside Paris in 1992.

Tokyo was the site of the first Disney theme park outside the USA. Disney's trademark castle pokes its spires up through the tangle of elevated highways and the gritty industrial wastes north of the city, attracting ten million visitors a year. But it is Euro Disney that points to the direction in which Disney is now moving under Eisner's leadership.

The company spent years looking at sites – from England in the north to Spain in the south – before choosing Marne-la-Vallée, within four hours' drive of 150 million people, as much for the financial inducements offered by the French government as its geographic location.

Well aware of both the fascination of the Europeans for Americana and the potential hostility towards cultural imperialism, Disney took a lot of time to make its mind up about whether or not to give the place an American flavour. Early on, Eisner took a troupe of architects to a weekend retreat to talk about strategy. Stanley Tigerman, Robert Stern, Michael Graves, Robert Venturi and Frank Gehry all took part, discussing the tone that the park should aim for, whether the hotels should be part of the fantasy as well as the theme park, what its character should be, and who should design it.

Robert Fitzpatrick, president of Euro Disney, explains that while 'The castle in California is based on Ludwig of Bavaria's Neuschwanstein, in Florida it's more like the middle ages. But you can't bring that sort of thing to Europe where the real thing comes from. I.M. Pei told me to look at the Très Riches Heures of the Duke of Berry for a model for France'.

To select architects to design the project, Eisner looked at the portfolios of 200 architects from all over the world and asked twenty of them, including Aldo Rossi, Rem Koolhaas, Bernard Tschumi, Jean Nouvel, Christian de Portzamparc, Hans Hollein and Arata Isozaki, to produce proposals for Marne-la-Vallée. Only James Stirling declined the invitation. What Eisner wanted was ideas more than detailed designs, a sign of the increasing sophistication of his audience.

It was the start of a long-drawn-out courtship ritual. With the exception of Frank Gehry, who designed the entertainment centre, all the designers who might be called modernists dropped out. Only the representational, themed hotels proved acceptable to Eisner's view of what Disney should

Walt Disney as a city planner

be. There will be five drawn up around an artificial lake, with a sixth forming a monumental gateway from the new stations for the TGV and RER lines to the park itself.

Robert Stern did the Hotel Cheyenne, a frontier town, with a Greek Revival city hall, a saloon, hitching posts and livery stables. His inspiration has been a careful scrutiny of stills from Westerns and the Lucky Luke strip cartoon, a French cowboy saga, a combination which Stern fondly imagines is his way of giving the place some Gallic resonances. Michael Graves is doing the New York Hotel, with its Midtown and Gramercy Park wings. Antoine Predock's Santa Fe-style hotel boasts an iconic drive-in movie screen.

Just as the expositions once offered escapist fantasies, Disney provides a complete fantasy world. But its economic power is real. It brings tens of thousands of real jobs, and not just for people who are prepared to put on a pair of Mickey ears. It offers not just an escape from the real world outside, nor even an adjunct to it, but an alternative model for the city.

As the international expos have grown more costly, and the chances of recovering the investments involved have receded, increasing attention has been paid to their catalytic impact on the shape of the city around them. It's an approach that has not always met with much success. Robert Moses managed to rid New York of the mountainous rubbish tips that stood on the site of the 1939 world's fair. But though he engineered its successor in 1964 with the deliberate policy of equipping the city with the maximum in the way of new infrastructure, there is little left today beyond a few ramshackle ruins, lost in the dereliction of Flushing Meadow. It's a fate that has often overtaken exhibition sites as once fashionable views of the world of tomorrow start to look dowdily outmoded as their monorails begin to rust away.

Few cities have been as ambitious in what they hope to extract from staging a fair as Seville, with its expo in 1992 marking the 500th anniversary of Christopher Columbus's discovery of America. A dusty city of just 650 000 people, Seville is planning the largest world's fair since Osaka, twenty years earlier, a longer than usual gap which is the result of President Mitterrand's unsuccessful battle with Jacques Chirac, the mayor of Paris, to stage an expo in Paris in 1989.

The site chosen is an artificial island once occupied by the fortified monastery of La Cartuja, isolated from the rest of Seville by a canal dug in the nineteenth century as part of the city's attempts to tame the unpredictable behaviour of its river, the Guadalquivir. Now the plan is to use the expo to build links between Seville's old centre and its new suburbs. At the same time, both provincial and central governments are spending billions of pesetas not just to emphasise Spanish emergence from the underdevelopment of the Franco years, but to put Andalusia on the international map.

Felipe Gonzalez, Spain's socialist prime minister, is determined to use the fair to pull Andalusia, one of Europe's poorest regions, up by its bootstraps. Along with the fairgrounds themselves, packed with the usual clichés of expo architecture, comes a whole shopping list of infrastructure investment. Manuel Castells, the Marxist sociology academic, commutes between Madrid and Berkeley to advise the Spanish government on how to use the expo to trigger off a rapid surge of development in Andalusia. The plan is to recycle the expo site as a science park, a base for biotechnology, medical and energy research. Seville's local university will move in, alongside a battery of international research and training centres. The usual litany of international high technology companies are being courted to establish themselves here.

The city is building a new railway station, Santa Justa, as the terminus for a cripplingly expensive high-speed rail link from Madrid that the Spanish are rushing to complete in time for the twenty-six weeks that the fair will be open – in the hope of bringing day-trippers from the capital. There will be 2000 kilometres of new motorways. And Seville's airport, where the passenger concourse had just three telephones in 1990, is being expanded with a new terminal designed by José Rafael Moneo to take intercontinental flights. There will also be a 4000-seat open-air theatre – replacing a stillborn plan for a full-blown opera house, and the city is installing a new digital telecommunications network.

The construction work clearly brings prosperity to developers and builders, but its long-term benefits are more nebulous. There are many who see the high-speed rail link in particular as a wrong-headed folly creating a vastly expensive line that leads nowhere, squandering money which would have been better spent connecting Madrid and Barcelona with France.

Seville's plans are an ambiguous mixture of old-fashioned pork barrel politics, involving a massive diversion of state funds by Madrid politicians anxious to secure re-election into the hands of local supporters, with sophisticated attempts to overcome the problems of economic backwardness. As a model for the new city, it is a synthesis of the Disney and expo traditions, a blend of escapism and cynicism that tells us all a great deal about the psychology of urbanism.

The architecture of consumption

11

Just at the point in the mid 1980s when it should finally have become clear to even the most myopic chauvinist that Japan was no longer content to prosper by relying on the low-budget recycling of other people's ideas, Seibu, the railway, hotel and retail chain, decided to underscore its prestige by building a new store in Tokyo. Completed in 1984, it is a lavish echo of the great nineteenth-century department stores of Europe and America, a species that has lapsed into self-parody in the West, but which is enjoying a late flowering in Japan.

It is sited in Yurakucho, the buffer zone that protects the relative calm of Tokyo's banks and corporate offices in Marunochi from the pedestrian-choked bedlam of the Ginza. Sprawling over two interlinked towers, the larger of which is all of fourteen floors high, it was a conscious attempt to show off, bringing together every new toy Seibu could find to sharpen the appetites of some of the most jaded and pampered consumers in the world.

The exterior is bland, despite its curved and finned facade which gestures feebly towards architectural restraint in a vain attempt to distinguish itself from its neon-festooned neighbours. As so often in Tokyo, it is the interior that really counts. Every morning the doors open with a flourish as teams of uniformed female employees in white gloves and boaters wait to greet customers with deep bows, treating the ritual with deadly seriousness, even as a humanoid robot cleaning machine potters back and forth behind them, clasping dust pan and brush in its mechanical grip.

It's a curious welcoming committee which oddly echoes a much earlier one at Aristide Boucicault's Bon Marché store in the Paris of the 1860s, described by Emile Zola in *Au Bonheur des Dames*, where 'each time a customer appeared, there was a stir among the page boys, lined up beneath the high porch, dressed in a livery consisting of a grey coat and trousers, and yellow and red striped waistcoat'.

Department stores were social, as well as architectural innovations. Unlike the specialist stores which they succeeded, the department stores did not bargain with their customers. Boucicault insisted on displaying clearly posted prices instead. With the grand courts, chandeliers, mahogany fittings and thick carpets that Zola characterised as democratised luxury, they aimed for a newly affluent clientele, one that needed both reassurance and guidance. Their elaborate displays were calculated not just to entertain and attract customers, but to advise and educate the socially anxious how to dress, and how to furnish their parlours.

In many ways, the Japanese stores play a similar role today. After spending most of the twentieth century in isolation, conditioned to work hard, live frugally, and save every penny they could, the Japanese need help spending their money now that it has become their patriotic duty to consume more to ward off the threat of a tariff war with the West.

Bon Marché and Seibu have each in their own way represented a significant shift in the definition of the city. They have become extensions of the public realm, places to eat and drink, to meet and to promenade.

In a society such as Japan's, in which even the relatively prosperous live in extremely modest homes, located in far distant suburbs, the department store is a genuine public space, with the room in which to be entertained and amused as much as to purchase domestic necessities.

On the ground floor of the Seibu store there are banks of touch-sensitive video screens which will guide you around all 122 of the store's departments. In three languages, they can advise you on the conversion of English collar sizes to their Japanese equivalents, the location of the fresh fish department, and the whereabouts of the Sotheby's office up on the seventh floor which offers Japanese bidders a satellite link to its London auctions. Should you tire of Seibu's own attractions, the screens can offer a selection of noodle bars in the neighbourhood, complete with menus and maps of how to find them, and a listing, updated daily, of the programmes at local cinemas.

Seibu entertains its customers with a continual flood of special events to ensure that they keep coming back. During Turkish month, the restaurant on the ground floor served food prepared by a chef flown over especially from Istanbul, while the furniture department upstairs was full of hand-crafted carpets, the wine and spirit department downstairs offered samplings of Efes beer, and the art gallery in the annexe staged a show of contemporary painting from Ankara. During Spanish month there was a selection of Rioja wines, contemporary Spanish fashion, design by Javier Mariscal, bespectacled creator of the mascot for the 1992 Barcelona Olympics, and a visiting Goya. There are exhibitions of avant garde furniture design, and arts and crafts architecture, impressionist painting and cartoons. You can find original chairs by Charles Rennie Mackintosh and paintings by Lichtenstein or Cy Twombley. It all adds up to a microcosm of the cosmopolitan city – the metropolis condensed into a consumerist spectacle.

The merchandise itself is treated with neurotic care and attention.

Throughout the year, the food hall in the basement offers meticulously wrapped bunches of perfectly spherical grapes the size of tangerines, at the price of dinner for two in a Michelin three-star restaurant. There are chiller cabinets packed with enough dry ice to send a mist of water cascading down over the green vegetables they contain, watched over by staff in rubber boots with the same tender solicitude they would lavish on a battery of incubators in a post-natal ward. Men in headbands bang wooden sticks to attract customers to their stalls of raw fish. There is tempura and eel and chicken yakitori to take out, and Aunt Stella's cookies and a pasta bar for those with more exotic tastes.

In the liquor section there are forty-eight different types of malt whisky, and as many bourbons as you could hope to find in a neighbourhood bar in Kentucky. There is a counter at which you can order a baguette and cheese, flown in daily the eight thousand miles from Paris, to accompany a glass of wine whose vintage the highly knowledgeable waiter will be happy to help you choose. Upstairs, the scent of freshly baked bread from the Le Notre bakery and the Fox Bagels stand percolates into the Café Kirn, with its selection of Alsatian sausage, before spreading out to the watch counter alongside, where cases full of antique Rolexes sit next to garish plastic Swatches. There is a department that sells only beige items – T-shirts, stationery, linen, trousers, pencils, piled up high in neat rows calculated to bring out the collecting instinct.

Up on the fashion floors, there are concession areas for Marithe Girbaud, Sonia Rykiel, Kenzo, Comme des Garçons, Issey Miyake, Katharine Hamnett, Jasper Conran, Ralph Lauren, part of a constantly changing litany of international fashion celebrities, from whose ranks the under-performers are quietly ejected each season to make way for fresher talent. Each of them has their own shop, actually more like a stage set since it is doorless and roofless, in which the designer's identity is signalled by a pyrotechnic display of shopfitting skills that must catch the split-second attention span of the crowds as they cruise up and down the aisles.

On the floor above you can buy European porcelain and jewellery from Van Cleef & Arpels and Garrards, or take tea and cucumber sandwiches served by a butler in tails. You can also find a serious bookshop here, selling French novels, poetry and art books, with jazz playing quietly over the loudspeakers.

This is by no means the only Seibu store in Tokyo, nor even the biggest. Seibu has a whole complex in Shibuya, the Ginza's younger rival as Tokyo's fashion centre. Another Seibu subsidiary in Roppongi, Wave, offers customers eight floors of records, a recording studio and a cinema, where there is no need to buy anything to spend an afternoon listening to music.

And Seibu's oldest Tokyo store at Ikebukuro now sprawls over 3.75 million square feet after forty years of continual extension – about the size of a major regional shopping centre in North America or Europe.

Seibu has a constant struggle in the highly competitive Japanese market to hang on to its reputation as the smartest of the department stores in the face of half a dozen other groups, all of which try to put on the same kind of spectacle. Nor do the department stores have a monopoly on retailing in Tokyo. The fashion building is a homegrown invention of the Tokyo real estate market, which brings together fashion shops and restaurants in miniature vertical malls. A Tokyo fashion building is a hallucinatory world that hovers between illusion and superrealism. On the ground floor of the Harajuku Quest, there is enough of a glimpse of green through the windows of the Ranarita restaurant to suggest that this could be a Milanese courtyard. Certainly the smells of garlic and olive oil are right. There is genuine Tiramisu on the menu. Even the round-shouldered, shot-silk dinner jacket the maître d' wears is Milanese. But the garden is actually a glassed-in box, like a squash court, which sits cheek by jowl with the unsightly backside of a Tokyo apartment block. Next door, the waitresses in C.H. Demmell, as the elaborate Edwardian gilt lettering on the door claims it is called, wear authentic maids' outfits, and dispense mountains of Sacher torte in a ceramic-tiled, stucco-ceilinged simulacrum of a Viennese coffee house. Both these alternative universes, contemporary Italy, and turn of the century Austro-Hungary, slotted into the framework of a sombre, grey-polished granite and fractured concrete structure, are here to divert shoppers on the way up to the Donna Karan store above, and all of them are owned and run by Asahi, the Japanese brewer.

This is a step beyond the fantasyland Englishness of Ralph Lauren's Rhinelander Mansion store on Madison Avenue in New York, where wooden toys, cricket bats, rowing boats and dried flowers scoured from English antique dealers have been shipped across the Atlantic by the containerload to festoon every square inch of wall and floor. In New York, it is the completeness of the illusion that is the point. The store panders to the fantasy that Lauren's customers could actually be the kind of person depicted in his advertisements. In Tokyo, it's the very dissonance of the alternate realities that the designer has created that gives the city the edge of strangeness which is part of its essential character. It's a fantasy that is so thorough and so businesslike that it transcends the limits of make believe and becomes a coherent and complete kind of urban reality. The city is experienced not at street level but in the stores.

The tireless attempts of Seibu and its rivals Tobu and Isetan to outdo each other in the lavishness of their displays in contemporary Tokyo

The architecture of consumption

echoes past rivalries. Stewart's Marble Palace in New York staged fashion shows and organ recitals to entertain customers in the 1850s. While Macy's imported mechanical singing birds from Europe, Gimbel's cleared out its entire fourth floor to stage an indoor golf tournament, and sponsored an aeroplane race between its New York and Philadelphia stores in 1907. Marshall Field, which with 8000 employees could handle 250 000 customers in a single day, claimed to have the biggest Christmas tree in the world. Another Philadelphia store opened its own radio station, while Hudson's in Detroit started a new tradition with its Thanksgiving Day parades.

The elaboration and scale of these enterprises kept on growing. New York boasted the first department store with a passenger lift, installed in one of James Bogardus's prefabricated cast-iron structures on Broome Street. Then in 1876 John Wanamaker turned what used to be a warehouse for the Pennsylvania Railroad in Philadelphia into an immense single-storey dry goods store. Under its trussed roof, it occupied no less than two acres of floor space, focused on a circular counter ninety feet across. Wanamaker opened a tea room in the store, which he boasted could serve 10 000 people in a day.

But it was Boucicault's Bon Marché in Paris that was the most successful and innovative of all the early department stores. Boucicault took over what had been a modest menswear store in 1852, and rebuilt it in considerable style in 1876 using Gustave Eiffel and Louis Boileau to design the new building. It was to be both the commercial, and the architectural model for the department store around the world.

Eiffel and Boileau got away from the warehouse origins of the department store and introduced the atrium to modern retailing, carving deep holes out of a glass-roofed, cast-iron structure to bring daylight down into the heart of the store.

Paul Sedille's Magasin Printemps of 1881-9, and Louis Sullivan's Carson Pirie Scott store in Chicago of 1900, followed in its footsteps, with imposing facades and ornate grand staircases. But it was Bon Marché's name that was appropriated by shopkeepers all around the world. And French associations are still important in retailing, from the Magasins du Nord in Copenhagen to Printemps in Tokyo.

In Chicago, each new store frantically tried to outdo its predecessors in architectural magnificence and the lavishness of its appointments. Henry Hobson Richardson reworked the Pitti Palace for Marshall Field in 1885. Shortly afterwards, Siegel Cooper claimed to have the largest retail floor area in the world, with more than half a million square feet of selling space. In 1892, Marshall Field used Daniel Burnham to build him a nine-storey new building. Louis Sullivan designed a store with a reading room, rest room, medical treatment suite, art galleries and restaurants.

By 1907, Field's main store sprawled across well over one million square feet. Its latest extension had been designed by Burnham in white granite, and featured a Tiffany mosaic dome, an indoor mall and a courtyard. Field even commissioned Alphonse Mucha to illustrate his newspaper advertisements.

Harry Gordon Selfridge – who went on to establish Selfridges in London – was Field's partner for a time. He came up with the idea of tying the store to events such as the Columbian Exposition, and was responsible for initiating the universal retail habit of counting down the days to Christmas. William Whitley pioneered the department store in London, opening his first establishment in 1880. Harrods' present home was built between 1900 and 1905, while Selfridges, architecturally the most grandiose of all London's department stores, began trading in 1909. Selfridge hired two American architects, Francis Swales and Daniel Burnham, to provide an authentically lavish transatlantic flavour to his enterprise in London.

Outside Japan, the city centre department store enjoyed only a brief hey-day of prosperity. It coincided with the peaking of the population of the central city. As the inner city went into its long, slow decline after World War One, stores which relied on large numbers of affluent consumers within easy reach began to suffer. In London, Whitley sold out to Selfridge in 1930. In New York, Gimbel's and Macy's were in trouble too. The Depression didn't help, but the longer-term threat came from the mush-rooming shopping centres designed for car-borne consumers, which were starting to appear on the edges of town.

The first modern out-of-town shopping centre is usually reckoned to be the Country Club Plaza, built in Kansas City by J.C. Nichols in 1922. Until then, the only retailing that took place on the edge of town had been the occasional strip of shops clustering around gas pumps or bus stations. The intensely conservative property business was convinced that successful shops depended on a high volume of passing pedestrians. In complete con-tradiction to that rule, Nichols set out to attract shops to the middle of nowhere, where there were no pedestrians at all. He established a highly successful formula for the shopping mall, making its stores visible from the street, and with an obvious car park a more important lure than a window display.

Nichols wrote a guide to mall design in 1947 in which he cautioned against 'extreme modernistic designs that may be quickly outdated' and suggested that 'second floors are seldom advisable'. It was to such places

The architecture of consumption

that the downtown stores moved quickly, turning into national chains in the process. Their downtown branches, whose fortunes were inextricably linked with their surrounding cities, meanwhile started on a spiral of decline, initially starved of investment, in some cases abandoned altogether. As the stores shut up shop, so the decline of the city became more and more obvious, and the less attractive it became to investors, and visitors. The more the city itself declined, so the less likely was the downtown store to survive.

The stores were of course well aware of what was happening. It was no accident that the Better Philadelphia Exhibition in 1947, which brought the message of urban renewal to the wider American public, was staged in Gimbel's downtown Philadelphia department store. More than 400 000 people visited the exhibition, attracted by a fourteen by thirty foot model of the city with removable sections to demonstrate how it could look after redevelopment.

But department stores are still in decline in America. Between 1985 and 1989 they lost five per cent of their revenues to speciality and designer stores and catalogues, the biggest shift in eighty years. Many of the best-known names – Saks, Marshall Field and Bloomingdale's – were all for sale, and Bonwit Teller and B. Altman were in difficulties at the end of the eighties.

As the traditional audience for the stores moved away, some found new ones in the tourist market. In London, Harrods provides a warning of the fate of the surviving city centre department store as it struggles to adapt to changing circumstances. They stretch a thick tasselled rope between sturdy brass posts across a corner of the meat department, the kind of arrangement normally deployed to hold back the crowds at cinemas. Here, in the heart of the store, it is guarding an array of pork chops and an artistically arranged wall of prime beef discreetly dripping blood into the parsley. Not the last line of defence against animal rights activists, it's there to prevent the hordes of back-packers and rubber-necks who pour into Harrods every day from reaching out to touch, just as zoos stop people pushing sweets through the bars. Elsewhere in the food hall, rippling matrons with the displacement of supertankers videotape each other buying cartons of yoghurt. Flaxen-haired Scandinavian teenagers clad from head to foot in stonewashed denim wander through the perfume department eating their sandwiches. Parties of Japanese in their Burberry uniforms are led through the crockery counters by flag-waving tour guides. Only the sensibly shod couples, up in town for the day, still maintain the hushed awe that Harrods once engendered. Though there is now an attempt to enforce a dress code.

Is it conceivable that back home people would behave in a manner that would require the same protection for the frozen turkey at Safeways as the chops get at Harrods? Would the matrons really want to capture a permanent record of themselves buying a doughnut at their local shopping centre? The reality is that Harrods has become a theme park in which the world wanders open-mouthed, chattering and pointing at the merchandise. This is no longer merely the top people's store, serving its Knightsbridge neighbours and their country cousins. It has become an attraction, an adventure playground. While the reality of shopping for the rest of the world becomes ever more standardised, people come here to gape at the sight of a meat pie or a side of stilton, a little like those interpretative centres where actors dress up as hollow-cheeked consumptive schoolchildren and turn-of-the-century grocers.

The result of all this has been a huge change in the way in which Harrods operates. To avoid being flattened by the hordes of locust-like visitors it has had to take defensive action. Harrods being Harrods, you would hardly expect to find it to be full of supermarket checkouts. But they are present all right, in the food hall, next to the bread counter, where large signs insist on the use of tongs while handling the croissants. But the checkouts here are like Ruritanian sentry boxes, manned by people in straw hats and salt of the earth aprons. Equally, the ground floor coffee bar now insists on cash on delivery, hardly the way that account customers would have expected to be treated in the old days, but essential now if the locusts are to be kept in check, as are the specially uniformed Harrods security forces.

Harrods is devouring itself. Larger and larger parts of the floor area of the store are devoted to selling Harrods merchandise: tea towels, jogging suits, clock radios that all bear the Harrods logotype, china mugs in the shape of Harrods door men, tea towels and bags, even fluffy mice done up as Harrods fishmongers. And the same products are taking Harrods to concessions in airports around the world, and into a licensing deal in Japan.

Meanwhile, the focus of innovation in retailing that used to come from stores like Harrods has moved to the edge of town. Ever since Nichols and shopping centre developers like him got going, retailers and the property business have had an intimate relationship, one very like that between the house builders and the suburban railways in London and Los Angeles, which shaped the face of suburban development at the turn of the century. The surge of suburban house building in the 1950s and 1960s, accompanied by the massive federal highway building programme, saw American shopping habits turned inside out as the department stores moved with their customers. The fact that developers depended on loans from pension funds, which insisted on protecting their investments by lending only to developers who could show they had pre-let seventy per cent of space in their developments to well-established retailers committed to taking substantial floor area, shaped the character and form of these places. Typically there would be two department stores, one at each end of the mall, with the smaller store units on each side. The restrictions imposed by the lenders drove out diversity and killed off the chances of smaller, more innovative stores opening up in malls.

To capture big national stores for their malls, developers were ready to offer them practically anything. So much so that the federal trade commission filed a series of law suits against what it saw as the unwholesomely close relationship between developers and big stores, charging that such practices as giving favoured retailers the right of approval on other tenants, and excluding discount stores were against the public interest.

The suits were eventually settled out of court. What the government could not do, however, was to persuade the developers to go back to the by now rotting downtowns. One big shopping centre developer, Edward De Bartolo, told *The New York Times* in 1973 'I wouldn't put a penny downtown. It's bad. Face it, why should people come in? They don't want the hassle, they don't want the danger. You would need fantastic government subsidies, amazing subsidies. No individual or corporate set-up can make a dent on these problems. So what do you do? Exactly what I'm doing, stay out in the country, that is the new downtown'.

What keeps the city centre department store in business in Japan is the efficiency with which it can offer home delivery, and the reliance of most Tokyo commuters on public transport. As a result, Japan has been slow to develop the out-of-town shopping centres and malls that have transformed the nature of city life in the West. Tokyo's newest ring of department stores is firmly located on the subway stations of the Yamanote loop line, allowing easy access for commuters, reflecting both the relatively low level of car ownership in the city and the commercial interests that the department store groups have in Japan's private railway system.

The original model for all the second generation out-of-town shopping centres was the Houston Galleria at Post Oak. Gerald Hines, who had opened the first phase in 1970 (where he crossed the Milan Galleria with the Magasin au Bon Marché), put the best face he could on the shopping centre phenomenon and its impact on the nature of the city. 'I was trying to define a new prototype, a whole new urban form that the American public doesn't know exists.'

The architecture of consumption

From the exterior, the Houston Galleria is all but invisible, dominated by the inevitable North American assembly of blank-walled parking structures. Exteriors hardly count when virtually all access is from the car park, and this is in any case a site that had no context whatsoever when Hines came here, beyond its convenience for the Houston orbital freeway, Loop 610. What makes it interesting is the way in which Hines tried to give the place more than the bare minimum of amenities. Planned around its famous ice rink, the Galleria is a place that people want to go to, if only because in Houston there isn't anywhere else to find the element of the unpredictable that city life is meant to offer.

Around the rink there is a tier of eating places, overlooked by shops and boutiques. And, contrary to conventional wisdom on mall design, there are three levels, with the lobbies from the hotel that Hines developed as part of the project feeding in as well. There is only one department store attached to the complex, Neiman-Marcus, which for once does have windows to the outside world.

There is an argument to be made that in Houston the Galleria actually *is* a downtown. Certainly there are more signs of life here on a Saturday morning than there are in the desolate streets of what is called the city. William H. Whyte, the indefatigable observer of life at street level, will tell you that shopping centres can never be real downtowns because in the last resort they are private, not public spaces. He has carefully documented the tendency of mall owners and their private security forces to harass anybody who doesn't look as if they are conventional consumers, to the extent of moving the elderly or the young off benches, and prohibiting leafleting, lobbying and casual street trading.

Whyte has a point. But the Galleria has genuinely helped to create a focus for Houston. Of course, by giving the Galleria a more memorable image than the average shopping mall, Hines is also protecting his own investment, raising the rents he can ask, and increasing the value of his land holdings around it.

By the standards of the larger and larger centres that followed, the Galleria is tame enough. The long, low-slung, glass-roofed aisles are actually more like Frank Lloyd Wright's roof-lit Marin Civic Center than its Milanese namesake. The ice rink, a conscious homage to the Rockefeller Center, is a strong attraction as a refuge from the punishing Texas summer outside. Post Oak, with its Philip Johnson fountain and its soaring Transco Tower, has become a significant office area for Houston, and as a result the Galleria is now a place where you might just about be able to go for a walk in car-dominated Texas without attracting too much attention. It's the birth of a new urban form. Post Oak-Galleria, as the area calls itself, is the urbanistic equivalent of an artificial intelligence machine. You start with the most basic circuits that simply distinguish between on and off – or in this case between building and absence of building. As you add more and more components, you eventually produce a set of circuits with the complexity to give the system the semblance of intelligence. Enough yes/no circuits, and you can eventually build a computerised chess player that will beat anyone but a grand master. So the accretion of urban ingredients, the hotel, the bookstore, the ice rink, the luxury shop, eventually creates something that transcends the poverty of the ingredients. Building/non-building may yet become piazza, square and forum. Meanwhile, the customers keep coming, even in the downturn that hit the Houston economy in the 1980s, lining up to buy shopping bags emblazoned with the Galleria name.

The other possibility, however, is not that the shopping centre is providing an equivalent to a traditional downtown, but that it is creating an altogether different kind of city around it. As the edge-of-town shopping centre has grown more elaborate it has taken on the functions and the scale that allow it to exist independently of a large city. A shopping centre giant, if it is on a motorway network that puts it within reach of two or three smaller towns, can prosper well away from a big city.

The biggest in the world in the 1980s was the West Edmonton Mall in Alberta, which blurred shopping and entertainment in a frankly disorientating way. Apart from its department stores and its cafés and its shops, the mall's centrepiece is a large-scale, three-masted replica of a man-of-war in full sail trapped in a pond. Its pneumatic figurehead has been inspired more by science fiction comics than the sixteenth century, but the vessel does float in perfectly authentic water, albeit surrounded by not quite such authentic rocks. In another pool, close by, hapless packs of dolphins are put through their paces, while the mall roof rears up at one point to accommodate a $9 million water chute that precipitates terrified small boys down through ten floors while their more timid siblings career up and down a miniature railway threading past the indoor hot-air balloons. Elsewhere in the mall there is the by now obligatory ice rink, the food court and hotel, along with a golf course. Here and there are stage sets that, with remarkable pathos, attempt to create the look of a traditional street, with sawn-off slate roofs, sash windows and shop fronts, all safely under cover. More than half a mile long, there is one primary axis, crossed by a major transept and a number of smaller cross-axes. Draw it on plan and you have what looks like a tangle of shopping streets, filletted out of a living city, dangling slippery entrails in all directions.

Some of the stores in West Edmonton complain that all the window dressing distracts their customers from their real tasks of shopping. But that hasn't stopped other developers from planning even more elaborate schemes. What they are offering is a fair which, instead of travelling the world to reach its audience, sits still on one permanent site and waits for its visitors to come to it.

In Bloomington, Minnesota, the first phase of the $600 million Mall of America has four big department stores, with four more to come in the second. There will be an enclosed entertainment mall based on Snoopy characters, eight hundred shops, eighteen cinemas, restaurants, nightclubs, a health club, three high-rise hotels, and a seventy feet high steel and concrete artificial mountain. With predictable bombast, the developer Melvin Simons, in partnership on the project with the team that built the West Edmonton Mall, calls it the ninth wonder of the world. It will have a total of 9.5 million square feet of enclosed shopping, entertainment and hotel space, twice that of a big city such as Glasgow. When the centre is completed at the end of the decade, retail downturns permitting, it will have to depend on pulling in shoppers from the entire Midwest. Because it will be too large to cover on foot in a single day, the planners expect that people will spend two or three days to see it all. There will be one thousand hotel bedrooms, as well as mobile home hook-ups in the car park (which will have 12 750 spaces). The designers are working on urban themes for the malls – one area will try to evoke Fifth Avenue, another will take its cue from Times Square, suitably sanitised, a development rather like the custom of international hotels in exotic locations to dress their employees in parodies of local costume and offer bowdlerised versions of local dishes on their menus and local dancing as part of their entertainment, while at the same time effectively destroying the culture from which they are derived by their very presence. The Mall of America offers a view of the big city without being threatened by it, just as you can enjoy India from the safety of the hotel pool.

The rush out of town in Britain finally took off in the 1980s – a product not just of car ownership that lagged behind America's, but also of the deliberate attempts to discourage developments that threatened the prosperity of the high streets.

Patrick Abercrombie's sentimental vision of London as a network of local communities based on the school and the local shop, which he mawkishly saw as the contemporary equivalent of the village green in his 1944 plan for the city, remained an article of faith for the British planning system. Abercrombie conceived of London as a shopping hierarchy with the corner shops at the base, the larger district centre with a wider range of shops in the middle, and city centre stores in Oxford Street and Regent

Street at the top. Planners automatically rejected any tendency which threatened to undermine that pattern. It was a cosy anachronism that died hard. Forty years later, they were still vainly attempting to impose precisely the same pattern on British cities.

But while the planning system could hinder the move out of town, it could not stop the growth in Britain of the multiple retail chain, which has had almost as much of an impact on the character of the high street. Multiples are taking a bigger share in every sector. The Office of Fair Trading in London found that while just under half of all food retailing was in the hands of the multiples in 1966, it had increased by nearly one third by 1982. In the clothes sector, sales by multiples went up from just under fifty to sixty per cent in the same period. The multiple chains are able to take over wholesale functions, using their own warehouses, which improves their margins and lowers prices to the consumer. That in turn contributes to the decline of the small independent store, since the removal of the multiples from the manufacturers' delivery networks raises the average costs for the rest.

For the city, the price to be paid is that the same names, with the same groceries or books or toys, will occupy most of the space in every shopping street from London to Glasgow. In the process, there is a reduction in the diversity that is supposedly the strongest counter the city centre has to the shopping centre.

The *coup de grâce* for city centre shopping in Britain came in 1984, when its leading high-street retailer, Marks and Spencer, a rather different kind of operation from the up-market American department stores, selling fresh food besides clothes and furniture, announced that it would be opening its first out-of-town store in the Gateshead Metro Centre. This was the first British attempt to match the scale of the big American regional shopping centres, and in fact it had started out as a much more modest affair until Marks and Spencer's decision to move in.

The centre, financed by the Church Commissioners, is built in an enterprise zone, an area of recently cleared derelict industrial land, on which the government offered large tax incentives and minimum development restrictions to encourage new development. They were incentives of the same order that the London Docklands Development Corporation offered developers at Canary Wharf, and they produced equally unexpected results. While Canary Wharf saw the conversion of derelict wharves into offices for international banks, in Gateshead, a declining area of unemployment and industrial decay, a site that was seen to be so lacking in attractions that it required special government assistance turned out to be the seed for a profitable shopping centre.

The architecture of consumption

Metro Centre's runaway success, together with the completion of London's M25 orbital motorway, triggered off a stampede of plans for similar developments around the capital with its far more affluent consumers. So eager were the developers to tap what they saw as a honeypot, that no less than seven proposals for large shopping centres on the M25 were put forward in 1988, each well over a million square feet. Clearly they calculated that the prize of a captive audience of wealthy metropolitan consumers would be enormously lucrative. To win it, they were prepared to offer millions of pounds in sweeteners. At Staines, just by the Junction 13 turn off on the M25, one firm wanted to turn a flooded gravel pit into what it called Knightsbridge-on-Thames – pulling shoppers from Kingston, Windsor and Maidenhead to an up-market mall modelled on the Houston Galleria. The site was right in the middle of London's previously sacrosanct green belt, but the developers were offering a 200-acre water park and nature reserve, with a trust fund with an annual income of £400 000 to manage it. At Richings Place, Country and District offered to widen more than a mile of motorway from three to four lanes at a cost of £12 million and, at the height of the Prince of Wales hiatus, produced a preposterous design for building the mall in the form of a Palladian country house with obelisks, rotundas and a symmetrical pedimented facade.

Neither was built – partly because the retail slump of the early 1990s intervened, but, more critically, because the government decided that the newest out-of-town developments represented a far greater threat to the town centre than superstores or small clusters of superstores on retail parks had. Based on North American centres, such places tend to turn into retail and leisure complexes that make for a day out, which, if they were successful, would rob the high street of not just its food shops and department stores, but its cinemas and restaurants as well, a development that would seal the fate of the town centre as a stable, secure entity.

Vetoing the M25 projects was certainly bolting the stable door much too late. The decade had already seen a huge boom in the building of shopping centres which amounted to nothing less than the complete reordering of British retailing.

The estate agents Hillier Parker calculated that there was a total of 28 million square feet of out-of-town shopping in 1980, with 9 million more under construction. In 1988, a total of 158 million square feet were complete, with 24 million more under construction. By the end of the decade there were seven regional out-of-town shopping centres and seven hundred new superstores. There was even a plan for a five million square foot development at Wednesbury, just north of West Bromwich, approaching the size of the West Edmonton Mall.

The architecture of consumption

These places are completely altering the grain of daily life. Asda's Watford superstore on the north-western edge of London, typical of the new breed, is not for the faint-hearted. Built in a crinkly tin box that feels large enough to generate its own microclimate, it stands on the site of the old Odhams print works. Where highly paid print workers once pursued their path to redundancy, Asda now recruits shelf-fillers and cleaners. Serried ranks of checkout tills stretch to the horizon, across a space large enough to swallow a traditional market square whole. In the distance, intersecting ramps glide up and down, insistently directing customers and their trolleys to and from the car parks.

The image is patently industrial, and it underscores the words of its designer, Graham Freeman of Fitch & Co, that 'this is where the house-wife goes out to work'. He explains his task in terms of organisation. 'The customers have an awful lot competing for their time and attention. We have to expose them to things that they didn't expect to buy, but to do it in a way that will not let them feel slowed down. I like to think of it as being organised, rather than manipulative.'

Few companies have bigger out-of-town sheds than Ikea, the Swedish furniture company. In Wembley, again on the north-west edge of London, it has a 240 000 square foot store which in its stock and arrangement is exactly the same as one of the company's stores in the USA, Japan, Hong Kong, France or Germany. On a Saturday afternoon, you will find twenty thousand people in here. This is less like shopping in the tradition-al sense than trying to embark on a package holiday with a bargain base-ment airline.

You start by driving to the edge of town, leaving the car in the long-term car park before setting off for the terminal building. You check in through a turnstile, and are issued with a chariot-sized trolley. Then you find your-self in what looks like an ideal home exhibition, a trade fair and a duty-free shop, all rolled into one.

It is full of people aimlessly looking at duvets, fingering quartz halogen light bulbs and working out how to open the sofa beds. All the traditional clues about shopping have gone. There are no shop windows, no conven-tional tills, and nobody to ask if they can help you. To pay for your pur-chases, you have to push your chariot through the warehouse, running the gauntlet of mountains of chairs and dinner plates, before reaching check-out tills that look like a row of motorway toll booths.

It takes twenty minutes to negotiate them. And it is only when you have parted with the cash that you discover that you have to wait anything up to half an hour on a good day for your bulk purchases to emerge from the bowels of the store. You wait in what looks like the baggage hall of a major

The architecture of consumption

international airport. You have to claim your purchases in person, a measure that seems to have been borrowed from the security procedures at Heathrow but seems of little relevance here. To keep you quiet there is a playground for infants, a restaurant, and even a stand-in for a duty-free shop, selling imported Swedish delicacies and Aquavit.

This is shopping on an industrial scale. And even the veneer of Swedish decency fails to mask the grim realities when, with the car park full to bursting and twenty thousand people in the store, the computer goes down and a delay of up to four hours in the baggage hall ensues as people wait for their sofas and bookshelves to materialise. Retailing on this scale brings choice, and important savings, but life has also been made just a little more brutish in the process.

Meanwhile, not content with the regional shopping centre, European developers are looking at the possibility of establishing vast, international shopping centres in northern France. Already planned is a huge auto shopping centre, in which all the European car manufacturers and supporting industries would come together under one roof. Another proposal is for the leading furniture manufacturers to be located in one complex, with large on-site central warehouses, with free one-way car trailers, and self-drive vans for shoppers to take their purchases home. When the channel tunnel opens, they would have a catchment area of 150 million people within four hours' drive. Like the vast American malls, these would be well on the way to becoming self-contained settlements in their own right.

The central question about shops is whether it is the form of shopping that dictates the nature of a city, or if it is the city's nature that dictates how shopping, its primary communal activity, is carried out. Perhaps the truth is somewhere in between; that the different incarnations of shopping, from the market to the department store, the high street to edge-of-town, are the signals that confirm the direction a city has taken. Vast shopping sheds that serve people from more than one city demonstrate that urbanism has already become an amorphous landscape in which mobility allows anything to happen anywhere. Paradoxically, while the city itself has decentralised, shopping has become ever more concentrated.

Success and failure

12

With a casual, brutal vulgarity, *Fortune* used its October 1989 issue to give flesh to the fear, usually left unspoken, that lies behind the struggle for jobs and investment now shaping the future of big cities everywhere. 'More than ever, where you are determines how you do', claimed the magazine. Below a photograph of the brittle glamour of Dallas's skyline, with the setting sun reflected in the blank, mirror-glass facades of its skyscrapers, their spires topped by blinking red aviation warning lights, it cautioned: 'Pity the poor fool with his headquarters in some mean streets town where office costs are out of sight, and only the reckless venture out after dusk. Say Amen for the chump with a big plant in some backwater where the workforce is riddled with thugs, druggies and thieves. The only answer for most companies stuck in the wrong place at the wrong time is to get out.'

Fortune asked the corporate relocation consulting firm Moran, Stahl & Boyer to look at the cities that were most likely to attract American businessmen who wanted to move offices or factories. They put Dallas at the top of the list – news which would no doubt have at least temporarily cheered the banks, tottering from shaky property loans on the 30 million square feet of empty offices in the Metroplex at the time.

But even *Fortune* conceded that New York and Los Angeles, for all their problems with high rents, taxes, poor school systems, crime and house prices, were still important places for any company hoping to maintain a world profile to have an office. How long they will keep that position has become the central question facing all the world cities, not just the American members of the club.

The drift from the countryside to the cities which gathered speed in the eighteenth century and turned into a rush in the twentieth has not, as some observers claim, been reversed by the decline of the population of the old city cores. Even if the cities are spreading themselves over ever larger areas, power is concentrating in fewer and fewer of them.

There is a widening gulf between the dwindling number of cities which are able to operate on a world scale and those that can't. London, Tokyo, Paris, New York, Los Angeles and, a few steps behind them, Frankfurt, Milan, Rotterdam, Hong Kong and Brussels thrive by attracting people and money from around the world. These are the cities in which the multinationals cluster together their so-called command and control functions. The media and communications companies, the corporate lawyers, the important bankers and the lobbyists all have to be in one of these cities. Their continued presence confirms the status of a world centre, just as the arrival of an emerging company or an ambitious individual in London or New York is a signal of intent. It is the airline hub and spoke system on an urban scale, the difference between Atlanta, with its vast traffic and business-generating airport, and increasingly marginalised New Orleans, out on a limb.

Cities depend for their very existence on the concentration of people and power that has always been the underlying theme of development in the industrial world. Despite appearances, that process of concentration did not end with the eclipse of the countryside by the town, which came in Europe and America with the industrial revolution, and in the years following World War Two in Asia and Africa. Cities have grown more diffuse since then as their historic cores and inner suburbs have lost population to their margins, but the dominant position occupied by a handful of them has become increasingly obvious. If anything, economic power in the post-industrial world has become concentrated in even fewer centres than it was a hundred years ago, sharpening the competition between the survivors. A few newcomers have joined the ranks of what Patrick Geddes called the 'world cities', but successful cities now achieve their success at the expense of other, no longer successful competitors. And that conflict has a direct effect on the quality of life in a city. In the nineteenth century, even the smaller European capitals all had a stock exchange, an opera house and an architecturally grandiloquent railway terminus. Now there are only three really important stock markets in the world, the vast majority of Europe's international travel is channelled through just three hub airports in London, Paris and Frankfurt, and most of its entertainment comes from California.

In the past, the competition for power and influence was between capital cities and their provincial rivals. One hundred and fifty years ago, Britain had five of the world's twenty largest cities. Manchester, Glasgow, Liverpool and Birmingham were all major forces in their own right, with their own standing on the world stage, independent of London. They had banks and newspapers, their own theatres and galleries. Their distinct cultures were strong enough not to be patronisingly dismissed by the qualification of 'local'.

In the eighteenth century, some of the greatest talents were happy to spend most of their lives living in provincial obscurity, where they prospered, free to pursue their ideas, to publish and to communicate with those few that they had to reach. But, in an ironic reversal, the picture has been completely inverted, despite the supposedly liberating potential of the ever more fluid nature of transport and technology. Only a handful of cities can offer the metropolitan qualities that keep provincialism at bay. Creative and economic power are concentrating ever more sharply. If you want to make a career in film, or music, or finance, or government, there are precious few choices about where you can do it.

The growing movements toward economic and political union in Europe have had similar effects. Whatever the opposition to centralisation and homogenisation, which in Ulster, Corsica and the Basque country and now the remains of Yugoslavia and the Soviet Union reaches as far as armed insurrection, the reality is that institutions are becoming more and more international. Money, power and culture is globalised, and is manipulated from fewer and fewer centres.

It's perfectly true that the fax machine and the word processor make it possible for the writer to retreat to rural isolation. And there are other jobs that can be done in this way, where location is immaterial. But the jobs that count are becoming more centralised and not less. More of the world is turning into a provincial backwater as power concentrates in ever fewer centres. The competition now is not so much between London and Manchester, or New York and Chicago, or even Osaka and Tokyo, but between the international cities. The alternative for a merchant banker is between London, Tokyo and New York. If London loses its place as the European leg of that tripod, it's not going to be replaced by Bristol or Milton Keynes. It will be supplanted by Frankfurt or Paris or Berlin, with effects for Britain's economy that would be nothing short of catastrophic. Not only would jobs and revenue vanish in the short term. But in the long term the talented would leave to find themselves a new arena that matched up to their ambitions.

The fact is that in a highly mobile world, traditional locational constraints do not apply in the way they once did. The choices that a corporation has to make about where to build its new plants or its headquarters can now be taken on what are apparently the most trivial of grounds – the quality of the restaurants, the size of the houses that middle managers can afford. Thus, it is very often the physically most attractive cities that prosper in this way. And the time-expired that do not. But these places lose their charms in turn as the roads start to clog up with traffic, international popularity pushes up local house prices, and the costs of paying for the infrastructure investments needed to support a growing population consequently increase property taxes. In the long term, the footloose companies will move on again, leaving behind the wreckage of their occupation.

Treating cities as disposable in this way is the most wasteful use of resources imaginable. At the same time, the globalisation of culture places increasing strains on the identity of peripheral societies. Denmark, for example, a nation with a population of just five million, is idyllic in some senses, but a difficult place in which to be a writer, or a film maker, if you intend to make a mark on the highest level of achievement – if for no other reason than that the critics, the juries that count, can't understand your work in its original language. When the Francophone world feels itself so threatened by the pressure of Anglo-Saxon international culture that Quebec goes to the lengths of banishing English-language shop signs, what hope is there for the Welsh or the Norwegians?

Nothing illustrates the competition between the major cities more clearly than the round of tooth and claw politics, arm twisting and out and out bribery that accompanied the last stage of the attempt of the International Olympics Commission to make up its collective mind about where to stage the 1996 Olympics. Despite the catastrophic history of violence, corruption and massive overspending that is the most lasting legacy of the modern Olympics, six cities – Manchester, Atlanta, Belgrade, Athens, Melbourne and Toronto – fought desperately for the chance to be allowed to mortgage themselves to the hilt to spend £2 billion on an event that will last just sixteen days. Enough money, should they have the mind to spend it differently, to build an international airport, fund a major subway line, put up the skyscrapers of Canary Wharf, or open Disney World.

Manchester, which was, as even its backers admitted, an outsider, spent £2.5 million on feasibility studies, advance planning, and flying in as many members of the IOC who would listen to march them up and down the banks of the Manchester Ship Canal on which the bid committee planned to stage the games. Despite starting off underfunded and understaffed, the bid committee, under the presidency of the Duke of Westminster, consoled itself with the thought that the mere fact of bidding was worthwhile 'because it would raise the city's international standing' and 'act as a catalyst for restoring pride and confidence', as its first bid document claimed.

Its rivals spent far more. Melbourne increased the capacity of its main stadium by building another stand, and poured £8.5 million into its bid for the games. Belgrade had most of the facilities needed to host the games by the time the IOC met in Tokyo to make up its mind in late 1990. So seriously was their decision taken that three prime ministers showed up to press the candidature of their respective cities.

What is it then that persuades ambitious mayors and hard-faced businessmen to open their chequebooks on such a scale, for what is essentially the most frivolous of pretexts – to allow a few thousand athletes to spend a fortnight running around a track?

In the past, the clearly understood subtext to every Olympic city's preparations was chauvinism, a force which has always had the power to loosen purse strings. The point of staging the Olympics was to demonstrate to the world that the host city was richer, more powerful, and more important than its predecessors. Building ever more elaborate stadiums and expressways was a kind of concrete and steel fireworks display, staged to dazzle the world. Ever since Tokyo built Kenzo Tange's great white concrete whale of a stadium in 1964, and Munich hit back two Olympics later with its high-tech Bedouin encampment, architecture has enjoyed the status of a semi-official Olympic sport, one that is played out years before the games themselves and for a much higher stake – prestige, an end that is used to justify all the expenditure, even if giant buildings are never used for their original purpose again.

There were, of course, nuances to the message that the games could be used to send to the world. Adolf Hitler's lavish spending on the 1936 Berlin Olympics, dedicated to the glorification of the master race, architecturally as well as on the track, was an extreme. At Tokyo in 1964, the Japanese had a gentler ambition. At last they had a chance to show that they were more than a nation of plagiarists, pirating transistors and living in shacks.

In fact the Olympics have very often managed with unexpected candour to put across precisely the opposite message about a city from that intended by its sponsors. The Mexico City games in 1968, for example, were meant to demonstrate that Mexico was part of the first world, but the violence that accompanied the event revealed that the army was ready to shoot anybody who got in the way of their vision of what Mexico should be like.

After the catastrophic overspending (the first budget was £150 million, the final costs £850 million), union troubles, corruption and construction delays that sank the 1976 Montreal Olympics in a sea of debt, the idea of the imperial games went into decline. So much money poured into so many empty gestures began to make people feel queasy. The Moscow games seemed to be treading water. Then came the Los Angeles Olympics, brought to you by Coca-Cola, American Express and Walt Disney, which showed that it was actually possible to make a profit if you applied a coat of paint to the facilities that you had already, built as little as possible, and struck a hard bargain over selling television rights.

Barcelona, which hosts the 1992 games, will be different again. It has pioneered the idea of the Olympics as a tool for urban renewal, a massive shot in the arm for a city emerging from economic decline. The mayor, his planners and architects have used the games as a chance to drive through the biggest restructuring of the city in a century.

Success and failure

Rather than banishing the Olympic village to some suburban precinct, it is being built in the heart of the city. The tracks leading into the city's main railway station have been torn up and buried, and the dense cluster of warehouses that once cut the city off from the sea have been destroyed to make way for the village. After the games are over, its 2500 apartments, built in city blocks like the rest of central Barcelona, will be sold. The layout of the village not only creates a new seafront, but it extends the Diagonal, the main thoroughfare of Barcelona's nineteenth-century growth, back to the eastern waterfront edge of the city. A high-rise hotel is going up, and the airport is being doubled in size. Norman Foster is building a communications mast the height of the Eiffel tower and the shape of a rocket on a hill top overlooking the city.

Architecturally, the Olympic village is a descendant of West Berlin's International Building Exhibition in that it attempts to create city fabric, rather than isolated monuments sitting in space. To avoid monotony, the project has been broken down into a number of different parcels, each with their own architect. These were allocated to the winners of the Catalan Architectural Institute's highest award, made annually since 1958, an idea which not only overcomes the ill feeling that usually goes with the allocation of such projects, but also ensures that the development, with its heterogeneous collection of designers, will have an instant sense of history, rather than be shaped in one, relentlessly up-to-the-minute, clean sweep. But each architect must work within the context of Oriol Bohigas's masterplan, and the majority of the new buildings will be in brick, to give some sense of coherence.

Manchester's bid for the 1996 games was trapped uncomfortably between the two extremes of Los Angeles and Barcelona. Its rhetoric was all about urban renewal, but its financial projections revealed that its strategy was to spend as little on the games as it could get away with, and to make as much money as possible from selling TV rights, sponsorship deals, Olympic coins and stamps. It talked about using the games to restore confidence in the city, but its planners failed to show the breadth of vision, and the ambition needed to pull it off.

The bid committee persuaded itself that it would only need to pay for building the £500 million main stadium itself. Everything else would be funded by private development, with the smaller halls leased for the duration of the games. Certainly this was no way to produce memorable architecture or to build a coherent masterplan. It predicted a surplus, as it was delicately called, that could be as much as £65 million. The early documents that Manchester produced to support its bid provide a remarkably frank insight into the motivations that push cities into making Olympic bids. Its brochures talked of a time 'in 1896 when the Olympic flame was rekindled in Athens, at the same time, the people of Northwest England completed an enterprise of equal magnitude. They excavated a giant waterway almost 40 miles from their city to the sea, the Manchester Ship Canal. In its past, its waters reflected the furnace fires of the world's first and greatest industrial landscapes. Now the time is right for the vision of the future, the Olympic renaissance of Northwest England'.

To support this toe-curling rhetoric, the committee produced an embarrassingly threadbare brochure, embellished with a collection of childishly crude watercolours, depicting all the time-expired clichés of Olympic architecture: monorails, waterbuses and tent stadia. Their first drawings depicted an Olympic village made up of wretched eight-storey-high prefabs, that looked as if they were made from bolted together segments of container lorry. Or, as the bid committee put it hopefully, 'a self-contained garden city accommodation in special temporary residential blocks', each with 'lounge and TV viewing areas and ample shower and toilet facilities', as they boasted proudly.

It is an Olympic vision full of the bathos that is part and parcel of Manchester's retreat from the assured grandiloquence of Alfred Waterhouse's monumental Victorian city to its present incarnation of trivial, crinkly tin sheds on suburban business parks. The old civic landmarks, the sandstone fire station, the insurance companies, the warehouses that shaped the city, are mostly empty now. The organisations that built them have moved on to shrunken, anaemic buildings on the edge of the city.

The contrast between Manchester and Barcelona, two industrial cities of similar size and spirit, provides a sharp insight into the way that life is lived in Britain, and the more civilised priorities that apply elsewhere in Europe. Narcis Serra, Barcelona's first post-Franco socialist mayor from 1979 to 1982, brought in his university friend, the architect Oriol Bohigas, as the city's planning consultant. Bohigas encapsulates his approach as 'monumentalising the periphery', that is to say bringing an identity to the sprawling, formless developments at the edge of Barcelona, closer in their character to the unplanned squatter settlements of Latin America than conventional suburbia, that eddied around the grid of the nineteenth-century city. The same idea motivated architects as disparate as Ricardo Bofill in Paris and Edward Jones in Toronto.

The campaign began with a series of low-budget, piecemeal projects that added up to a hundred new squares and parks, scattered here and there over this formless periphery. They formed the starting point for Pasqual Maragall, Serra's successor as mayor, who continued to encourage

Bohigas's policies and took rapid steps to increase greatly their scope. It was only in 1986 that Barcelona's bid for the Olympics was finally successful, and what had begun as small-scale interventions turned into a huge restructuring to reshape the whole of Barcelona. Nor was the reconstruction confined to a single site. The Olympic village at Poblenou formed one centre while the sports facilities on Montjuïc, the site of the still-born 1936 Olympics bid, is the other main focus.

The fight for the Olympics lays the competition between the world cities out in the open. For other, even more important urban prizes, the competition is seldom quite so public but many of the same weapons and strategies are used. London's increasingly shaky claims to be the natural financial capital of Europe, if not the world, are based mainly on its time zone, the English language, and its liberal banking laws. But now Frankfurt, Paris, and in the slightly longer term Berlin, are pressing hard from behind. Frankfurt, home to the mighty Deutsche Bank and the country's massive pensions and insurance business, as well as the focus of a domestic economy that is far larger than Britain's, has signalled its ambitions through the simple-minded symbolism of the Messe Turm tower, designed by Helmut Jahn to be even taller than Canary Wharf's largest.

Meanwhile, in the five years to 1989 New York completed 39 million square feet of office space in Manhattan alone. In Paris, plans were drawn up to extend La Défense still further into the suburbs, and to build a new financial district at Bercy on the other side of the city. It all amounted to a building boom that looked like a re-run of the years leading up to the First World War, when the race to build iron-clad battleships threatened to bankrupt the great powers. Possession of a conspicuous homage to finance such as Canary Wharf has become the price of entry to the economic superpower league. Like huge aircraft carriers, or battleships moored in harbour, these self-contained monoliths are in the city, but not of it. Aspiring cities with pretensions to the big league try to emulate them, the way that the Third World buys airliners and Mercedes limousines, so that even Dublin wants a Canary Wharf, and Sydney is looking at building its own 10 million square foot financial services centre in Pyrmont.

These are developments that have a symbolic as much as a practical role, just as the towers of San Gimignano were built to symbolise the power of their owners as much as for practical purposes. They are both signs and substance. Just like nuclear weapons, they signify power because none but the powerful can afford to build them, but they also represent actual power.

There remains the nagging doubt that the world doesn't actually need three full-blown financial markets. The American banks and brokers in

London have been consolidating, or even pulling out altogether, while cutting back in New York too. Citicorp, for example, acquired the old Billingsgate fishmarket, converted it into a dealing room, then put it on the market without ever having occupied it. All the predictions point to a glut of office space through the first half of the 1990s, though optimists profess to see another upswing in demand in the later years of the decade. But with a massive 3.5 million square feet of office space coming onto the market each year, London runs the risk of ending up like one of the US sunbelt cities, their ranks of empty skyscrapers reminders of a boom that has turned to bust, an experience that could turn out to be even more damaging than the disaster of 1973, when the Bank of England was pressured into launching a rescue for over-extended secondary banks in the wake of the collapse of the property market, all in the name of maintaining confidence in London.

Paris meanwhile is driven by a haunting fear that it is in the wrong place. French government researchers keep producing worrying interpretations of the shape of urbanism in Europe, which they see as a long, curving dorsal spine that arcs down from London, through the Netherlands and Belgium, the Rhine conurbation, and down to Milan. Roger Brunet, in a study prepared for the French state planning agency DATAR, suggests that a new economic axis is being created, one that runs along the northern shores of the Mediterranean, stretching from Barcelona to Toulouse, Munich and Milan – a stronghold of vehicle manufacturing, aerospace, electronics and research, Europe's California, where new growth is being attracted at the expense of some of the less favoured northern cities. These are the cities that are commonly presented as the economically buoyant, progressively organised.

Similar predictions about the American sunbelt, Atlanta, California and Texas, were made in the 1980s and demonstrate the caution that needs to be exercised before it is accepted that these shifts are permanent or as far-reaching as is sometimes claimed. The low-wage, non-unionised areas of the United States, with their higher quality of life for the affluent, lack of congestion, lower house prices and relative absence of crime, attracted both migrants and employers in search of motivated, docile workforces.

Yet the energy price slump of the early 1980s showed how vulnerable many of the new cities were to a downturn. Houston, which grew prodigiously after 1973, with the gas shortages and plant closures in the Northeast spurring the arrival of thousands of newcomers, went into an equally sharp decline after oil prices fell.

In this context, Paris, crucial though it is to France, is out on a limb in the midst of what the French élite call the French desert. And the position, as far as the French see it, unless they take steps to remedy their isolation, is likely only to get worse as the pull of Eastern Europe starts to divert the future growth of the conurbation towards Berlin.

In some ways it's a construct which is meaningless. Contiguous urbanism is not nearly so contiguous as the diagrams suggest. Nor does the fact that cities are cut off from each other by large swathes of empty territory necessarily isolate them. But it is a very real fear in the French mind. Just as Louis XIV centralised his emerging nation with the most grandiloquent of gestures, endowing Paris with a court magnificent enough to ensure that the nobility had to be there or become marginalised, so modern France is ensuring that Paris does have a place at the centre of European life, by investing vast sums in high-speed railway lines, motorways, airports and museums, by encouraging Disney to go to Marne-la-Vallée, and attracting as many international organisations as it can. Louis did it to protect his throne by distracting the nobility from building up regional power bases, Mitterrand does it for the country's economy, but the means and the ends are very much the same.

London has lost its empire, it's no longer a major industrial power in the way that it once was, but it is still a crucially important transport interchange for air travel, it's at one end of the dorsal spine that shapes the European conurbation, and it is still the pre-eminent European financial centre.

New York may have lost some of the big companies that once made their headquarters there, its population has thinned out, and its fiscal future is uncertain, but it too is still the most important financial centre in America.

Los Angeles is a new addition to the list of world cities – a city that hardly existed in the middle of the nineteenth century, which is on course to become the largest in the United States, a key focus of the Pacific economy, a city that is still growing with the frenetic speed of the Third World. Equally, it is a city that is peculiarly geared to the fragmented shape of the post-industrial economy, a place which is a key centre simultaneously for low-skilled, low-wage manufacturing and the highest of high technology, as well as for what some at least would say is the most important of all, that is the Hollywood image manufacturing industry, with its power to tap deep-seated emotional responses to the Los Angeles way of life.

Tokyo is not only home to the world's largest banks and many of the world's most important industrial concerns, but, since the end of the Second World War, has taken a leading role in the service economy as well, a centre of education, advertising, engineering and design.

The end of the same war saw West Germany back, more or less, to the state it had been in the eighteenth century, when there was no single, cen-

Overleaf: The struggle for ascendancy by Europe's big cities was complicated dramatically by the re-unification of Berlin. The breaching of the wall ended forty years of isolation, and turned what had been an urbanistic freak, into a leading contender for the role of newest metropolis. The derelict heart of the city, an empty void for so long, began to be snapped up by developers convinced that they stood to make substantial profits

tral, dominant city, rather the country was a confederation of self-govern-ing cities and provinces. Parliament, the ministries and embassies set up in Bonn, and the banks returned to Frankfurt, which they had left in 1860 for Berlin. The West German cities stretched in a long arc from Hamburg in the north to Munich in the south, and they fought it out for supremacy. Frankfurt in particular poured billions of marks into an attempt to make itself a plausible centre for West Germany as a whole, well aware that despite its prosperity, it was popularly regarded as one of the dullest cor-ners of Europe.

Berlin, divided into two unequal halves by twenty-nine miles of wall, was less than the sum of its parts. It added up to nothing much more than two provincial backwaters, squashed uncomfortably close together. But united as the capital of eighty million Germans, it mounts a serious chal-lenge to both London and Paris as Europe's leading metropolis. After three decades of fossilisation, Berlin is emerging from the chaos of reunification. In 1990, it was a city that felt much as it must have done in 1945, full of the dispossessed, left in limbo by the collapse of an unchal-lenged order. With the tearing down of the wall, however, the streets were full not of Germans bartering wedding rings for food, but of Poles scav-enging the discount stores to buy instant coffee, fresh fruit and video recorders to lug back to the Polish border, fifty miles east.

The urban landscape, fractured by the wall, still looked the same even as Checkpoint Charlie was winched away to disappear into a museum. But its meaning has changed out of all recognition. What were the edges of two distinct cities were suddenly transformed into the centre of a single entity once more.

The world city needs far more to fuel its growth, and its continuing eco-nomic health, than homespun remedies. The critical mass of a major metropolis with more than ten million inhabitants is extraordinary, demo-graphic and technological change at even the most apparently minor level having enormous consequences when applied at the scale of the whole number.

The global economic shift of the post-war years has seen industrial manufacturing restructured in the most radical fashion – from the old industrial heartlands of Northwestern Europe, and the Eastern seaboard of the United States, manufacturing migrated first to the emerging economies of Mediterranean Europe – France, Italy and Spain – and, still more crucially, to the Far East – Japan, followed by the other Pacific Rim nations, Taiwan, Thailand, Hong Kong and Korea. At the same time, the vast majority of urban growth has taken place in Asia and Africa. So far,

few of the new multi-million population cities have established themselves as globally significant in the way that their size would once have suggested.

The impact of this shift on the cities of the West and Japan has been mixed. The old industrial cities suffered badly of course. The manufacturing bases of Manchester, Birmingham and Glasgow, Detroit and Pittsburgh were decimated. But the shift also took place within areas as well as across the globe. Crucial to the relative position of the major cities is the determination of their governments to maintain them. In this sense, Paris and Frankfurt have taken a strategic view of their position in the European and the world contexts. To retain their grip on the control and command functions, they have invested heavily in the infrastructure of their cities, in culture, transport and education. At one level, you could say that they have tried to make their cities pleasanter places in which to live. At another, it could be that they have spent money on persuading employers to relocate their factories to within their boundaries.

Without the economic buoyancy that makes a city a desirable place, it's very hard for a city administration to achieve much. A mayor can try to put in place the funding for a hotel to be built, or persuade the government to put up the cash for the construction of new warehouses, but he can't get the employers to occupy them. He can fund convention centres in the hope of attracting high-spending businessmen, but the solutions of the 1980s, a festival market, a convention centre, an atrium hotel, don't amount to a very great deal as an economic turn around.

The freeway versus
the metro

13

The 1980s saw an explosion of investment in public transport as the world's cities rediscovered mass transit. But whether all the money was spent wisely or not is debatable. The tram, optimistically rechristened the light railway, shed its time-expired, battered Art Deco image and suddenly became as much a part of the repertoire of every modishly ambitious city as its festival market and conference centre.

Not every mayor can persuade his electorate to foot the bill for a subway, but for a fraction of the cost a light railway can be just as conspicuous a prize. Much of the technical inspiration has come from the smaller European cities where the trams never went away. Cities such as Hanover, Grenoble and Lille upgraded and automated their systems using computers, and carefully integrated buses, trams and railways. Following in their tracks, born-again tramway systems appeared in Atlanta, Miami and Baltimore in quick succession. Even in car-dominated Dallas, the twenty-mile first leg of a similar system linking downtown to the mostly white northern suburbs is due to open by 1995, and there are plans to treble that distance. Houston is also thinking about a commercially financed light railway.

Even Britain, which for ten years had a government that took a jaundiced view of any kind of investment in public transport, started to rediscover the tram. Light rail lines were planned for Manchester, Birmingham, Sheffield, Leeds and London.

Despite the enthusiasm for them among politicians, many of the new lines have turned out to be of only marginal utility. Just as sandblasting the brick walls of Boston's Faneuil Hall and London's Covent Garden created the impression of activity without making much real impact on the underlying health of their respective local economies, so light rail has had as much a symbolic as a practical role.

In London, the tilt back to public transport came too late to secure a rapid reverse of forty years of chronic lack of investment. As early as 1949, London Transport had accepted the need for a major expansion of the system to catch up with London's growth. But of the eight new subway lines proposed, only the Victoria Line got the go-ahead, and even that took twenty years to complete. At the same time, the system faced serious labour shortages. Recruitment campaigns in the Caribbean and the Indian subcontinent that provided labour in the fifties and sixties had become politically impossible, and the resulting unfilled vacancies caused continual disruption to services.

London Transport began the 1980s overwhelmed by geriatric rolling stock, inadequate equipment and squalid stations. During the morning rush hour, which new fare policies succeeded in spreading well into the afternoon, trains already full to bursting were subject to protracted halts in claustrophobic tunnels. On top of this, a series of accidents, culminating in a catastrophic fire that killed seventeen people at King's Cross, raised genuine fears over the system's safety.

From its elegant heyday in the 1930s, shaped by the progressive taste of its patrician chairman Frank Pick, London's Underground had deteriorated into a squalid, graffiti-scarred world stinking of urine, crowded by buskers, drunks and the mentally disturbed. It was a picture that came close to the popular view of the New York subway, where vigilante patrols, random violence, and crime have scared away all those affluent enough to have a choice of transport. And one which the new Jubilee Line east into the docks, due for completion in the mid 1990s, will have to overcome.

For all the excitement about public transport, the reality of the 1980s in most cities was the troubling combination of ever larger numbers of private cars coupled with a drastic cutback in road building. Roads were not the vote winners they had once been, they involved recasting the city in ways that were no longer palatable, and governments became much less enthusiastic about building them, especially in urban areas. The shift was triggered in large part by the widely held belief that, past a certain level, building more roads does little to decrease congestion. Just as massive investment in public housing had failed to end homelessness, so fifty years of building urban motorways had achieved little more than gridlock.

Road building was a god that had spectacularly failed, nowhere more obviously so than in Los Angeles, a city whose freeways with their multilevel intersections and spiralling clover leafs were once the very image of the modern world. But their attractions quickly faded in the face of deteriorating concrete, gridlocks and the smogs that appeared as early as the 1940s.

Between 1961 and 1979, years that saw the frenzied peak of the freeway building boom, the number of cars in the five Los Angeles counties doubled to almost nine million. California's Department of Transportation declared that the city's freeways had reached saturation point in 1978. The older, central parts of the system, the Harbor, Hollywood and Santa Ana freeways, are thick with traffic all day long, just like the streets that they

The freeway versus the metro

were built to replace in the first place. The newer freeways sprawl across ten lanes in an effort to keep the cars moving, but as traffic multiplies year after year, they too are clogging up. Downtown gridlocks so regularly that the helicopter could soon overtake the limousine as the primary form of local transport for the over-privileged. Many of the city's other office centres, such as Westwood, suffer from the same congestion problem.

In London and Los Angeles, the switch in attitudes against roads came with particular suddenness. Supported by both main political parties, the idea of building a three-tiered ring of orbital motorways for London had been on the agenda since 1965. But despite initial enthusiasm, the plan provoked the sharpest conflicts over road building that Britain had ever seen. At one point the Labour-controlled Greater London Council actually considered building roads that would have cost 100 000 people their homes, then precipitously changed its mind and won the 1973 elections with a commitment to drop its earlier plans. Only the M25, the outermost ring, was built. Yet this road exceeded its design capacity almost as soon as it was completed.

In Los Angeles, voters managed to stop the freeways in their tracks. The power of their revolt was dramatically symbolised by flyovers ending in mid-air in a tangle of twisted reinforcing steel, reflecting a sudden change in policy. It was only at the end of the 1970s, as the freeways began to buckle under the sheer weight of traffic, that Los Angeles finally spread beyond the boundaries set by the railways and street cars which had originally defined the city. At its peak in the 1920s, the 1100 miles of the Pacific Electric Railway system had carried 100 million passengers a year across a vast area stretching eighty-seven miles from east to west, and fifty-eight miles from north to south. At the same time, the street cars covered a 123-mile diameter area with a dense web of lines, carrying more than 225 million passengers in 1924.

By the 1980s, however, the tract house builders were uprooting Joshua trees and filling up the remotest corners of the desert as far away as Palmdale and Antelope Valley, where the railways had never penetrated, places so utterly dependent on the motorcar and built to a density that they precluded any other form of transport but the car. The extra traffic they generated placed an intolerable burden on the freeways, yet as suburbs they could not exist without them. Los Angeles, along with many other cities, is beginning to consider more and more moves to discourage drivers with direct charges on road usage, severe parking restrictions and all out bans.

Despite Los Angeles's image of endless sprawl, of all American cities only New York has higher densities. Its built-up areas average 5200 people to the square mile. The city core – the strip from downtown to Santa

Monica, for which Wilshire Boulevard is to Los Angeles what Broadway is to Manhattan – averages 12 000 and peaks at 28 000 people to the square mile. Enough people to keep the almost forgotten buses of the Southern California Rapid Transit District busy. The figures underscore the problem that faces Los Angeles. It has grown too big and too dense to function as a car-based city, as Houston and Phoenix still can, but at the same time it is too spread out for a new mass transit system to provide an alternative without a drastic change of heart by the city's electorate, who like higher taxes even less than they like jams.

Along with its massive aqueduct schemes that fill the city's reservoirs with water from as far away as Colorado, Los Angeles's original railway network made the city what it is. The railway allowed a scattershot of towns and cities to coalesce by reaching across towards each other along the tracks, in sharp contrast to the steady outward growth from a single centre of the classic European cities.

San Pedro, Los Angeles's original port, was linked to the city by a steam-powered railway as early as 1869. Its route was closely paralleled 120 years later by the new light rail system which started construction in 1986, the first step in a Long Beach to Los Angeles line. There were horsedrawn trams in Los Angeles from 1874, when it was still a small town with less than 6000 inhabitants, and the Spring and Sixth Street Rail Road Company, Los Angeles's first cable car line, went into operation from 1884 on a section of Second Street that was too much for the horses. Two years later the first electric trolley car line opened, and by 1896 the lines to Pasadena, Hollywood and Santa Monica were electrified, their gantry masts and overhead cables weaving north through the empty poppy fields as far as the San Gabriel foothills.

It is not simply the location of development that is dictated by transport systems. Until the start of the twentieth century, road layouts directly created the shape of the urban environment. This connection was cut in the twentieth century by the apparently humane ambition of planners and architects to segregate traffic from people. Housing areas were to be defined by a hierarchy of roads that had pedestrianised areas at one extreme, and motorways at the other. In between were local and district distributor roads which had no built-up frontages. It was a configuration that has become one of the most crucial factors affecting the character of the modern city.

In the same way, the trams of Los Angeles dictated not just the location of the boulevards, and in turn the form of the freeway network, but their architectural form as well. They allowed clerks to live in sight of the orange groves, and in walking distance of a trolley line that could whisk them downtown in twenty minutes. It was a pattern that created strips of tall commercial buildings on the boulevards, rising like icebergs out of the seas of bungalows that lined the streets immediately behind them.

But the more that California took to the automobile, the more the street cars found themselves competing with the tens of thousands of motorists pouring onto the dusty roads. The average journey time for the tram ride down to Long Beach dragged out from thirty-six minutes to a full hour, and as the service became less and less reliable even more people switched to their cars, which in turn increased congestion and lengthened journey times.

Los Angeles started talking about following the example set by London and New York and building an underground railway of its own as early as 1906. Work actually started in 1925, but the graffiti-daubed portals of the Belmont tunnel at First and Glendale are all that is left of the single mile of track built before the money ran out.

The project was blocked by the refusal of the voters to back the heavy spending that would have been involved. Measures to approve the bond issues needed to finance construction were defeated in 1925, and again in 1935. Meanwhile the road lobby, led by the Automobile Club, was already agitating for a freeway system – modelled on the parkways that Robert Moses was building in New York. Construction of the Arroyo Seco parkway to Pasadena, the first segment of the Los Angeles motorway net, began in 1938. Unlike the European model of concentric motorway rings, the pattern for Los Angeles was a net, spreading in all directions. It's that grid that gives Los Angeles such an apparently distinctive character. People from concentric cities find it very hard to orientate themselves.

There was more at stake in the decision to build the freeways instead of a subway than dispassionate policy making. Just as the railways had gone to court to fight off the threat to their monopoly from the jitneys, so the naked self-interest of the oil and auto companies led to a concerted campaign against railways. In 1930, General Motors, Firestone and Standard Oil of California formed National City Lines, which began buying up municipal trolley lines and forcing them to switch to diesel buses – manufactured not uncoincidentally by GM. These moves finally collided with the anti-trust laws. In 1949, a federal jury in Chicago convicted the three companies of criminal conspiracy, but the court confined itself to the gentlest of taps on the wrist, a $5000 fine. By that time, NCL had taken over transit systems all over America. An NCL subsidiary, Pacific City Lines, had acquired control of the Los Angeles system in 1939, gradually replacing trolley services with diesel buses and pulling up the tracks. The last Pacific Electric tram ran in 1963.

The freeway versus the metro

Though the war between the private car and mass transit may have been an unequal one, it went rumbling on. Even in 1970 a coalition of car makers, oil and tyre companies was funding a campaign against using California's state gasoline taxes for rapid transit and air pollution control measures.

The mass transit programme that finally made a fitful start in Los Angeles at the end of the 1980s certainly had its green aspects. The city talked about eliminating the internal combustion engine from downtown by the end of the century as part of the fight against smog, and electric trains will certainly help. But it is the downtown business community that has lobbied hardest for a subway, for reasons that have predictably little to do with environmentalism. They see the lack of a mass transit system as undermining property values in the city centre to the benefit of landowners on the edges of town. Christopher Streart, president of the Central City Association in 1984, told the *LA Times* 'We're simply trying to protect the investment that is already here'. Big developers such as the Irvine Ranch have been putting money into the transit campaigns. Parochial suburban homeowners, on the other hand, have seen no reason to pay higher taxes by voting for transport projects that seem to offer them very little practical benefit.

Tom Bradley, in his attempt to be all things to all constituencies, ran for mayor in 1973 promising that he would begin building a subway within eighteen months of being elected. He was not the first to make such bold promises. In 1954 there had been a serious proposal for a Los Angeles monorail, followed in 1960 by another for an ambitious high-speed train system. But bond issue proposals for mass transit systems were defeated by the electorate three times in the sixties and seventies. And even a relatively modest scheme for running buses down the middle of the Hollywood freeway failed.

In the very different climate of the late 1970s, the voters at last approved a 0.5 per cent sales tax in 1980 to pay for a long-planned $3.3 billion, 18.6-mile subway line, intended as the first leg of a 150-mile system. Legal challenges delayed the imposition of the tax for two years. And even then, the money went on buying more buses. Only in 1985 was $100 million a year made available for rail construction. The money is being matched by the federal government, but Washington refuses to come up with enough to pay for the project in full. So the first segment, now under construction, was cut back to 4.4 miles, just half the 'minimum operable' system originally defined by the Rapid Transit District, which estimated just 55 000 daily boardings in this segment, a five-station fragment that runs from Union Station, through three downtown stops, and terminates in low-income, inner-city Westlake. The 1986 estimate of the cost was $1.25 billion, raising the awful possibility that the new Los Angeles subway will turn out to be an even more expensive fiasco than the abandoned mile of underground track laid sixty years earlier.

The tortuous route it follows bears all the signs of the horse trading needed to get the system off the ground. Accommodating every important political interest group meant taking 18.5 miles to cover just 11 miles. The line starts logically enough, crossing downtown, and heading off under Wilshire Boulevard, but rather than running direct to Beverly Hills or any of the other obvious places, Century City, Westwood, Brentwood or Santa Monica, it shoots off to North Hollywood, the southernmost corner of the San Fernando valley, as a sop to suburban voters who saw the rapid transit plan as benefitting only the central city.

A much cheaper light rail line linking Long Beach with downtown on what was once a Pacific Electric right of way is also under construction. Its promoters claim it will attract 54 000 passengers every day. But Peter Gordon, a professor at the University of Southern California, claims that they will be lucky to get 10 000, far too few to make economic sense.

Gordon claims that encouraging commuters to share cars to and from their workplaces would do far more to reduce traffic congestion and pollution, for a fraction of the cost of the construction of mass transit lines. At the end of the 1980s, it took ten cars to get every eleven commuters to work in Los Angeles, while in Washington DC, they would have carried fourteen, and the national average was more than twelve. Simply matching the average figure could take half a million vehicles off the roads.

There is a continual tension between the sense of freedom the motorcar brings its owners, and the sense of grievance that crowded roads bring against other car drivers who are seen as limiting that freedom.

The convenience of being able to complete the whole journey from door to door without having to worry about timetables, set against the perceived inconvenience of changing from one means of transport to another, gives the motorcar an unbeatable psychological advantage over public transport. Though the environmental costs of the internal combustion engine clearly put its future in doubt, the hostility to the car is as much ideological as it is pragmatic. Even electric cars can still cause traffic jams, and would be out of financial reach of large numbers of people. The restrictions being introduced against cars in the city centre have already given the arguments for traffic management a political tinge.

In California, the green revolt has caused stringent conditions to be imposed, in theory at least, on the siting of new housing and factories to minimise the new traffic that results on the freeways. It is too early to see much impact on the layout of settlements. Petrol shortages have been shrugged off, speed limits have come and gone. And while the road building schemes of the post-freeway era were met with a slow-growth, anti-highway revolt, no convincing alternative has yet been formulated. Meanwhile, the pattern of development in the last two decades has only gone to reinforce dependence on the motorcar. Business parks, out-of-town shopping centres, and more and more dispersed housing settlements can only work with the networks of roads and car parks that go with them.

All the improved insulation standards in the world, all the worthy attempts to replace tungsten lights with miniature fluorescents are futile in energy terms if they are applied to a building sitting in the midst of a beautifully landscaped car park full of vehicles which, even at their most fuel efficient, have consumed several barrels of oil to bring their occupants to work.

But there is scope for the introduction of technology to ease traffic congestion, not simply such measures as the moving map guidance systems which are already commercially available to direct subscribers and their cars around slow-moving traffic. If Hertz can manage to provide computerised maps and lists of names for the drivers of the shuttle buses which take customers to their preassigned cars at Los Angeles airport, then it should be possible to match car pool members.

The form of a city dictates what kind of transport system is feasible. But transport itself is in turn a major determinant of the shape that a city takes. The relationship between the two is a complex blend of cause and effect. Big cities in general tend to have significantly lower car ownership than smaller ones. In 1985, sixty per cent of British households as a whole owned a car, compared with fifty per cent in small towns and just forty-two per cent in London. London's comparatively low car ownership could be explained by the concentration of the poor in the inner city, but equally London's public transport network, and the measures taken by the police to discourage motorists, makes car ownership less attractive than in a smaller city. Thus public transport could be seen as simultaneously improving the quality of life in a city, and making possible an intolerable concentration of people in claustrophobic proximity.

In Tokyo, for example, where roads occupy just 12.7 per cent of the city's land, there are only 1.7 million cars, while in the considerably less populous Los Angeles with 9 million cars, roads have encroached on the city to account for 30 per cent of its land area. London, with 23 per cent of its area devoted to roads, and Paris with 26 per cent, come somewhere between the two extremes.

Variations from city to city reflect not just degrees of affluence, but also their relative densities. In 1979, Japan still had the lowest number of cars – 226 for every 1000 people – of any of the advanced industrial economies. The United States by comparison had 540.

What in retrospect turn out to have been key turning points in the shaping of a transport system, such as the way in which the railways were built in the nineteenth century, are seldom recognised as such until it is too late for their effects to be remedied without enormous cost. Thus London's north/south divide along the Thames was made permanent by the positioning of the Victorian railway terminals, which precluded the possibility of running through trains across the city. In Los Angeles, the pattern of freeways is still shaped by the memory of the tramlines that the city built in the last quarter of the nineteenth century.

Where mass transit routes go, and how they cover their costs, are critical issues in determining the character of a city. Without efficient late-night transport, for example, the public life of a city atrophies very quickly, even for those affluent enough not to have to worry about bus fares and the time of the last service. Waiters, stage hands and firemen all need to be able to get home at a price they can afford.

Transport is an essential part of the well-being of the poor. It allows them to reach jobs and low-price shopping centres, rather than being forced to rely on expensive ghetto stores. Yet very often it is the well off who benefit most from the massive investments in rapid transit. Washington's subway, for example, has been of greater benefit to affluent suburbanites than to the majority black population of the District of Columbia. Similarly, there are no early plans to extend the Los Angeles metro system east of downtown into Watts, or the other blue-collar ghetto sections of the city. Rather, it has been shaped by the need to placate the tax-paying suburban lobby.

To such people, the mass transit system can seem like an extension of the inner city, a conduit for bringing threatening outsiders into their neighbourhoods. Yet the physical characteristics of a transport system – the red buses that are vanishing from London, the art nouveau Parisian metro station entrances, the elevated railway in Chicago, are among the most potent means of establishing the identity of a city.

Transport is much more than a technical issue. It is a political and economic issue too. The policies of the Labour-controlled GLC at the start of the 1980s showed just how sensitive ridership levels are to fare prices. In 1981, a heavily subsidised zonal fares system, with discount travel cards, immediately produced a massive increase in ridership. Faithfully echoing the downtown versus suburban divide of Los Angeles, the outer borough of Bromley went to court rather than pay a share of the subsidy.

While Los Angeles developed a sophisticated public transport system very early on and then destroyed it, Paris, which was forty years behind London in starting to build its system, is now a world leader in transport planning. Since 1961, massive investments have created a modern suburban railway network which has tied together the metro and the mainline railway, a move that has coincided with the building of the high-speed mainline rail links that Paris sees as reinforcing its claims to be the natural centre of Europe.

Like London, Paris is at the focus of a national network of railway lines that radiate out from a ring of termini. Built piecemeal by highly competitive private companies, they have made through rail traffic difficult in both France and England. The Paris metro is doubly flawed. Its tracks are laid to a different gauge from the main lines and could never link the main stations as the government had wanted. And its very dense network of stations and short lines makes journeys slow and complicated.

The idea of building a suburban rail network in Paris, partly underground, partly on the surface, was first formulated as part of the plans to make La Défense into a new office centre and to link the city system with the ring of new towns being planned for the suburbs in the 1950s. By 1977 it had become a real network, with a 32-mile line running all the way from St-Germain-en-Laye in the west, through the centre of Paris, and on to Boissy St Leger in the south-east. At the centre of the network is the new interchange of Chatelet, scooped out of the hole in the ground left by the demolition of Les Halles, which claims to be the largest and busiest underground station in the world. A second line running north to south from Charles de Gaulle airport at Roissy to St Remy and Evry was also built. And, unlike London and Los Angeles, public investment went into both roads and railways. The RER network was being built at the same time as the expressways on the Seine and the périphérique orbital motorway.

Its approach to transport is one of the things that makes Tokyo different from the other cities in this book. In the past twenty years its public transport system has grown enormously while road traffic has proportionately declined. According to the Tokyo Metropolitan Government, subways accounted for six per cent of traffic in the twenty-three wards of metropolitan Tokyo in 1960. Twenty years later the percentage had quadrupled, from 865 000 passengers transported in one day to 5 377 000: that is three times the all-time high recorded by London Transport in 1948. While bus traffic declined, and the trams all but vanished, daily traffic as a whole grew from 15 million passengers to 22.5 million passengers, an extraordinary, daunting wave of people that would be unimaginable in any society less disciplined than the Japanese.

The freeway versus the metro

Tokyo built its first expressways for the 1964 Olympics, to show the world that it was a modern city, and for a few years the idea of hurtling around the metropolis after dark, the lights of the city's new skyscrapers coming and going as the concrete ribbon unwound its way through the city, was one of the key images of its identity. Now Tokyo's roads are so badly congested that it is common for those stuck in jams in taxis to abandon them for the subway. And the vertiginous escalation of land values has made it too expensive for the government to build new roads. Car ownership in Tokyo is now prohibited without an off-street parking place. Instead, the subways have been continually expanding. Tokyo opened its first line in 1927 between Ueno and Asakusa, with women in kimonos moving from carriage to carriage selling refreshments. Even today the system bears little resemblance to the western legend of stuffers paid to cram the cars to sardine-can capacity. You can buy magazines and noodles on most platforms. The trains operate with astonishing punctuality, thanks in part to an enormous staff, from the ticket collectors who man every barrier, clippers clicking like rain, to the flag-waving station masters.

The most notable feature of Tokyo's mass transit system is the Yamanote line, which circles the capital in a 21-mile-long loop. Its twenty-nine stations intersect with all ten of the capital's subway lines, and the mainline stations. The loop has played a vital part in shaping the capital's growth, allowing for the development of alternatives to the old downtown between the Ginza and Marunouchi, with new commercial and office focuses located next to the key stations at Shinjuku, Ikebukuro and Shibuya.

Both for residents and visitors, the identity of a city is shaped by the means by which they move in and around it. The subways, airports, highways and mass transit systems become a key part of the city. What, for example, would Houston be without Loop 610, both scenically and in terms of the definition of the city? It is from the vantage point of the road, dipping up and down through the trees north of downtown and then plunging into the industrial landscape south of the city, continually revealing fragments of the central high rises, that Houston is given its identity. To understand the city's geography is to find the quickest route from home to the loop, then a circumnavigation clockwise or anticlockwise, before taking off again at the exit nearest to the destination. It's a perception that imposes order on the fundamental disorder that underlies the loop.

Without a degree of legibility, any transport network loses the sense of being an ordered system. Its complexity in a modern city of any size is enough to turn it into a baffling landscape of signs and anonymous platforms. Making sense of the system is an essential rite of passage

for any adolescent growing up in a big city.

A great deal of academic argument has been expended over the sub-text of mass transit system maps in advanced cities, especially in London, which was the first to build a complex underground railway system, opening from Paddington to Farringdon in 1863 and starting on its deep lines in 1890. Adrian Forty, in *Objects of Desire,* and others have argued that distortion of distances on some parts of the London Transport map was the product of a deliberate, manipulative move to encourage passengers to travel more, and to persuade people to live in the outlying suburbs, around the stations, by minimising the apparent distances to the centre.

It's not necessary to subscribe to this slightly paranoid view to see the conceptual importance of the underground map to the city – and it is the difficulty of providing a bus map of equal clarity for a city that has played a real part in the relative decline of these services, coupled, of course, with ever increasing journey times as buses have to fight their way through the heavy surface traffic. The difficulty in making new routes comprehensible to users, not just through route maps, but also numbering systems, and not just to citizens of the city itself but to visitors as well, has meant that bus routes have remained static despite changing needs. In London there are routes operated today that have exactly the same stops and route numbers as those operated by long-vanished companies with horse-drawn services 150 years ago.

New York has had similar problems. Its new subway map in the 1970s was beautiful but incomprehensible, so it was withdrawn to overcome the confusion. Its bright colours were an attempt to update the terrible image of the system, which was a Victorian survival in many places, the product of bankrupt companies and ancient rolling stock. Investment since then has been minimal. New York does not even have a direct subway link to its three major airports.

The sense of space that the mass transit system creates is a vital ingredient of the cityscape. The subway station, and its presence at street level, is a civic space of a kind, a fact that city planners have clearly been conscious of. Washington's metro system went out of its way to monumentalise the subway. Vaulted concrete and careful lighting reflected the city's imperial self-image in a conscious echo of the marble halls of the Moscow metro system.

The role of design – stretching from architecture to typography – in the great days of the London system is famous, and is now equally infamous, a grim reflection of the shifting values of British society. In Britain, the railway station is now all but indistinguishable from the shopping centre, and the Victorian stations are bit by bit being transformed into malls where fast

The freeway versus the metro

food and niche market stores attempt to distract the passing 'customers' from their journeys.

The physical form of the city is clearly shaped more and more by the need to accommodate the vehicle. The way buildings are now experienced, entry first involves warehousing a large machine: a far more complex and nuanced business than is conventionally realised. Once the car is parked, the interchange between people is entirely determined by the relationship of street to car park to entrance to buildings.

On the wider scale, it is these interchanges from one form of transport to another, and to buildings and public spaces, that are what really create the public life of a city. Both in terms of movement across a city and the quality of life within it, the nature of a civic transport system is the starting point for building a sense of civic cohesion.

Looking at the world through inverted commas

14

It was only some time in the late 1980s, when Heathrow began to clog up with Jumbo loads of Koreans, and out-of-the-way Cotswold tearooms started to accept Japanese credit cards, that Britain found itself facing tourism from the wrong end of the telescope. It had taken twenty-five years from the birth of mass tourism for the country to become what the travel business calls 'a major destination', with approaching sixteen million foreign visitors a year. The UK, in 1991, ranked fifth in the world tourism league, ahead of Germany, Switzerland, Belgium, Greece, Portugal and the Netherlands. The number of overseas visitors has increased by twenty-five per cent in the last ten years, and the money they spend – £6.2 billion in 1989 – has become an important part of the economy. That growth is showing no sign of slackening, even in spite of the temporary hesitation caused by the Gulf War. The British Tourist Authority forecasts more than twenty million overseas visitors a year.

In its early days, tourism was something that affluent northern Europeans and North Americans did to other people. They put on brightly coloured clothes and wandered around the world as if it were a zoo, chattering away in front of the natives, scattering sheaves of local currency that they did not need to bother to understand because they could buy so many with their dollars and pounds, confident that they were watching a spectacle mounted entirely for their benefit. Now the compliment is being returned. The British could tolerate free-spending Americans with large hats asking for directions to Fortnums, or Australians colonising the pavements at the Aldwych to sell their campers, but when the Arabs started to turn the lower reaches of the Edgware Road into souks, lined with stalls offering Lebanese sweetmeats and shops which stayed open until midnight selling white slingback shoes for men, tolerance started to wear thin.

In Hong Kong, the tourist board goes to great pains to persuade tourists that they will not be cheated by the merchants in the air-conditioned, but still humid shopping malls that run from one end of Kowloon to the other. In the French countryside, the government runs campaigns to persuade the farmers to smile at the tourists. In New York, they run charm schools for taxi drivers – albeit to no great effect. But in London, the English Tourist Board feels it necessary to offer leaflets to the *tourists* advising them

High rise hotels are indistinguishable one from another, from Tokyo to the Spanish beaches. Tourism has changed the life of cities; from active participants, the buildings occupying the great public spaces have been turned into passive spectators, the landmarks stripped of any other significance, but that of draws for the coach parties on how to behave if they are to avoid offending the British.

The more squeamish of northerners used to deplore the plight of noble Catalan fishermen and proud Turkish farmers reduced to waiters and bus drivers, but the idea that Britain or America or Australia might one day find themselves just as ambivalently grateful for the foreign currency tourism brings never occurred to them.

What has only recently become clear is that the tourist phenomenon goes far beyond international travel. The city is now a large enough place for tourism to be just as much what happens when a family from Queens rides the subway to look at South Street Seaport, or a couple of pensioners in Paris take the RER to La Villette, as it is to do with foreign travel or two weeks in the sun. The same impulse to look for the spectacular, for the exotic and the entertaining, is at work.

As a force for social change, tourism has had an impact of the same order as the industrial revolution. In less than three decades, tourism has transformed the way that the world looks, and works. A decade of packaged holidays to Spain weaned the British from a thousand-year preference for warm cloudy beer and introduced them to cheap wine, topless beaches, and restaurants where you didn't have to pay at the same time that they delivered your food. The remotest Greek islands have had their social fabric torn apart by northern European sex tourists. Now affluent Indians in Bombay pore over brochures for tours to London and New York. And in Australia, trips to the Micronesian islands are sold just like weeks on the Costa Brava. Yet Australia sees itself as under threat from a Japanese invasion, in the shape of the Tokyo property companies investing heavily in Gold Coast hotels for honeymooners from Honshu and Kyushu.

Tourism has the power to reduce the most potent of symbols to an empty cliché. The pyramids, St Peters and the Kremlin are principally tourist icons now, invoked to persuade people to travel. Religion, culture, art and history are all reduced to a spectacle. Tourism puts the seedy blocks on Hollywood Boulevard on either side of Grauman's Chinese Theater, full of bus loads of visitors aimlessly looking for something that makes this place special, in exactly the same category as Windsor Castle. Walk around Windsor on a summer weekend and you find yourself in a world which exists solely to cater for people who never spend more than a few hours in the place. To buy everyday groceries, you have to drive to the shopping sheds of Slough. Windsor's high street contains only fast-food restaurants to feed the hordes who have just finished the tour of the castle. Groups of Italians, Spaniards and Americans cross and recross on their way from Pizza Express to McDonald's, attempting in vain to stave off that sense of emptiness which comes with the realisation that travel and movement cannot provide more than a temporary distraction. In their bleached denims or their fake Burberrys, they sit in the pubs, nursing their beers, waiting for something to convince them that they are somewhere different from where they came from. You can see the same scenes in Amsterdam or Venice, or any of the other cities where a crust of old buildings still keeps the shoe box hotels out of sight, where people go in search of experience, and find only reflections of themselves.

We long for 'authentic' experiences, the café that only local workmen go to, the restaurant that sells local cuisine which nobody else knows about, the bar in which you can meet real people. It's a curious dream of the thinking classes, which exerts just as powerful an influence on the way that the big cities are seen as it does the resorts. And it is that idea of authentic spontaneity which is behind the idealised view of the city.

Raw history is hardly enough to satisfy the appetite for sensation of a generation reared on perceptions of reality fractured by television into easily digestible chunks. To make up for the fact that most visitors to Windsor will never get even a glimpse of Her Majesty in the royal apartments, Madame Tussaud's thoughtfully provided a waxwork tableau of the arrival of an earlier queen at the railway station.

The picture is no different in the heart of London, Paris or Vienna. On any summer weekday, the most conspicuous component of the foreground to the heroic view of St Paul's Cathedral, looking up towards the dome of Christopher Wren's masterpiece from William IV Street, is the file of eighty-seater buses parked in a line that starts almost level with the steps at the west front and swings out around the south transept before eddying out to fill the car park to the east.

They come in their scores each day, from all over Britain and the Continent, with their chrome trim and their proud back-window boasts of air brakes, TV and on-board WC. These are the pride of the Volvo and Mercedes coach fleet. And they are now as much of a fixture at the cathedral as the merchants who used to set up their stalls in the churchyard three hundred years ago. Surprisingly, English Heritage hasn't as yet asked for them to be repainted to match the colour of the stone, nor has it insisted that they have their windows redesigned in classical style. From them issue crocodiles of orderly Japanese, following the little flags flown by their guides, and the parties of Scandinavian students who photograph each other from every angle. Throughout the day, they wash back and forth through the doors of the cathedral, 2.5 million of them every year. The first thing they see as they spill through the nave is a stall selling post cards. Some venture up to the whispering gallery, and a few make it down into the crypt, before they filter out again, but fewer still think about taking the slightest part in the religious purpose of the building.

Yet when the subject of modern London rises to the surface of contemporary debate, its shortcomings are seen entirely in terms of how the new buildings around the cathedral *look*. The Prince of Wales compares them to a scrum of American football players, crowding out the classic views of the cathedral. It's hardly an apt metaphor, given that ever since Wren's time, St Paul's has been surrounded by a dense thicket of buildings. More importantly, to see the city in this way is to be hypnotised by appearances, and to ignore the substance of the situation.

The problem for those who long to see the modern setting of the cathedral demolished and replaced with what they call a more sympathetic backdrop, one which some architects believe should be a Georgian caprice, with brick-faced low buildings, sliding sash windows, rubbed-brick soldier courses over their heads, and elegant carved door cases, is that this will not bring back the Paternoster that has disappeared. The essential difficulty for those who want the area restored to its pre-war condition is that St Paul's is no longer the symbol of national and religious unity that it once was, nor the heart of a bustling city economy, surrounded by working wharves, skilled workshops and printers. Its primary civic purpose now is as the backdrop for the television set pieces – royal weddings, victory parades – and as the focus for those continual snaking parties of tourists, drilled by their guides, who recite the litany of its history. It may or may not be possible to create a more attractive environment than that which now exists. But it would be wise to think long and hard before setting about yet another clean sweep of all the existing buildings. They are not the brutish concrete that some short-sighted observers claim, but are actually faced with costly roach bed Portland stone and slate. Nor is Paternoster Square as it is presently disposed in reality the bleak, windswept space that it is constantly presented as being. It is actually two interlinked spaces, which do a reasonable job of balancing the conflicting needs of simultaneously containing the cathedral and giving it room to breathe.

No amount of stagecraft or architectural mouth-to-mouth resuscitation will bring that vanished past back. That society has gone. If we build a network of narrow lanes around the cathedral, if we make the buildings look as if they have been there for four hundred years, we will still not recapture the lost life that the London of the seventeenth century had. Nor, if we had it, would we be so keen to experience it. Yet the hope that things need not change is a powerful impulse, one which it is foolish to ignore. Particularly since the late 1960s, Europe has seen a strong current of nostalgia for a lost urbanism, a sense that the European cities had a natural organic quality which they are in danger of losing, and that newer,

Looking at the world through inverted commas

supposedly 'artificial' cities, have never had.

Venice, of course, has lived out a prosperous twilight for the past three hundred years or so based on an entirely 'artificial' economy. From a worldwide trading empire, with the political and financial clout to go with it, which has a good claim on having invented mass production with its galley-building factories in the Arsenal, Venice declined into a gilded tourist honeypot. It survived not because of its banks or its global traders, but as an essential stop on the grand tour, a place in which the leisured aristocrats of France, Germany and Britain would spend a month or two, visiting the theatre, commissioning Canaletto, or one of his followers, buying silver and glass, and looking at churches. What had been a vigorous, thriving, cosmopolitan society atrophied and turned in on itself, becoming more interested in form than substance. Venice played Dorian Gray, retaining its sublime beauty, while Mestre, its mainland twin, was ravaged by heavy industry. At first the appearance of privileged Venetian ease was not hard to maintain. But by the 1980s, the illusion became increasingly threadbare amongst the flood of mass tourism which turned the twisting streets into thoroughfares as crowded as the Tokyo underground system, and which saw St Mark's Square overrun by backpackers, clustering outside the faded Edwardian elegance of Florian's.

Its significance as a cultural centre had all but vanished. Once Venice was an artistic powerhouse, a focus for some of the greatest talents in architecture, painting and music. Now it is a museum piece lost in dowdy provincialism which the Biennale does little to change.

It's a phenomenon that is hardly confined to Venice. When the Ritz in London becomes a package holiday hotel, when the Parisian boulevards are taken over not by a community of café-goers who share a culture, but by temporary visitors, looking for instant gratification, the sense of a city is lost. Tourism has eaten away at various aspects of London life, from the overcrowding of the pavements, to the monotonous diet provided by theatres only too well aware of the income generated by American tourists unlikely to relish being jolted into wakefulness by anything too demanding.

It is futile to bemoan what Venice has become. The gondolas, the pensiones, the Murano glass workshops have been the mainstays of the Venetian economy for so long that it is absurd to see it in any other way. The struggle now is to ensure that the place goes on being attractive enough to bring in tourists, the only economic asset it has left. The narrowly averted plan to hold an exposition in the city at the end of the century, shelved only after vigorous protests from those who saw the idea as finally tipping the fragile equilibrium of the city from over-ripe but picturesque decay to tawdry squalor, shows how much is at stake.

Managing Venice is an impossible attempt to square the circle. Its very attractiveness to visitors tends to destroy its charm. Since it has been selling itself to all comers for three hundred years, it is only logical to put up turnstiles to limit admission on summer weekends, when the place finally threatens to sink under the weight of humanity attempting to visit it.

The decay that threatens so many modern cities is not so different from the long-drawn-out decline that has reduced Venice to a stage set. Tourism has become an increasingly important part of government strategy in Europe and America, for the urban basket cases as much as the moors and beaches. When there are no attractions to appeal to the crowds, money can be found to fabricate them. After the huge financial success of the Jorvik installation in York, which purports to recreate the life of a Viking settlement, and where the souvenir shop does business as brisk as Marks and Spencer's Oxford Street store, Britain has been deluged by similar attempts at capitalising on heritage.

Dover District Council, for example, in an attempt to fight the economic and social damage caused to its port by the opening of the channel tunnel, has built a £14 million tourist attraction they describe as The White Cliffs Experience. 'Jorvik helped put York on the map,' claimed the council leader, Paul Watkins. 'The same expertise will help breathe new life into the Dover area.'

The 'experience', built on a derelict tip near the town centre and in the form of a Martello tower, is expected to attract 280 000 visitors a year. They will find a recreation of a Dover street of 1940, alongside the inevitable 'themed' shopping. Visitors will be attacked by woad-painted ancient Britons, there will be an artificial beach, overlooked by an artificial cliff. This mechanical foreshore will literally come alive as seagulls and crabs discuss momentous events of the past.

It's the latest incarnation of what has become an increasingly common phenomenon. In Los Angeles, even if you leave aside the film studios with their sets looming over Hollywood, it goes back to at least 1930, when the city manufactured its own view of its past, turning Olvera Street into the Pueblo, a highly sanitised version of a colonial Spanish street market. As the difference between a high-rise social housing block in northern Europe or America and a Yugoslav or Thai hotel complex has narrowed, so it has become commonplace for a cosmetic layer of design to be applied to heighten the tourist 'experience', for example by adding just enough local colour to a prefabricated concrete hotel to allow the guests to see the world through inverted commas. Design is used to fabricate attractions: to create products to take home, and to persuade visitors to open their wallets to buy them. It's inescapable everywhere you go. At York Railway Museum, they offer a range of toiletries as used in GWR sleeping cars. The Ironbridge Gorge shop – the spot at which the first shots in the industrial revolution were fired – is second only to Harrods in sales of Coalport China.

The potential revenue at stake has lead scores of cities with the most unlikely track records to start gearing themselves up towards marketing themselves to tourists, and those who already have them to polish their appeal to bring in more. New York commissioned Milton Glazer to produce the I♥NY campaign, depressed mill towns in Europe and America set out to sell themselves. Even the antiseptic city-state of Singapore has begun to rebuild its gamey past of transvestite bars and flea markets that it cleared away less than a decade ago in an attempt to restore tourism to its economic base alongside banking and electronics.

As a building type the hotel is curiously undervalued, perhaps because – with a handful of exceptions, such as Frank Lloyd Wright's Imperial Hotel in Tokyo – it has produced few architectural masterpieces. Yet its nature is crucial to understanding much of the nature of the modern city.

The hotel, especially in America, has become part of the credit card culture. You can hardly check in without surrendering an imprint, any more than you can hire a car without one. It's an inextricable part of the convention centre/tourist nexus which is a vital part of the strategy of every hard-pressed mayor attempting to talk their city out of a recession, oiling the wheels of commerce by attracting free-spending visitors. It's the equivalent, but at the scale of a city, of believing that the poor can all prosper by taking in each other's washing.

The hotel is not simply in the business of providing beds. The revenue that an efficiently run hotel can make from the other services it provides, from food to conference and shopping facilities or, usually less explicitly, from sex, is substantial.

The modern hotel is primarily a nineteenth-century invention – pioneered in America, where the room with bath became customary far earlier than in Europe – and it has created a way of life that is geared to the ceaseless movement that is an essential characteristic of the modern world.

The hotel is caught between two impulses, the first is to do everything it can to minimise the sense that the constant traveller has left home. The international hotel chains, franchise operations most of them, have grown enormously by offering the same-sized room, the same menu, the same fittings in the bathroom, everywhere the traveller goes, to provide the sense of reassurance that, whatever the chaos of a city outside the hotel door, once he has got back past the concierge he is in a world that is once more familiar, controllable, understandable.

The other impulse is to glamorise the basic functional necessities of carefully standardised bedrooms into something else. In the nineteenth century it created the remarkable splendours of the Ritz in London and Paris, as well as the astonishing resort hotels, at spas, mountains and lakes, and their urban equivalents the Plaza in New York, the St Francis in San Francisco and the Biltmore in Los Angeles, full of polished marble and luxuriant plasterwork, adding up to a deliberate creation of ostentatious luxury.

The present day still sees attempts in this direction. John Portman appropriated the nineteenth-century department store atrium and put it to new use as the centrepiece of the new-wave hotels of the 1970s and 1980s as a crude, but effective way of turning banality into spectacle. It was a strategy that worked extremely well for a while. But the atrium, and the glass wall-climber lift, have now become as inevitable a part of the hotel that is trying to impress as cocktails in the lobby and the notice in the closet that offers to sell you the bathrobe.

After the atrium came the design-conscious hotel, the Paramount in New York, La Villa in Paris, il Palazzo in Fukuoka, where Philippe Starck, Ettore Sottsass and André Putmann have created the fashion-conscious equivalent of the Holiday Inn. The world outside is still dangerous, but at least you can come home to a Michael Graves kettle at night.

It's not just the hotel that is tailored for the visitor. The fabric of the city itself is being recast to cope with the fleeting attention span of the visitor. An early example of this phenomenon was the case of the Ghirardelli chocolate factory, overlooking the Golden Gate Bridge in San Francisco.

Between 1900 and 1916, Domingo Ghirardelli built his red-brick factory on San Francisco Bay at the end of the trolley-car line. The complex sprawled haphazardly around a rectangular block that stepped, in San Francisco style, steeply downhill towards the sea. The Ghirardelli redevelopment in 1964 was significant, not so much for the fact that it involved the recycling of a number of not particularly interesting old industrial buildings for retail use, but because of its pioneering role in the development of the now ubiquitous festival market, the prefabricated Venetian experience. The sandblasted brick walls, the hanging fern baskets, the bars and restaurants, the shops selling posters, earrings and Peruvian sweaters that have since spread around the world, as the mark of modern consumerism, all originated here.

In fact, Ghirardelli has very little to do with conventional retailing, and is much more concerned with providing a place for people to spend time, and money, with the lure of a spectacular view over San Francisco Bay. Architecturally, the first conversion at Ghirardelli was no great shakes, a series of glumly municipal structures tacked on to the humdrum industrial buildings. But it had never been done before, so the whole world came and looked. And they found that all the formulae regarded by shopping centre developers as holy writ stood revealed as empty superstitions. You did not have to put all your shops on one level, you did not have to have a single clear route all the way through, and you did not have to have a single department store anchor to bring in the customers. Ghirardelli certainly had none of these supposedly vital features. Its sixty-eight shops, fifteen restaurants and three hundred underground parking spaces rambled over ten distinct buildings in a maze of twisting corridors, up and down staircases and split levels, in and out of the open air.

The complex has grown old since it first opened. It has been revamped by its new owner, an insurance company, to shoehorn in even more bars and restaurants – eating and drinking now accounts for almost half of Ghirardelli's space. The ubiquitous franchise chains such as Benetton have arrived, and some of the larger stores have been replaced by smaller, more profitable operations. It's hard now to remember that the place once seemed subversive and fresh, but it still looks busy, and on a sunny afternoon is as good a place to spend an hour as any.

Building on the precedent of Ghirardelli, Boston's Faneuil Hall Market, developed by the Rouse Corporation and designed by Benjamin and Jane Thompson, made the festival market into a religion. James Rouse had previously amassed a considerable fortune from mortgage banking, house building, and developing conventional shopping centres. The Thompsons brought him to Boston when their scheme to refurbish Faneuil Hall and turn it into a shopping centre looked like foundering in the face of sceptical bankers. With substantial subsidies from the city and the federal government, and Rouse's bullish self-confidence, the scheme eventually got built and, as everybody knows, turned out to be a huge popular and financial success. The market is made up of the heavily restored eighteenth-century red-brick Faneuil Hall, and the three parallel terraces that make up Quincy Market, designed in 1826 by Alexander Parris, a neo-classical *tour de force* in granite. With the exaggerated ruggedness of its cobbled surfaces and its permanent crowds of visitors, looking for all the world like a soft-focus Pepsi-Cola commercial, it has become the embodiment of the much-advertised inner city revival, decked with banners, awash with frozen yoghurt stalls, batik and deep-pan pizza, followed closely by London's Covent Garden and a dozen virtually indistinguishable city centre developments.

Ben Thompson's conversion of the buildings is cavalier and highly theatrical. All the accretions that erupted from the Parris buildings over the years have been stripped back to return the complex to the ruthless symmetry of its earliest years, ostensibly in the interests of authenticity, though much of what you see now dates no further back than 1976. While the chimneys remain, all the original sliding sash windows have been removed and, instead of the small panes, windows are now all single pivoting frames. Inside, Thompson delights in ostentatious juxtapositions of plaster with exposed brickwork. The place is full of enamel industrial lamp shades and festoon blinds, and gilded and carved pastiches of Victorian signs. Of course, it's not really a shopping centre, any more than Ghirardelli Square is. Half of the market's twelve million visitors a year are tourists or conventioneers, and despite the continual attempts of Rouse's staff to police the terms of leases which forbid fast-food stores and prohibit tenants from using 'coy, rustic or unnaturally antiquated names, or use imitations of old English or similar scripts, or affectations of spelling', florists keep slipping in soft drink sidelines, and the butchers end up selling take-away slices of salami. In fact, sixty per cent of sales are accounted for by food, most of it scoffed by the hordes as they march to and fro among the stalls, looking for something, anything, to prove that they have been to Boston.

Thompson and Rouse were touted as the international saviours of the inner city, adulation which has clearly gone to both their heads. Rouse now goes about calling himself the Robin Hood of real estate – despite having sold a hefty stake in his business to the giant developers Olympia and York, who, whatever else they may be, are certainly not in the business of charity, while the Thompsons have started to sound more like new-age missionaries than architects. 'The marketplace offers intense sensations and deep sensory involvement,' burbles Jane Thompson. 'Visitors are surrounded by smells, colour, movement, things to touch and taste, all experienced at a high level of intensity. The full and free exposure of foods, flowers and goods, so different from the plastic-wrapped displays of the contemporary retail environment, act on some people almost as a shock that brings the senses to heightened awareness,' she says, making it all sound like a drug-induced hallucination.

'The marketplace, with food as the common denominator, is a mothering place, welcoming and supportive, a source of sustenance. Its visual abundance gives assurance that growing, harvesting, preparing of food is celebrated on a daily basis. It tells us that the food we eat is the same as that grown and brought fresh to the market. The sense of healthy spontaneity of eating is close to natural supply sources.' It's a claim that sounds more than a little hollow at the end of a Saturday afternoon as the garbage

Looking at the world through inverted commas

trucks cruise by filled to the gills with styrofoam packaging.

It's true that a good building has been saved, and it's equally true that Boston has the appearance of life again on its streets, but it has become increasingly apparent that burgeoning festival markets are simply the other side of the coin to the monster middle-of-nowhere malls like West Edmonton and Bloomington. Both offer a theatrical, and highly artificial environment. The involvement of the same developers simply serves to underscore the point.

The most curious aspect of all is the way in which desperate city authorities from all over the world have taken to calling in Rouse and/or Thompson as the only people with the power to save them. In Manchester, the mayor actually claims 'it is a coup for Manchester to have Rouse interested in the city and its people'. In America, Rouse and Thompson have worked in Baltimore, Toledo and New York, at the South Street Seaport, and also in Australia, where the same formula came out yet again at the Festival Market in Sydney's Darling Harbour, opened in time for the bicentennial celebrations of 1988, where they worked with the Australian Hayson family. Rouse and Hayson subsequently extended their operations into Britain, where they have looked at a scheme for Brighton Pier, at another in Glasgow for a still-born fashion centre, and in Manchester, where they are involved with Central Station Properties and Commercial Union to develop twenty-seven acres of the Manchester Festival Market. Thompson is working on a scheme for Dublin's Docks where he claims, in prose as purple as his wife's, 'The departure of commercial shipping activity from the River Liffey and the adjoining canals has left ribbons of water streaming through the city. The river is a stage waiting to be animated with colour and movement and daily drama.'

But the formula is running out of steam. Darling Harbour and New York's South Street Seaport have a grim familiarity about them, the artful choreography has started to feel as monotonous and inevitable as the international hotels, airports and mirror-glass skyscrapers once did.

New York's old market at South Street and Fulton is a goldfish bowl surrounded by a stockade of Wall Street skyscrapers, most of whose occupants are too self-consciously smart to come down to the market's unsubtle delights – the usual giant graphics, the Italian market umbrellas, the Benetton and Laura Ashley outlets – despite views towards Brooklyn Bridge that are truly spectacular. South Street is in the limbo land of the Brookstone catalogue store, the Sharper Image, and the Banana Republic store. It's the kind of place that offers unlimited Californian champagne and bloody marys with the $26.50 Sunday brunch. It's a place where the only person tentatively sampling the wares of the Seaport Fries Stall,

The recycled industrial market hall has become as much part of the repertoire of the developer as the financial centre and the convention hall. Shopping, the owners hope, is turned into entertainment. But while the boosters eagerly claim that such places recreate the vital street life of the traditional city, they are in reality just another form of giant out-of-town shopping mall

offering fifteen different kinds of chips, is a clergyman in a dog collar.

On busy weekends, Covent Garden's lovingly restored old vegetable market looks like nothing so much as the departure lounge of Gatwick Airport caught in the middle of a Spanish air-traffic control strike. It is full to bursting with sullen visitors, longing for a good day out, but signally failing to find anything more exotic than shops full of neon sculpture, and stalls selling the by now traditional busts of Elvis and ceramic ice cream cones.

Undaunted, developers for such diverse projects as Liverpool's Albert Dock and Glasgow's Merchant City continue promising to build new Covent Gardens, every time they come across a redundant warehouse or superfluous tram shed. The idea of a recycled industrial building, filled with clever little shops, wine bars, and romantic pavement cafés, has become one of the inescapable clichés of urban renewal, the soft-focus inner city that takes over where the Martini umbrellas of the 1960s left off.

Yet pavement cafés run by multinational food chains never provide quite the same intellectual nourishment that took Sartre to Les Deux Magots. Rather than being the haunt of bright-eyed students arguing about existentialism until dawn, Covent Garden is a place where people queue ten deep at the baked potato stand. They circle the benches, waiting to pounce as soon as a seat on which to eat their sandwiches becomes vacant. Entertainment of a kind is provided by the same buskers hired by the British Airports Authority to distract the tourists long enough to prevent an open mutiny.

The crowds are preyed on by itinerant traders who know a captive audience when they see one. The sandwich bar has displaced the wine bar as Covent Garden's dominant life form, while the atmosphere has changed dramatically. In the Neal's Yard Wholefood Warehouse, last refuge of the brown rice eater, the management has had to install security turnstiles and post private security guards. Even Terry Farrell's garden centre for Jacob Rothschild's Clifton Nurseries has been gutted and turned into yet another sandwich bar.

Meanwhile the ominous march of pedestrianisation spreads relentlessly across the whole of Covent Garden, bringing with it that curious sense of unreality that comes with street furniture, chunky bollards made out of railway sleepers, and herringbone-pattern clay paving. The same process is now threatening to spill over into Soho, where the sex industry was temporarily driven out, not so much by moral outrage, but by the greater profits to be made from turning legitimate, and opening modish neo-fifties hamburger bars, and shops selling imported second-hand jeans and Japanese electronics.

Looking at the world through inverted commas

The saddest thing about Covent Garden's plight is its inevitability. It has followed exactly the same trajectory of rise and fall that fashionable thoroughfares from Carnaby Street to Melrose have had to endure since the 1960s. Even before the refurbished market reopened its doors in 1981, the planners behind the project had seen the awful fate that had overtaken Carnaby Street and vowed to prevent it from happening again. Just like Covent Garden, Carnaby Street had gone from being a quiet, but pleasant backwater, to being fiercely fashionable. And just like Carnaby Street or Broadway, Covent Garden looks in danger of deteriorating into squalor.

The market's original landlords, the Greater London Council, outlawed shops that sold cheesecloth shirts and denim jeans. Strict rules were drawn up about how frontages could look, and attempts were made to encourage useful shops rather than simply relentless fashion – just as they were in Boston. All of it was done with the best of intentions, but the effort failed, the area falling victim to the economics of a cycle of rise and fall. The antiquarian bookshop carved out of a vegetable wholesaler's store in Long Acre now belongs to a multinational American company selling sweaters. The friendly store that once specialised in European magazines and newspapers is now the branch of another large chain, staffed by uniformed and uninterested employees rather than enthusiasts. And the whole complex is now in the hands of an insurance company,

Over and over again the same pattern has been repeated, from Broadway to Les Halles, from King's Road to Brompton Cross. Stage one is low rent cosmopolitanism. Junk shops and working men's cafés, specialist bookshops and scruffy but interesting street markets cling together. Then the low rents and the relaxed ambience start pulling in the impecunious but creative. Stage two sees the newcomers starting to crowd out the older, established occupants. An antique shop can manage on higher overheads than a junk shop, a shop that sells walnut oil and fresh coffee beans will push out the corner grocer. Quickly, the balance tips towards the newcomers, who find themselves in the majority. But the pioneers are then driven out of the area too. Like the original residents, they reach the point when they can no longer afford the ever higher rents that come as landlords begin to extract a slice of the profits from the upturn in the area's fortunes. The lucky ones sell on the tail ends of their leases, for a quick profit. Rents go so high that the only stores that can afford them are, on the one hand, those that are too snooty to want to stay, and on the other hand, the low-overheads, high-return shops selling snacks and T-shirts. Stage three sees the smart shops move out and on to the next up-and-coming area, while the tat takes over. The next stage is harder to predict.

Sometimes the decay is terminal and irreversible. In other cases, such as

Looking at the world through inverted commas

Carnaby Street, the whole cycle eventually starts up all over again. The place becomes so seedy that the rents fall to the point at which a new generation of bright young things starts to move back. Alternatively, the institutions take over and freeze the process of change.

The city has always been a spectacle. It has grown in part because of its very attractiveness, its sense that it has something special to offer. And this spectacle has always been consciously manufactured, from the circuses of ancient Rome to the more recent inventions of the tourist industry. They have become an essential part of the economy of cities. But the last two decades have seen the process whipped up to fever pitch in the world cities, where the impact of mass tourism has started to bring about structural changes. As long as travel remains widely available, the change is likely to be irreversible.

The myth of community

15

The most cherished of contemporary myths is the recurring dream of community. Half rose-tinted Frank Capra, half *Passport to Pimlico*, it's a fantasy that celebrates the corner shop, borrowing a cup of sugar from the neighbours, and all those other unimpeachable suburban virtues that range from motherhood to apple pie.

The myth acquired a gloss of credibility from the short-lived burst of academic interest in urban sociology in the years after World War Two. A stream of sociologists and social anthropologists descended on London's East End and America's burgeoning Levittowns with the same wide-eyed but uncomprehending wonder with which they had once clambered over the Yucatán and New Guinea. Long after they moved on to more promising genres, their influence in vulgarised form is still pervasive. Peter Willmott and Michael Young's *Family and Kinship in East London*, the product of what they called 'three years' field work' in Bethnal Green and on a new housing estate in Essex, was typical. The two researchers presented their findings in what they believed was scientific and objective language but which today reads more like a querulous wail about modern life and the subversion of the proletariat by consumerism. They shook their heads about the proliferation of television sets, they deplored the lust for expensive consumer goods, they worried that there were no corner shops and pubs in the suburban Essex to which the old residents of the East End were moving in ever larger numbers in the 1940s, as if these were all part of a natural habitat under threat in the ecological sense.

In a case study worth quoting for the flavour it gives of their work, they cited a family they called the Harpers. 'Mrs Harper, a stout, red-faced woman in her late thirties, had, like her husband, always lived in the same part of Bethnal Green, before she went to Essex in 1948. She came from a large family – six girls, and two boys – and she grew up amidst brothers, and sisters, uncles and aunts and cousins. When she married at 18, she went on living with her parents, and her first child was brought up more by her mother than herself. As the family grew, they moved out to three rooms on the ground floor of a house in the next street. Their life was that of the extended family.

'That busy sociable life is now a memory. Shopping in the mornings

In the 1930s, the most exotic building in Southall, a respectable lower-middle class suburb of London, was the Pagoda roof of the Liberty Cinema. The wave of migration that has changed the face of all the major cities of the world since those days has brought with it the surreal sight of authentic Hindu temples amidst the nineteenth-century terraces, just as many of the strip malls of Los Angeles are now awash with neon in Korean and Iranian scripts amidst the chromium and tiles of the Parade is a lonely business, compared with the familiar faces and sights of the old street market.'

What Young and Willmott don't discuss is the question of where that extended family came from *before* they had lived in the East End. The chances are high that they were part of the huge influx of people that London experienced from the early nineteenth century onwards, and for them Bethnal Green was no more than a temporary stopping off point, with nothing to mark it out as any more essential a part of the family's background than anywhere else.

By the 1990s, when the 'new' Essex of the post-war years had acquired its own myths and folklore, a new generation of observers was already contrasting the cultural poverty of hypermarkets equally unfavourably with the unpretentious virtues of chromium-plated parades. Yet Young and Willmott treated what they saw in the 1950s as an enduring model for urban life, one which municipal architects, backed up by sociologists and social workers, attempted to reproduce in the new housing projects of the 1960s.

Peter Townsend, a founder member of the Institute of Community Studies, wandered the streets of Bethnal Green in the 1940s evidently under the impression that he was looking at exotic primitives. He claimed to have found that the streets of the area reproduced themselves spontaneously in informally demarcated areas of the underground bomb shelters of the Blitz, and that local loyalties were given physical symbolism, just like the turf signals of Renaissance Siena, or the Los Angeles crips gangs. 'In one street is a row of six houses with an aspidistra in each front window, rarely found elsewhere; in another street a line of four alsatian dogs and in a third, a succession of curtains of a particular hue, dark blue, rose pink, yellow ochre.' No doubt Townsend would today read as much significance into the shape of the satellite dishes lashed to the facades of working-class houses.

Once you look past the astonishingly condescending view that the academics had of their subjects, you find a fundamental misapprehension about the nature of city life, one that is inextricably tied to the lasting grip of the countryside on the Anglo-Saxon imagination. The model for the 'natural' order of urban organisation that is the tacit assumption behind the community myth is the farming hamlet and the fishing village, where everybody knows everybody else, where people stay close to home and families keep in touch.

The comforting conviction that there is an underlying sense of continuity, of collective memory and shared experience to give meaning to the aimlessness of everyday urban life was an essential part of the repertoire of the more sentimental writers on urban affairs, long before Jane Jacobs. Even Steen Eiler Rasmussen, London's otherwise highly perceptive Danish biographer, claimed to see the city as a network of villages, whose residents have always identified with their community, not with the city as a whole.

That is of course exactly the shape that Los Angeles has taken on in the last years, as homeowner groups build walls around their communities to defend themselves against the outside world, and especially against the demands of City Hall for taxes. But, underpinned by ethnic antagonism and anxiety about crime and property values, it is hardly a reassuring model. Substitute the word ghetto – or fiefdom – for village, and the whole idea acquires a more sinister resonance.

The idea of community has been used to underpin the abiding hostility of the intellectual for suburbia, a stick for metropolitans to beat the backs of the hicks, rather than to get to grips with the actual nature of the city. Suburbia is held to lack the sense of community that 'authentic' cities have.

To argue that 'community' does not exist – as Margaret Thatcher once did – does not necessarily imply the acceptance of her own brand of neo-conservatism. Nor does it rule out the possibility of collective action and shared responsibilities. But the concept needs to be subjected to rather sharper scrutiny than the sentimentality with which it is usually discussed. Like the territoriality which underpins the defensible spaces doctrines of geographers such as Oscar Newman and Alice Coleman, the idea of community has its roots in behavioural and anthropological studies. But this is an inadequate basis on which to build a theory about the nature of the city. It fails to deal with the nuances that are involved in the continual movement that is an essential part of urban life, especially so in the United States, but also in the big cities of Europe.

Yet the more that the world retreats, for better or worse, into privacy, adopting starter homes, personal headphones, pot noodles and portions for one, so the idea of community is celebrated by popular culture with ever more elaboration. As people come to regard their neighbours, and even their increasingly hard to control offspring, with growing suspicion, so the myth is burnished to perfection. The western economy is inextricably linked to the extended family, the present giving of Christmas and Mother's Day, Father's Day, Thanksgiving and Easter, even as the 3.2-person household becomes an increasingly irrelevant model. In fact these are the most stressful moments in the year for many people, breeding domestic violence and tension. For other festivals, the ideal collides with the alternative myth of romanticism and travel to far-off places that finds its most poignant expression in the solitary couples who fly to tropical islands to go through conveyor-belt wedding ceremonies surrounded by strangers with only a video tape to take home for their families.

Television promotes beer with images of slow-motion good fellowship in the local park. It sells hamburgers by showing the neighbourhood football team getting together for a Saturday kickabout, then adjourning for a shared meal. It depicts bars as being centres of local life, not grim fleapits full of derelicts. It shows shared experiences and extended families, roots and continuity. Meanwhile, voting with their feet, those who can afford to leave the old neighbourhood do so, not just because they fear that it is about to be swamped by undesirable newcomers, nor because they are forced to move under pressure from urban renewal, but just as often because they see themselves as simply outgrowing their former contemporaries and surroundings. There are the die-hards who refuse to quit under any circumstances, the hold-outs who cling to the home in which their parents were born in the face of dereliction all around and threats or bribes. But these people are the exceptions, untypical and extraordinary.

The so-called community does not necessarily hold the same attraction for all its members as sentimental outsiders might think. It is only those who feel some overwhelming sense of shared threat who have a need to gather together for protection from racism or economic hardship. Of course there are sadnesses about the decay of neighbourhood institutions, the closure of churches or synagogues, the subdivision or consolidation of homes, the departure of the younger and more ambitious residents, leaving the sick and the old. But the alternative is a kind of tribalism, a freezing of the status quo in a way that is the very antithesis of the dynamic qualities that make the city what it is.

The mismatch between the increasingly solitary, fractured and private way of life in the cities and the idealised vision would be a harmless enough fantasy were it not for the fact that even policy-makers have been seduced into believing that the myth is real. Community has become the basis for a whole raft of muddled and confused policies. It was behind the well-intentioned but catastrophic idea of closing Victorian institutions for the care of the insane and returning their confused and helpless patients to the care of the 'community', which in practice turns out to be costly and insanitary single-resident-occupancy hotels and lodging houses, or even the streets. It is perfectly true that there are many selfless people who are prepared to devote their lives to the care of aged relatives, and a smaller number ready to extend this care to neighbours or even strangers for whom they feel a sense of responsibility. But all the evidence suggests that they are a tiny minority. For many more people, the freedom from obligations and ties that comes with modern city life, whether it is consciously admitted or not, is a liberating development. The hundreds of thousands of people who deliberately choose to go missing each year, cutting themselves off from friends and families, point to the mobility and anonymity that is the reality behind the fantasies of domestic harmony. These are genuine aspirations, not the product of malevolent intervention or manipulation.

For the affluent, the dream of domesticity represented by the family kitchen remains an important symbol, even as they eat in restaurants six nights a week, and on Sunday lunchtimes. In the same way that Ronald Reagan talked constantly about the importance he placed on religion, without ever attending a regular act of worship, still less anything that could be called a parish church, so the idea of community as a desirable, but essentially abstract quality is much more powerful than its reality.

We talk of neighbourhoods, and the need to design housing to encourage a sense of community, even as dismaying reports appear in London and New York newspapers of neighbours stepping over victims struggling with rapists in lift lobbies. It's commonplace in some housing estates for parents to hurl discarded nappies from upper floor windows. It is absurd to blame architecture, concrete construction methods, or even housing management for these things. Affluent homeowners are likely to be suspicious of their neighbours, intolerant of their pets and their late-night parties, their early-morning bonfires and their blaring record players, rather than to feel a sense of solidarity. The poor bar their doors and shutter their windows against their neighbours.

In planning policies, the 'community' has been elevated to the point of a fetish. Its preservation has become an all-embracing preoccupation, a cloak for all kinds of motivations which, while perfectly understandable, would be far less acceptable if more openly expressed. From homeowners who want to build a wall around their suburban enclaves to exclude newcomers with different skin colours, to the rallying cry of middle-class activists who want to preserve working-class communities against the depredations of mercenary property developers, community is presented as desirable in itself, a reflection of a natural order of life that is tampered with at society's peril. Thus in the 1960s the road building and urban renewal programmes were seen as 'destroying' communities, with a resulting breakdown in social order. To the Jane Jacobs camp, urban motorways produced broken families and fractured family life, leading to crime, drugs and gangs. The equation was as simple as that. By that definition, community was apparently a form of social control.

All this is based on a carefully fabricated image of neighbourhoods as the anchors of social stability. But it is fundamentally a myth. Life in the city has never been stable. Given the extraordinarily rapid turnover of people and households of the last century, urban communities are more symbolic expressions than physical realities. The ideal urban community is presented as if urban families occupied a dynastic homestead for life which they would pass on to their children, and their children's children. It presupposes a Mediterranean fishing village social organisation, with land held in common, and a strongly hierarchical social structure in which elders are natural leaders, deferred to by their younger contemporaries. Even if the kind of stability on which a community of that kind depends did exist, it is by no means clear that it would present a desirable option for most city dwellers.

All the evidence is that this is the very form of social organisation that, given the choice, the vast majority of the motivated and the ambitious are only too eager to leave behind. The emptying of the countryside and the enormous growth of the cities that continues in the developing world is based precisely on the attractions of social mobility that the city offers. What we call urban communities are by no means the static, homogeneous places that we assume. Even without undergoing the massive physical transformations that characterise comprehensive redevelopment or gentrification, areas of cities go through enormous changes while looking outwardly the same. From generation to generation, families move up and down the economic scale, they come and go, lose touch and reform. Parents attempt to pass on their skills to their children, but do not always succeed, siblings drift apart. Family concerns and preoccupations change, and inevitably their horizons are not bounded by the horizons of neighbourhood and turf, a fact that is ignored by the naive propagandists for the community, with their impossible dreams of creating the social structure of a Sicilian hill village in the heart of the city.

The population structure of a big city goes through almost continuous change, through immigration, through economic prosperity or decline. The single most arresting feature of life in all developed societies has been the dramatic decrease in the size of the average household, which in significant areas of London and New York is already less than two. This can be explained partly by an ageing population, partly by the weakening of the institution of marriage.

The fact is that the idyll of the community fostered for commercial and political ends does not accord with the increasingly private world sought for a variety of reasons by an ever increasing proportion of the population. The massive shift of people away from the inner city provides ample evidence that the old idea of urban community does not exist. It's a construct which is essentially fleeting, a snapshot that freezes time for a moment, providing a partial clue to the character of an area at a particular time. But

The myth of community

cities are in reality constantly fluctuating places, with people moving in and out, forming, breaking and reforming households.

Homeowners in America move on average every four years, in Britain every six. The difficulty that the British government experienced in administering the ill-fated property tax levied on individuals – the so-called community charge, or poll tax – because so many people were continually moving, provided ample evidence of the quicksilver nature of life in the modern city. In Oxford, eighty per cent of all the names on the register moved in a year. In London, it was around forty per cent. At the same time, house sizes are constantly falling, suggesting that homes are designed to be much less flexible, and therefore to encourage people to move as their demands for space fluctuate, and mortgage lenders continually revise the terms of their loans to cope.

The idea of urban communities as something to be regarded as solid and fixed is misleading. They are continually being redefined by the people in them, and their particular needs and preoccupations. Nowhere is this clearer than in the impact of the increasing internationalisation of the world's greatest cities. The migrations of the industrial revolution of the nineteenth century are still underway. But with Europe now almost completely urbanised, the successors of the country people who flocked to London and Paris in the nineteenth century, to Tokyo after World War Two, and to Los Angeles since the 1970s, come from the other side of the world. They are from peasant villages in India, Pakistan and Bangladesh, the Philippines and from the *barrios* of Latin America. There are wealthy refugees from Iran, and boat people from Vietnam. In the process, they have triggered off a bout of urban restructuring just as sharp as that which changed the face of Manhattan with the arrival of the Europeans at the start of the century.

According to the 1981 census, the 700 000 people of Indian origin then living in Britain made up the largest single immigrant group. There were 547 000 West Indians, 406 000 from Pakistan, 99 000 from Bangladesh, 122 000 Chinese and 100 000 Africans. The census showed that people who were not born in the UK made up eighteen per cent of London's population. But their distribution was very uneven. The borough of Brent in the northwest of the city was the most diverse, with more than a third of its residents non-white and thirty-seven per cent born outside the UK. In Havering, however, a long way to the east, the non-white total was less than three per cent. The figures conceal highly intricate ethnic geography. The British race relations industry adopts some unusual ethnic definitions. Cypriots, for example, would hardly be counted as 'non-white' by most cultures.

The myth of community

The number of foreign-born people living in France at the beginning of 1981 was more than four million, eight per cent of the population, not counting an estimated 300 000 illegal immigrants. Portugal provided the highest number, closely followed by Algeria. People of North African origin accounted for one-third of the total.

There are 1.35 million foreign-born people living in the Paris region, who have now mostly moved on from the shanty towns of the 1960s. In the inner suburb of Nanterre, targeted for the next major extension of the office complex of La Défense, a quarter of the residents are foreign-born, and immigrants account for up to three-quarters of the population in some schools.

Changes of this sort have had conspicuous effects on the fabric of London. When it was built in the 1930s, the Liberty Cinema was the most exotic structure in Southall, a humble nineteenth-century suburb. The ceramic Chinese dragons on its lurid yellow and green roof tiles injected a little second-hand Hollywood glamour into the borough's monotonous terraced streets. This was John Betjeman's London, created by the Great Western Railway and peopled by clerks and postmen.

The cinema is now the Liberty Shopping Centre and bears witness to the tide of rather more authentic exoticism which has made Southall Britain's best-known Asian suburb. The auditorium has been converted into a network of souk-like alleys. In one of them there is the office of a broker who can arrange a marriage. There are stalls selling saris and bangles, ticket agencies offering seats for the next Asian superstar spectacular at Wembley Stadium, and butchers who stock neither pork nor beef.

Metroland Southall's boundary is marked by the railway station, with its incongruous French château roof. To the south is Heathrow Airport – source of large numbers of low-skilled jobs – and the more familiar face of London suburbia. Asian Southall starts in the goods yard of the station, immediately to the north. Here, the peeling 1960s factory units, built in the hope of attracting plastics manufacturers, provide the headquarters for one of the fiery local Sikh political organisations. Indian conflicts have erupted bloodily here – the storming of the Golden Temple in Amritsar by Indira Gandhi's commandos in the early 1980s provoked more than one political murder in Britain.

A little way down the road is a chemist's shop, whose window is filled with an enormous colour photograph of the Golden Temple. Beyond is a curious little ziggurat rising from the scaffolding that shrouds an otherwise anonymous hall, a memory of the Hindu temples that can be found all over the subcontinent. Around the corner in the high street, purposeful Sikhs in their improbably cantilevered turbans move about their business, taking

286   *The myth of community*

tea in the tandoori houses or pausing for glutinous sweetmeats. The religious rub shoulders with secular businessmen, who cruise back and forth in second-hand BMWs equipped with tinted windscreens, and stereos booming Asian pop music.

Women in tunics and trousers linger in jewellery shops that compete to present the lushest interior. One, looking like the inside of a box of chocolates, has its walls entirely lined with turquoise silk offset by chandeliers dripping crystal beads. In the grocery stores, alongside the mountains of Kleenex boxes and tins of spaghetti soup, there is rack upon rack of Indian essentials. You can stock up on the products of Nogi & Co of Bombay, whose pride and joy is Monkey Brand Black Toothpaste – 'avoid worthless imitations', the pack cautions – and Tibet Snow hair oil, its pre-Raphaelite wrappings a tribute to the enduring vigour of the Victorian printers' art in the more anaemic world of contemporary British consumerism. In the Oberoi stores, six armed elephant gods in cast brass marked down to bargain prices stand on the shelves next to cooking pots and kitchen knives, alongside a whole wall of gold bangles.

Next door in the greengrocers, there are trays of nameless, shapeless vegetables beside the bananas. You can buy bargain five-gallon drums of cotton seed oil, and huge packs of poppadoms: all that is needed in fact to keep a thousand Asian restaurants in business. In the clothes shops, dhotis and saris fill the windows and spill out on to the pavement on mobile racks. In Southall, those few national chains that do set up shop here learn from the way that the locals do things. The Burton clothes store is crammed to the roof with racks of shirts, and defended with roller shutters, and the Bank of Baroda makes a bigger showing than Barclays.

The area is not sustained simply by importing the old way of life. The number of shops advertising tax-free facilities for visitors point to the fact that it is very much a two-way trade. Many of the Asian products on the shelves of Southall are made in Britain, from the Kingfisher Beer, brewed in north London under licence from its Indian owners, to the extra spicey Kassava crisps. And in the sari shops, there are Schwarzenegger T-shirts alongside more traditional embroidered tunics. Southall's streets have the diversity and life that recall shopkeeping the way it used to be, before Britain's high streets were frozen into conformity by the chain stores, exactly in the same way that Latino Los Angeles has made Broadway into a flourishing shopping street much closer to the European than the American model.

According to the UK census, approaching one-third of Southall's residents were born outside Britain. Two wards in the borough of Ealing, of which it forms part, are more than seventy per cent black. In some of its schools, whites are even more heavily outnumbered by children of Asian origin. Southall's transformation from its nineteenth-century form is a product of the wave of immigration from Asia to the cities of Europe and America from the 1960s to the 1980s. Immigration by this time was no longer a phenomenon dominated by the very poor, but a more complex and diverse process. Unlike the millions of destitute Europeans who crossed the Atlantic to pile into the slums of the East Coast cities of America, a significant proportion of the migrants of the 1970s were well-educated and prosperous. They were able to by-pass the inner city for suburbs like Southall and Brent, circumventing the conventional route through the inner city that has been the traditional path for the assimilation of the immigrant.

Equally, there are enormous differences between the various sections of London's immigrant population. The Sylhetti villagers of Bangladesh, far poorer than the traders who are prominently represented in Southall, are among the most recent groups to have settled in London, and have concentrated themselves almost entirely in the borough of Tower Hamlets. They were farmers from one of the poorest and most overcrowded parts of the globe. Following in the footsteps of colonial sailors who established a tiny community in London's East End in the early part of the century, the Sylhetti villagers came to London in the 1970s. They came not from the poorest families, but from those with enough land to raise money for the fare. And they came to London, like the gastarbeitern of West Germany from Yugoslavia and Turkey, or the Central Americans in Los Angeles, to earn enough to send money home to help support an extended family, and if possible to raise enough cash to be able to buy more land. As the community established itself, it changed from a predominantly male one, characterised by young men working in the restaurant and garment industries, living in hostels or shared houses, saving as much as possible, and living a life remote from the British community around them. In the 1980s the picture changed rapidly, as stricter immigration controls made many Bangladeshis decide to bring their families to London to join them while they were still able to. As the Bangladeshi women and children arrived, the housing problems of the Spitalfields area in which they concentrated grew acute. In the face of the threat of violence from the poor whites of London's East End, who found themselves competing for jobs and homes, and the refusal of the local authorities to provide suitable housing, tension grew sharper.

The pressure from the expanding city fringe to turn parts of the area into office developments threatened to make matters worse. The Bangladeshis, especially the newly arrived women who rarely spoke English, had the

288   *The myth of community*

traditional need of immigrants to live close together. As the size and confidence of the community grew, the state began to make more provision for them. The housing associations, largely financed by exactions on commercial developers, began to build houses and flats suitable for the much larger families that the Bangladeshis still had. And the Fieldgate mosque was built with £2 million in donations – including a substantial one from King Fahd of Saudi Arabia.

Not all immigrant groups are at a social disadvantage. There are small, but extremely significant groups of foreigners whose presence in London is essential to its role as a world city. The Americans are in London in substantial numbers, including bankers, diplomats and military personnel. Far less conspicuous, but equally significant, are the Japanese, with their school – whose move from Camden Town to Acton detonated an upheaval in the property market in affluent London suburbia – their supermarkets in Golders Green and St John's Wood which import Lucky 7 cigarettes and sell the previous day's *Asahi Shimbun*. There is the Japanese hair salon for the corporate wives who don't feel confident about their English, the hostess bars in Piccadilly basements, the sushi delivery services and the golf clubs, which all add up to a hermetic world, almost a parallel city. The Japanese in London, and for that matter in Frankfurt and Düsseldorf, tend to stay for shorter periods than the Americans. In many ways they regard London as a hardship posting, to be endured as a patriotic chore.

Almost alone among the major Western metropolises, Los Angeles has continued to increase its population, even in its central core, a growth that has been fuelled by migration from the rest of the United States, and from Asia and Latin America. The number of whites living within Los Angeles's city limits declined by 27.5 per cent from 1960 to 1980, or almost 500 000 people. But despite this exodus, the city experienced a net gain of nearly 700 000 in the decade to 1980, made up of Hispanics, Asians and even Pacific islanders. In Los Angeles County, whites declined by thirty per cent, an absolute loss of more than one million. As with most of the big cities, the majority stayed close to the areas they had left. In the four counties around Los Angeles, which must now be counted as part of the city for all practical purposes, if not political ones, there was a population growth of one million whites.

The five counties of the Los Angeles area had 11 332 400 inhabitants in 1980, of which nineteen per cent were foreign-born, fewer than half were born in California, and only twenty per cent were from Los Angeles itself. Los Angeles, settled first from the rest of America, has become an even more ethnically diverse city than New York. More liberal immigration laws since 1968 allowed a new wave of immigrants from Latin America and

Asia into what was of course once a Mexican settlement. With between 400 000 and 1.1 million illegal immigrants, the Mexican and Central American population increased by at least 1.5 million in the decade to 1980. While the Mexicans got caught in the inner city, the Asians moved to the outer ring, educational and financial advantages getting them straight into Orange County, where the Vietnamese worked in electronics manufacturing.

The ethnic diversity has also allowed a sweat shop economy to exist side by side with some of the most advanced technology in the world. Of the 2210 garment firms in LA County only ten per cent had union management agreements, and sixty-five per cent of the employees in these places, mainly Mexican women, their employers Hong Kong Chinese and Taiwanese, Koreans and Latin Americans, had no work papers. As one American commentator put it, Los Angeles has within it a Singapore and a Managua, a Boston and a Detroit: rust belts, Third World sweat shops, and the highest concentration of PhDs and engineers in the world.

The ethnic diversity has created new and complex antagonisms. Asian-owned stores have prospered in areas of the city core abandoned by the national chains, where their customers are mainly the poorest members of the black underclass, who sometimes see the shopkeeper as a parasitic outsider. Ethnic tensions have become far more tortuous than simple issues of black against white. Asian suburbs in Orange County saw petitions from both anglo and black locals trying to ban foreign-language business signs, as a rash of exotic alphabets began to spread over the city's strip malls. Given the Spanish origins of the city, it was a curious response.

To argue that communities should be petrified, unchanging in their social composition, is unrealistic and unjust. It is only the very poor, who have no freedom, who need the security of a tight-knit community around them, but why should their dependence on this be reinforced by the deliberate construction of ghettos? What, for example, will happen to the carefully won, larger than average housing built for the Bangladeshis in Spitalfields when they more closely match the fertility of the rest of the British nation? Have these people come to be defined only in this way?

The very nature of the city since its earliest incarnation as a trading post or religious centre has always implied a degree of internationalism. Athens and Rome were places that sat at the centre of imperial networks which made the cities which were their focus quite different entities from the countries in which they were located. The city, early on in its development, was a place to escape the parochialism of the country, a place with a level of freedom that peasant communities could not cope with.

Since the middle ages, that pattern established itself in the major

The myth of community

capitals of Europe, with Amsterdam, Paris and London, which each built up communities of foreigners, initially bankers, traders and seafarers, later refugees and religious communities, all adding to the mixture.

A phenomenon that was born of colonialism has been transformed in the post-colonial era into something else. The nineteenth century saw the country move into the towns, abandoning the farms for the first factories. In turn, in search of the prosperity and freedom that the cities seemed to offer, peasants from Bangladesh, Hong Kong computer programmers and chefs, and Caribbean bus drivers began to pour into London. Greek and Turkish Cypriots, and South African political émigrés all followed. Clearly a large part of this was the inheritance of empire, the inextricable relationship between the colonial centre and its dependencies. But it is a phenomenon that is common to all the international cities, and in fact those cities which do not have an ethnic mixture are now the ones which seem provincial and backward in some ways.

It is Tokyo's ethnic homogeneity, for example, only now beginning to break down, which marked it out as not yet a true world city. Paris, on the other hand, has very much the same ethnic diversity as London, for very much the same reasons. It is also the place which has been the sanctuary for European refugees, a place in which a whole alternative life goes on, from the exiled Khomeini and Ho Chi Minh to the Kurds and Romanians of recent times.

New York and Los Angeles developed in different ways, but are now perhaps the most ethnically diverse cities in the world. New York grew from a few tens of thousands to tens of millions of people as a result of a massive wave of immigration from Europe.

These immigrants have changed the demographic characteristics of the big cities. Without them, the inner cities would be empty indeed, and they have provided the workforce that has allowed the cities' services to survive. But the internationalisation of the modern city goes beyond the arrival of low-paid immigrant guest workers, prepared to carry out the dirty jobs that native citizens are not prepared for.

When Hong Kong millionaires buy themselves apartments in Los Angeles, go shopping in New York and invest their money through London, while they remain in the Far East, they are drawing each one of those cities into an internationalised network. The metropolis has become a part of other places, as well as part of its host country, and in a sense it is that new character which is a far more significant part of the city's new identity than the way in which London's Chinatown has been transformed with Chinese-charactered street signs, and pagoda-topped telephone boxes.

The myth of community

New York now has its botanicas and its Spanish TV and newspapers, its Irish parades and its Russian communities, following in the pattern established by the Chinese and the Eastern European Jews. Conventional wisdom once held that these groups have always been assimilated into the mainstream after a period. The experience of the second generation in the school system, and the army, has cemented them as New Yorkers first, Americans second, and whatever their roots are third.

But that comfortable picture could be breaking down. The evidence so far is mixed, but the signs are that emigrant groups are now building communities which maintain more of the characteristics of the old country. In London, for example, the immigrants from the Indian subcontinent continue to show higher fertility rates than the rest of the community, which calls for the construction of housing far larger than the standards for the rest of the community, the money that they earn still goes back to Asia to support poor communities, and they continue the tradition of arranged marriages.

And New York, a city that is becoming steadily poorer and blacker, provides little hope for a gradual achievement of majority standards of living by minorities. In 1900, blacks made up two per cent of the New York City population, in 1950 it was ten per cent, in 1990 it was at least twenty-five per cent, while 1.2 million whites have moved out of the city since the 1970s. In New York, Puerto Ricans earn half the all-household average while whites are fifty per cent richer than the all-household average.

If this is one end of the spectrum, the other is the affluent: the diplomats, the businessmen, the academics, the consultants, who form part of the international flying circus of the perpetually jet-lagged who have become an essential part of the landscape of the modern city. In some places the two strands meet, in Los Angeles's Japan Town for example, where the descendants of the migrants who helped build the railways, and who were drawn to the gold rush, now inhabit a downtown ghetto that has been tranformed by the investment of large sums of money from the modern Japan in hotels and office blocks. The tensions between different ethnic groups has been at the essence of big city life for three thousand years. By definition, cities are places that attract outsiders, and which form a meeting place between different cultures. From Alexandria to Venice, from Palermo to London, from Sydney to Los Angeles, it is the exoticism of scores of different cultures, sometimes in conflict, sometimes coexisting, which shapes distinctive urban cultures and underpins their economies.

Clearly the understanding of how a city functions must be based on a sense of the people who live in it. But those kinds of definitions are far subtler than the primitive notion of community. The same phenomena of internationalisation are overtaking the world's largest cities, which has led to the creation of new versions of the old idea of the community. It is too early yet to say how they will evolve and develop. It is entirely possible that they will once more dissolve, just as Little Italy in Manhattan lost its original ethnic character, and as the Jews of Spitalfields in London gave way to the Bangladeshis.

It may, on the other hand, be that some ethnic communities become more entrenched, in the way that contemporary Los Angeles suggests, where it is not just Koreans and Iranians, but the homosexuals of West Hollywood and the affluent whites of Beverly Hills who are retreating into defended compounds.

In the long term, however, it is a tendency which seems to be cutting across the most universal tendency of all, the decentralisation of the city. Clearly, the amorphous suburb, and the sharply focused ghetto, look set to coexist for a considerable time to come. Their meanings, however, are not to be found in sentimental visions of community.

The image of the city

16

Pinning down a city with statistics is a notoriously difficult undertaking. There is no international yardstick to define a conurbation, and some countries don't even have a national standard with which to do it. In the absence of shared assumptions, even the most basic question of whom to count as living in a city and whom to regard as a suburbanite is in doubt. The published figures on the population of Milan, for example, vary from 1.6 million to 4 million. Frankfurt by some estimates is a city with just 600 000 inhabitants. But if you count in the small towns such as Offenbach and Hanau, which are functionally if not administratively part of the city, the total is almost one million. And getting on for 1.6 million people live in a twelve-mile ring around the cathedral.

This lack of definition helps to perpetuate myths about cities. *Time* magazine will tell you that New York has twice as many people as Los Angeles, even though the US does have carefully worked-out definitions of standard metropolitan areas which show that the two are level pegging. *Time*'s figures reflect arbitrary and outdated political boundaries, but simply by publishing them they affect perceptions of both cities. Similarly, most accounts of inner city decline begin with a barrage of statistics that show how far and how fast the population of a given city has fallen, without pointing out that what might actually be happening is a reconfiguration rather than an absolute decline.

London, as defined by the boundaries of the old Greater London Council area, for example, lost 739 000 of its seven million people during the ten years to 1981. But seventeen million people live in a continuously urbanised area within a fifty-mile radius of Oxford Circus, and logically, the entire area must be considered as much London as Santa Monica, Pasadena and Irvine are counted physically, if not politically, part of Los Angeles, or Tsukuba and Yokohama are part of greater Tokyo. Defined like this, far from losing population, London has actually been growing.

The major invention of urban historians of the 1960s was the idea of the megalopolis, introducing a perception of great cities metamorphosing into amorphous urban regions spreading halfway across an entire country. But continuous urbanisation does not always satisfactorily define a city. There is, it is true, a built-up strip running all the way from Boston to

It is contemporary Tokyo that has provided much of the imagery for the cinema's new-found view of the city of the future, from 'Blade Runner' onward. It is Tokyo's apparently anarchic juxtaposition of shacks and high-rises, its rippling neon, and the diversity of its street life, that has shaped ideas of what the city can be

Washington. But even if they are physically contiguous, its constituent parts still have quite distinct economies, defined by smaller cities that maintain their own identities.

The Bos-Wash corridor remains little more than a figure of speech. But Dutch claims for the existence of the Randstad megalopolis – the ring of cities that takes in Amsterdam, Utrecht, The Hague and Rotterdam – amount to a deliberate political statement, an attempt to turn what would otherwise be regarded as a nation of extremely modest size into a very large city. If it actually existed, Randstad would be vast. More than eight million people live amidst its baroque steeples, prefabricated concrete housing estates and bulb fields. But the Randstad, unlike London, is less than the sum of its parts. It is Amsterdam, Rotterdam and The Hague that are important, and they are still distinct cities, even if they are only half an hour apart. In the same way, the sprawling Ruhr conurbation stretching across Northwest Germany has ten million people, enough to be counted in the same league as Paris. Yet the complex of German cities lacks the stature of the French capital, or even of the far less populous Berlin.

Large numbers of people living in close proximity do not in themselves constitute a city. But when a conurbation does have a sufficiently strong focus, then the whole sprawl takes on its identity. There is, for example, a continuous carpet of blue-tiled factory roofs, pylons and concrete spreading all the way from Tokyo to Osaka. But it is still Tokyo that is the focus and Osaka which has to struggle against the drain northwards of company headquarters and ambitious young talent.

The impression persists that the central city and its satellites, such as the Parisian new towns, are experienced entirely separately one from another, that there is an experience of Paris that is one thing, and that there is another, it goes almost without saying, vastly impoverished one elsewhere. It's a perception that applies equally strongly to other major cities. There is a contrast drawn between the Sydney of the harbour, the bridge and the opera house, and the endless ring of suburbs in which the vast majority of that city's two million people live with their barbecues and their shopping malls, just as there is a gap between the skyscrapers of Manhattan, and the Levittown suburbs of New Jersey.

It is a view that is inadequate on at least two counts. For a start, it is wrong to see the five Parisian new towns as distinct entities in their own right. Rather, they are essential parts of the city itself. They could not exist without the network of motorways, airports, and above all metro lines that constitutes Paris just as much as the picturesque crust of masonry buildings of Haussmann and his predecessors. It is not just that you can get from one part of Marne-la-Vallée to another by train that counts. The fact that you

The image of the city

can get to the shopping malls of Les Halles in less than twenty minutes, and on to the other new towns on the far side of the city without changing platforms, has transformed the mental map of the city that Parisians carry in their heads. Equally, New York is not just Manhattan. The skyscrapers make themselves felt as visual eruptions in the flat lands of New Jersey, just as the presence of the Bridge and Tunnel world underpins the hysteria of Manhattan.

To make sense of this kind of city it's important to grasp the new land-marks that define it. The airliner door has become the city gate. It is through its duralumin frame that visiting celebrities are photographed. It's here that teeny-boppers flock to meet their idols, and it's from an Alitalia Boeing that the Pope steps out to kiss the tarmac.

The public realm of the city is no longer defined by the church, the leg-islature, the market or the agora, but is now the restaurant and the bar. In Los Angeles, the most pretentious specimens actually have unlisted tele-phone numbers. In Barcelona and Tokyo, they are constantly rebuilt in ever more lavish and sensational style. These are places to which people go to see each other, to hold court, to play, as far as they can, a public part in city life.

Reaction to these shifting definitions has, to say the least, been mixed – just as was the response to the no less dramatic transformations that London, Paris and New York went through in the nineteenth century. Victorian critics attacked what they saw as the lifeless, spirit-diminishing industrial city. And a hundred years later, in the closing years of the twenti-eth century, equally bitter polemics were focused on the state of the metropolis. The world, it was said, faced an irreparable loss: the extinction of the traditional European city, mankind's most precious artefact.

It is true that in its new incarnation the diffuse, sprawling, and endlessly mobile world metropolis is fundamentally different from the city as we have known it. But for the architect and the urbanist to turn their backs on this new form, which is the backdrop to everyday life for the vast majority of people, is both condescending and self-defeating. This new species of city is not an accretion of streets and squares that can be comprehended by the pedestrian, but instead manifests its shape from the air, the car or the mass transit railway. Landmarks are reduced to flashes of slow-moving traffic, glimpsed from above on elevated highways amid a glittering river of red stoplights, or famous place names translated into the illuminated sta-tion signs that punctuate the darkness of metro tunnels.

But the equipment we have for making sense of what is happening to our cities has lagged far behind these changes. Both the popular and the academic views of what the city is, are coloured more by historical perceptions than by present-day realities. Painfully little work has been done on what it is really like to live in such a city, with its diffuse focuses, and its enormous distances. Instead, the image of London that persists is the historic crust that tourists see, defined by the area between Tower Bridge and Marble Arch that they can comfortably cover on foot or negotiate by bus and taxi in the interval between breakfast in the hotel and lunch in the mock-Edwardian pub. Of course, this definition of a city is in its own way just as valid as any other, but it is by no means adequate as a complete explanation. It neglects the more fundamental truth that the modern city is a collection of landmarks that have different meanings to the different people who live in it or who use it, some shared, others with more private significance.

The geography of New York, as understood by a Haitian or a Korean immigrant, describes a different place to that experienced by an expatriate British banker living on Central Park West, or a native-born Jewish American on the Upper East Side, just as London is a collection of landmarks that have a different significance to a middle-class family in Clapham, a Bengali immigrant in Southall, or the child of East Enders transplanted to Essex. It is in fact an essential property of the authentic metropolis that it can support this complex, overlapping set of meanings. The language used by twentieth-century critics is often much the same as their nineteenth-century predecessors', but the very city that the Victorian reformers denounced is now seen as an ideal model, to be preserved at all costs and, if possible, recreated in new developments.

But were the changes of the 1980s, for better or worse, the outcome of the conscious application of will or merely the product of circumstance? The literature of town planning used to be dominated by those who saw the physical form of the city as being of primary importance. A newer generation of urban economists and geographers see things in different terms, primarily demographics and land values. But both groups have attempted to explain the shape of the city in terms of the application and pursuit of particular aims and theories.

The sharpest question, however, is how much does planning philosophy shape the outcome of development? It is perfectly true that large areas of the cities discussed in this book have been rebuilt in the last four decades in a manner which conforms more or less to the plans put forward by the modernists of the 1920s and 1930s. And it is possible to argue that what happened during the 1980s is at least in part a reaction to that legacy. But did Le Corbusier's vision of the towers in a park of *La Ville Radieuse* really determine the form of the suburbs of Paris, and the housing projects of

New York, or was it simple expediency that allowed them to happen? Is it the process of industrialisation itself that is responsible, or is it the philosophies that emerged from out of that process, of which modernism is the most prominent?

The changes that have taken place in the world's mature cities go beyond appearance. It is not the fact that buildings look different, that they have plate glass or stone facades rather than concrete ones, nor even that they are configured in different ways, that has caused the underlying changes in the way that life is lived. It is the affluence of the society that builds them, the patterns of living that its citizens adopt, and perhaps most critically, the struggle for economic advantage by one city over another that have been the driving forces behind change.

Architectural and planning philosophy may provide retrospective legitimisation, but is seldom in the driving seat. It is rising land costs and the greater mobility of their workforces that have propelled businesses out to the edge of town; and retailers who cater for car-borne consumers rather than pedestrians have caused the eclipse of main street by out-of-town shopping.

The drive to construct new developments in the image of the classical city will do nothing to change those basic patterns, unless their inhabitants are parted not just from their motorcars but from their taste for supermarket shopping and exotic imported products.

The image of the city is simultaneously endlessly attractive, and threatening and repellent. It's a place where the poor can make their fortune, it's a honeypot for the adolescent looking for excitement, it provides the freedom of the bachelor for the suburban husband escaping his responsibilities, it's sex and glamour. It's also poverty and menace, beggars and muggers, dirt and squalor.

Writing about cities is full of this sense of threat, the attempts of the reformers to impose order on it, and their subsequent protestation of horror as they find their order crumbling in front of them.

Hardly surprisingly, the city in the nineteenth century, just at the moment that it was embarking on the greatest burst of growth in its history, provided one of the great themes of literature. Seeking to make sense of this astonishing change in the human condition that overtook enormous numbers of people translated suddenly from the country to the town, Zola and Dickens made it the focus of their work, both as observers and polemicists. Dickens's picture of the teeming slums of London was a powerful weapon in the campaigns of the Victorian reformers to banish the squalor and degradation that seemed an inescapable part of the city.

Early black and white photography captured the physical quality of the city. Lyonel Feininger's image of New York's cliff-like streets stepping down to the piers along the Hudson as the *SS America* slips past evokes the gritty, smoky metropolis, a city of possibilities and grey sadness, as nothing else can. It's an image that Woody Allen brought to life in the first frames of *Manhattan* to the accompaniment of George Gershwin. These were more than distinguished photographs, they helped to give the city an image of itself.

New York now is a fractured, incoherent place, still surprisingly nineteenth-century in the flavour of its great set pieces, in which the impact of over-development is making itself felt in the form of great canyons of anonymous high rise office towers in midtown. So striking and so sensational is the image of downtown that it has eclipsed everything else to become the embodiment of the city, in the same way that the set-back skyscraper did in the 1920s and 1930s. And just as the set-back tower was the unexpected outcome of the zoning regulations intended to bring sunlight into the streets, so the current form of New York is the result of the neurotic over-building of the city, an unintended by-product of the unfettered play of market forces, tempered by the bribery of the air-rights system, inspired perhaps by Fritz Lang's *Metropolis*. There are other New Yorks, the rolling green suburbs as well as the grim wastes of the Bronx. But Manhattan is so powerful, so sensational, that it has set the agenda for all other cities in America. Without the towers, these places still feel that they aren't 'real' cities. Yet this image of the city is a very recent one, the product of the constant, frenetic remodelling of the skyline that makes New York look entirely different from what it was just twenty years ago. The office core leapt from the financial district up to midtown, so that there are now two clumps of high rises, one around Wall Street, the other stretching across from the Rockefeller Center. The most desirable area for development since then has been the strip on Madison Avenue above the smart shops, where architectural fashions have switched from stone to glass, and now back to stone, while the buildings have got taller and taller and more densely packed.

Clearly, the current shape of Manhattan – a city where some children now attend school in bullet-proof flak jackets – has had a large part to play in the formulation of the urban dystopia that has haunted the imagination of the popular cinema, represented in particular by Ridley Scott's *Blade Runner*. Few film-makers, however, have been able to get to grips with the suburb in the way that *Blue Velvet*, David Lynch's hallucinogenic *film noir* – if that is not a contradiction in terms – has done.

Blade Runner's view that the future was going to be grubby and dripping steam, messy and criminal, rather than orderly and hygienic, touched a

Overleaf: The biggest shift in the popular perception of the city has been the realisation that the city of the future is unlikely to be sleek and streamlined, but will have a messy edge of decay to it, one that will offer vitality as well as a sense of threat

chord around the world. With its synthesis of actual developments – the noodle bars and neon of Tokyo, with the high rises of Los Angeles – it has turned into a self-fulfilling prophecy clearly influencing the collage architecture of Nigel Coates and others.

The film directors have not been slow in capitalising on the sense of threat many feel from the city. John Carpenter's series of films, including *Assault on Precinct 13*, an update of John Ford's *Stagecoach* to the setting of an abandoned police station in East Los Angeles's gangland wastes, and *Escape from New York*, which envisaged the complete abandonment of a Manhattan ringed with wire and watchtowers to the criminal underclasses, have also had a powerful impact.

Of course, these films are simple entertainment, but they help to convey a sense of what the city is, or can be. The cinema plays up the idea of the metropolis, of light and dark, of high density, of vital urbanism. Yet the cinema has also played its part in attempting to convey some of the complexities of what is happening. *Chinatown* was Roman Polanski's powerful investigation of the darker side of the city's history, and the corruption that shaped the continual struggle for water that led to the building of aqueducts striding all the way across California.

The myth-making of film, of urban outlaws and of community, has been crucial. But so also has been the view of the camera moving around the city – which has done as much as anything to convey the sense of the modern city, of how the landmarks of a city read in actual use. Reyner Banham confessed the feeling of familiarity that Los Angeles had for him when he first arrived in California, because of the frequency with which its suburbs appeared in the background to Hollywood's films. Curiously, Los Angeles, as far as film was concerned, had very few identifying landmarks, with the exception of the freeways which, owing to the difficulty of telling one from another, contributed to the general sense of placeless rootlessness. It is a situation that has started to change with the building of the new downtown skyscrapers.

Individual buildings and building types have also been subject to the explorations of the cinema. *Die Hard* painted a portrait of the high-tech skyscraper every bit as revealing as *Towering Inferno*. The image of the city is created by its architecture. You can see it in the staccato fragments of mirror glass and flamingoes that flicker past as the background to the rolling credits for *Miami Vice*.

This televisual acceptance of the vitality of the city, reminiscent of the over-excited futurist poetry of midnight railway stations, is in sharp contrast to the conventional contempt of western literature for the new incarnation of the city. The camera provides a moving view, yet one which can

also be carefully framed to look composed and considered, which has had a very large part in creating the image that we have of specific cities. The neon and heat haze and aerial photography of *West Side Story*, filmed from a helicopter shooting along the avenues and diagonally down Broadway, provides an image of extraordinary power.

The architectural historians have only just begun to get to grips with the way that the modern city functions, to be able to formulate as multilayered a view of the city as that which the cinema has always been able to offer. It took Reyner Banham to point out that the freeway is as much a part of urban space as the civic square, and Venturi's book on Las Vegas tried to do the same for the strip. But the message is put across far more effectively in the cinema. It reveals just how irrelevant is the city-beautiful idea of vistas and sequences of spaces unfolding at pedestrian pace to a city that stretches from Bournemouth to Ipswich, or from Marne-la-Vallée to Cergy-Pontoise.

In such cities, the centre still plays an important symbolic role. Without the historic crust, the city would not have existed. Without the two thousand years of economic importance of London, the prosperous corridor on either side of the M4 motorway to Bristol, the ever expanding ring of settlements that may be leaving the centre denuded of jobs and investment, could not exist. In Manhattan, Broadway slashes across the grid, a memory of the Mohawk trail that it once was.

The specifics of place and climate are still crucial – Los Angeles is not yet New York. London is not New York. Each has its differences in the way in which people live determined by the grain of the city – the size of the average home, its configuration, and the rest. Yet, as this book has argued, the world's cities are inextricably linked as a single system, one which demands sharper and sharper competition between them.

The vision of cities in the twentieth century as having fallen from grace is fundamentally misconceived and implausible. The cities of the past that we admire were themselves characterised by poverty, suffering and disease, no matter how splendid their facades. And if the purpose of urban reform is to improve the lot of the broad mass of people, then the apparent horrors of life in such cities must be approached with caution, for they may themselves be the engines of change.

The hundred-mile city

17

Imagine the force field around a high-tension power line, crackling with energy and ready to flash over and discharge 20 000 volts at any point along its length, and you have some idea of the nature of the modern city as it enters the last decade of the century.

The city's force field is not a linear one, however. Rather, it stretches for a hundred miles in each direction, over towns and villages and across vast tracts of what appears to be open country, far from any existing settlement that could conventionally be called a city. Without any warning, a flash of energy short-circuits the field, and precipitates a shopping centre so big that it needs three or five million people within reach to make it pay. Just as the dust has settled, there is another discharge of energy, and an office park erupts out of nothing, its thirty- and forty-storey towers rising sheer out of what had previously been farmland. The two have no visible connection, yet they are part of the same city, linked only by the energy field, just like the housing compounds that crop up here and there, and the airport, and the cloverleaf on the freeway, and the corporate headquarters with its own lake in the middle of a park.

Somewhere, in a remote corner, there is no doubt a little enclave of pedestrian streets, a fringe of terraced houses that circles the crop of office towers that marks downtown. There will be a sandblasted old market hall recycled for recreational shopping. And somewhere else, there will be the social derelicts, the casualties, trapped in welfare housing or worse.

The energy that powers the force field is of course mobility. The wider ownership of the car that has come since the 1960s has finally transformed the nature of the city. The old certainties of urban geography have vanished, and in their place is this edgy and apparently amorphous new kind of settlement. The chances are that the force field couldn't have come into being without a downtown, or historic crust, because massive amounts of resources are needed to achieve the critical mass required by this kind of city as a trigger. But in its present incarnation, the old centre is just another piece on the board, a counter that has perhaps the same weight as the airport, or the medical centre, or the museum complex. They all swim in a soup of shopping malls, hypermarkets and warehouses, drive-in restaurants and anonymous industrial sheds, beltways and motorway boxes.

Previous page: The old idea of the city focussed only on the picture post-card landmarks, and the central crust of buildings and spaces. But it is clear that the present day city has long-since outstripped those limits. The new incarnation of the city is an endless, amorphous sprawl, within which outcrops of skyscrapers, or vast shopping malls can appear almost anywhere

The words to describe it vary in different cultures, but the pattern is no longer confined to North America. You can see the same phenomenon around Atlanta, or in the stretch of France that connects Barcelona with Milan, or along the M4 motorway running westward out of London. As Europe has become more mobile, so it too has taken on the same characteristics, despite its older city centres and their traditional patterns based on the pedestrian.

At first sight, all sense of coherence has gone. In this new city, it's no longer necessary to go to the centre to work or to shop. So the geography becomes disorientating, especially to newcomers who need far longer to pick up the signals that we all need to make sense of an unfamiliar city. Some traditional functions have been taken out of the equation altogether. In many cities there is no main street that anybody would care to visit given the choice. So there is Disney instead, already installed on both sides of America and in Japan, and due to arrive shortly in Paris, which offers the trappings of the convivial old city, instantly available for pilgrims and free of the sense of threat that is a constant subtext to the big city as we know it.

In the force field city, nothing is unself-conscious, any urban gesture is calculated.

For the affluent, the home is the centre of life – though given the astonishing increase in household mobility, it's not likely to be the same home for very long. From it, the city radiates outwards as a star-shaped pattern of overlapping routes to and from the workplace, the shopping centre, and the school. They are all self-contained abstractions that function as free-floating elements. Each destination caters to a certain range of the needs of urban life, but they have no physical or spatial connection with each other in the way that we have been conditioned to expect of the city.

Architecture and urban space has been overwhelmed by the sheer scale of new buildings. A new race of giant boxes has descended, warehouses, discount superstores, shopping malls and leisure centres that it is hardly possible to differentiate one from another. Despite their anonymity, they have swallowed up most civic functions.

Mobility means overlapping force fields. Cities compete with each other in a grimly determined struggle to maintain the energy that keeps them working. But the lives of their citizens take in other cities to an extent that is unparalled in history. They move from one to another constantly, to live, to visit, to do business.

In most economic areas, one or two individual cities have come to monopolise the world market. So New York, Tokyo and London are the world's financial capitals, Los Angeles is its entertainment centre. Perhaps the hundred-mile city has already become the thousand-mile city.

The hundred-mile city

The other side to the equation is the widening gap between those cities that are successful, and those that are not. Some cities are clearly failing. Their treasuries teeter on the edge of bankruptcy, they fail to attract new employers, they have little to recommend them culturally. But beyond that there is the widening difference between metropolitan cities which draw in the ambitious and the gifted, and provincial cities which lose them.

The hundred-mile city is a model of urban life which many people find threatening even as they embrace it. By and large, those who have a choice do not care to live in cramped city centre homes, nor do they see much economic future in the old downtowns. The historic pattern of the city is undoubtedly a high point in civilisation, one that is worth preserving. But even if masonry endures, its meaning has been irrevocably altered.

There are many issues posed by this new kind of city. The most alarming of course is the prospect of what happens if the supply of energy is shut off – if the private car on which so many cities depend is made obsolete by future energy crises. Will exurbia have to be abandoned just like the empty Indian city of Fatephur Sikhri? It's an issue that is already preoccupying the most notorious car-orientated city, Los Angeles. It's not just the prospect of shortages that is worrying the city, but the more immediate prospect of gridlock on its freeways. Clearly there are many settlements which it is already too late to do anything about, but any responsible planning system must address the issue, which is at its most acute in the location of housing. But what the planner cannot do is to cut across the direction of events. The only plausible strategy is to attempt to harness the dynamics of development to move things in the direction that you want. For the planner or the architect to ignore the currents that are shaping the city is clearly futile. Enormous amounts of energy have been expended on means of reconstructing the traditional European city, as if this were possible by the simple exertion of will.

To accept this image of the city is to accept uncomfortable things about ourselves, and our illusions about the way we want to live. The city is as much about selfishness and fear as it is about community and civic life. And yet to accept that the city has a dark side, of menace and greed, does not diminish its vitality and strength. In the last analysis, it reflects man and all his potential.

Bibliography

Alexander, Christopher: *The Production of Houses* New York (OUP 1985)

Banham, Reyner: *Los Angeles: The Architecture of Four Ecologies* London (Penguin 1973)

Brunet, Roger: *Les Villes Européennes* Paris (Reclus 1989)

Coleman, Alice M.: *Utopia on Trial: Vision and Reality in Planned Housing* London (Hilary Shipman 1984)

Collins, George and Crasemann, Christiane: *Camillo Sitte: The Birth of Modern City Planning* New York (Rizzoli 1986)

Le Corbusier: *The City of Tomorrow* translated by Frederick Etchells; London (Architectural Press 1987)

Dogan, Mattei and Kasarda, John: *The Metropolis Era: Mega Cities* Newbury Park, California (Sage Publications 1988)

Fishman, Robert: *Urban Utopias in the Twentieth Century: Ebenezer Howard, Frank Lloyd Wright and Le Corbusier* Cambridge, Massachusetts (MIT Press 1982)

Forman, Charlie: *Spitalfields, A Battle for Land* London (Hilary Shipman 1989)

Frieden, Bernard and Sagalyn, Lyne: *Downtown Inc, How America Rebuilds Cities* Cambridge Massachusetts (MIT 1989)

Gans, Herbert: *People and Plans* abridged edition (Penguin 1972)

Hall, Peter: *Cities of Tomorrow, An Intellectual History of Urban Planning and Design in the Twentieth Century* Oxford (Basil Blackwell 1988)

Hall, Peter: *London 2001* London (Unwin Hyman 1989)

Hall, Peter: *The World Cities* Third edition; London (Weidenfeld and Nicolson 1984)

Harvey, David: *The Urbanization of Capital: Studies in the History and Theory of Capitalist Urbanization* Oxford (Basil Blackwell 1985)

Hebbert, Michael and Nakai, Norihiro: *How Tokyo Grows: Land Development and Planning on the Metropolitan Fringe* London (LSE 1988)

Howard, Ebenezer: originally published 1898 as *Tomorrow, A Peaceful Path to Real Reform.* Reissued as *Garden Cities of Tomorrow* Bluith Wells (Attic Books 1989)

Jacobs, Jane: *The Death and Life of Great American Cities* British edition, London (Peregrine 1984)

King, Anthony D.: *Global Cities: Post Imperialism and the Internationalisation of London* London (Routledge 1990)

Mumford, Lewis: *The City in History* London (Penguin 1966)

Pawley, Martin: *Architecture Versus Housing* London (Studio Vista 1971)

Power, Anne *Property Before People: The Management of Twentieth Century Council Housing* London (Allen & Unwin 1987)

Rowe, Colin and Koetter, Fred: *Collage City* Cambridge, Massachusetts (MIT 1985)

Savitch H. V.: *Post-industrial Cities: Politics and Planning in New York, Paris and London* Princeton (Princeton University Press 1988)

Schickel, Richard: *The Disney Version* London (Pavilion 1986)

Smith, Neil and Williams, Peter (editors): *Gentrification of the City* Boston (Allen & Unwin Inc 1986)

Thompson, Jane: 'Boston's Faneuil Hall', *Urban Studies International* December 1979

Venturi, Robert; Scott-Brown, Denise and Izenour, Steven: *Learning from Las Vegas* Revised edition, Cambridge Massachusetts (MIT 1988)

Wakeford, Richard: *American Development Control: Parallels and Paradoxes from an English Perspective* London (HMSO 1990)

Whyte, William H.: *City: Rediscovering the Center* New York (Doubleday 1988)

Willmott, Peter and Young, Michael F. D.: *Family and Kinship in East London* London (Penguin 1962)

Zukin, Sharon: *Loft Living: Culture and Capital in Urban Change* London (Century Hutchinson 1988)

Index